THE BEST
PLACES
TO KISS™
IN SOUTHERN CALIFORNIA

A Romantic Travel Guide

COMPLETELY REVISED
4th EDITION
AND UPDATED

by

Caroline O'Connell with Megan Davenport

BEGINNING
PRESS

OTHER BOOKS IN THE

BEST PLACES TO KISS™

SERIES:

The Best Places To Kiss In Northern California, 4th Edition $13.95

The Best Places To Kiss In The Northwest, 6th Edition $15.95

The Best Places To Kiss In Hawaii, 2nd Edition $12.95

ANY OF THESE BOOKS CAN BE ORDERED DIRECTLY FROM THE PUBLISHER.

Please send a check or money order for the total
amount of the books, plus shipping and handling
($3 for the first book, and $1 for each additional book) to:

Beginning Press
5418 South Brandon
Seattle, Washington 98118

All prices are listed in U.S. funds.
For information about ordering from Canada or to place
an order using Visa or MasterCard, call (206) 723-6300.

Art Direction and Production: Studio Pacific, Inc.
Cover Design: Studio Pacific, Inc., Deb McCarroll
Editors: Miriam Bulmer and Laura Kraemer
Printing: Publishers Press
Contributors: Paula Begoun, Deborah Brada, Elizabeth Janda,
          and Rachel Permann

Copyright 1990, 1992, 1994, 1997 by Paula Begoun

First Edition: June 1990
Second Edition: June 1992
Third Edition: June 1994
Fourth Edition: March 1997
1 2 3 4 5 6 7 8 9 10

BEST PLACES TO KISS™

is a registered trademark of Beginning Press
ISBN 1-877988-20-0

This book is distributed to the U.S. book trade by:
Publisher's Group West
4065 Hollis Street
Emeryville, CA 94608
(800) 788-3123

This book is distributed to the Canadian book trade by:
Raincoast Books
8680 Cambie Street
Vancouver, B.C.
V6P-6M9
Canada
(800) 663-5714

"As usual with most lovers in the city, they were troubled by the lack of that essential need of love—a meeting place."

Thomas Wolfe

Publisher's Note

Travel books have many different criteria for the places they include. We would like the reader to know that this book is not an advertising vehicle. As is true in all *The Best Places To Kiss* books, the businesses included were not charged fees, nor did they pay us for their reviews. This book is a sincere, unbiased effort to highlight those special parts of the region that are filled with romance and splendor. Sometimes those places were created by people, such as restaurants, inns, lounges, lodges, hotels, and bed and breakfasts. Sometimes those places are untouched by people and simply created by God for us to enjoy. Wherever you go, be gentle with each other and with the earth.

The publisher made the final decision on the recommendations in this collection, but we would love to hear what you think of our suggestions. We strive to create a reliable guide for your amorous outings, and in this quest for blissful sojourns, your romantic feedback assists greatly in increasing our accuracy and our resources for information. If you have any additional comments, criticisms, or cherished memories of your own from a place we directed you to or a place you discovered on your own, feel free to write us at:

Beginning Press
5418 South Brandon Street
Seattle, WA 98118

We would love to hear from you!

"*What of soul was left, I wonder, when the kissing had to stop?*"

Robert Browning

Table of Contents

The Fine Art of Kissing

Why It's Still Best To Kiss In Southern California

It must be the constant sunshine that affects the heart so warmly here in Southern California. There is a passionate attachment to this region that is evident in both the density of population and the vast number of tourists who visit each year. From the village of Cambria in the north to the flawless scenery that surrounds San Diego, there is enough amorous territory here to ignite romantic fires in the most cynical among us. Encounter the elite beach enclave of Santa Barbara, experience the intense love/hate relationship with the urban paradise/blight of Los Angeles, take in the towering San Bernadino Mountains, or navigate the flat parched desert that leads to the urban oasis of Palm Springs. From the pristine shores of Catalina to the snowy peaks of Lake Arrowhead and Big Bear to the arid bronzed landscape of Death Valley, your options are vitually limitless.

If you've ever longed for a magical place where you can share closeness and private moments, you will find it in Southern California: silky white beaches, crashing surf, state-of-the-art wineries, hot-air balloon rides, stunning bed and breakfasts, enticing restaurants, enthralling vistas, lush country hikes, and hidden parks—all accompanied by sparkling blue skies. Southern California is not a secret, but the extraordinarily romantic parts of this region can be difficult to uncover. Now that most of the lip work has been done for you, the only challenge left will be to find the lovable niche in which your hearts fit best.

You Call This Research?

This book was undertaken primarily as a journalistic effort and is the product of ongoing interviews, travel, thorough investigation, and critical observation. Although it would have been nice, even preferable, kissing was not the major research method used to select the locations listed in this book. If smooching had been the determining factor, several inescapable problems would have developed. First, we would still be researching, and this book would be just a good idea, some breathless moments, random notes, and nothing more. Second, depending on the mood of the moment, many kisses might have occurred in places that do not meet the requirements of this travel guide. Therefore, for both practical and physical reasons, more objective criteria had to be established.

You may be wondering how, if we did not kiss at every location during our research, we could be certain that a particular place was good for such an activity? The answer is that we employed reporters' instincts to evaluate the heartfelt, magnetic pull of each place visited. If, upon examining a place, we felt a longing inside for our special someone to share what we had discovered, we considered this to be as reliable as a kissing analysis. In the final evaluation, we can guarantee that once you choose where to go from among any of the places listed, you will be assured of some degree of privacy, a beautiful setting, heart-stirring ambience, and romantic accommodations. When you get there, what you do romantically is up to you and your partner.

Rating Romance

The three major factors that determined whether or not we included a place were:

- Privacy
- Location/view/setting
- Ambience

Of these determining factors, "privacy" and "location" are fairly self-explanatory, but "ambience" can probably use some clarification. Wonderful, loving environments are not just four-poster beds covered with down quilts and lace pillows, or tables decorated with white tablecloths and nicely folded linen napkins. Instead, there must be other engaging features that encourage intimacy and allow for uninterrupted affectionate discourse. For the most part, ambience was rated according to degree of comfort and number of gracious appointments, as opposed to image and frills

If a place had all three factors going for it, inclusion was automatic. But if one or two of the criteria were weak or nonexistent, the other feature(s) had to be superior before the location would be included. For example, if a breathtakingly beautiful panoramic vista was in a spot that's inundated with tourists and children on field trips, the place was not included. If a fabulous bed and breakfast was set in a less than desirable location, it would be included if, and only if, its interior was so wonderfully inviting and cozy that the outside world no longer mattered. Extras like complimentary champagne, handmade truffles, or extraordinary service earned brownie points and frequently determined the difference between three-and-a-half and four-lip ratings.

Romantic Note: If you're planning to celebrate a special occasion, such as an anniversary or birthday, we highly recommend telling the proprietors about it when making your reservation. Many bed and breakfasts and hotels offer "special occasion packages," which can include a complimentary bottle of wine, breakfast in bed, fresh flowers, and special touches during turndown service, like dimmed lights and your beloved's favorite CD playing in the background to set the right romantic mood. Restaurants are also sometimes willing to accommodate special occasions by offering free desserts or helping you coordinate a surprise proposal.

Kiss Ratings

The lip rating following each entry is our way of indicating just how romantic we thought a place was and how contented we were during our visit. The number of lips awarded each location indicates:

No lips	=	Reputed to be a romantic destination, but we strongly disagree
💋	=	Romantic possibilities with potential drawbacks
💋💋	=	Can provide a satisfying experience
💋💋💋	=	Very desirable
💋💋💋💋	=	Simply sublime
Unrated	=	Not open at the time this edition went to print, but looks promising

Cost Ratings

We have included additional ratings to help you determine whether your lips can afford to kiss in a particular restaurant, hotel, or bed and breakfast. (Almost all of the outdoor places are free; some charge a small fee.) The price for overnight accommodations is always based on double occupancy; otherwise there wouldn't be anyone to kiss. Eating establishment prices are based on a full dinner for two, excluding liquor, unless otherwise indicated. Because prices and business hours change, it is always advisable to call each place you plan to visit, so your lips will not end up disappointed.

Restaurants

Inexpensive	Less than $30
Moderate	$30 to $50
Expensive	$50 to $80
Very Expensive	$80 to $110
Unbelievably Expensive	More than $110

Lodgings

Inexpensive	Less than $95
Moderate	$95 to $115
Expensive	$115 to $155
Very Expensive	$155 to $250
Unbelievably Expensive	More than $250

Wedding Bells

One of the more auspicious times to kiss is the moment after wedding vows have been exchanged. The setting for that magical moment can vary from your own cozy living room to a lush garden perched at the ocean's edge to a grand ballroom at an elegant downtown hotel. As an added service to those of you in the midst of prenuptial arrangements, we have indicated which properties have impressive wedding facilities. For more specific information about which facilities and services are offered, please call the establishment directly. They should be able to provide you with menus, prices, and all the details needed to make your wedding day as spectacular as you have ever imagined.

Romantic Note: If wedding bells aren't in your near future and you are going to an establishment that specializes in weddings and private parties, call ahead to ensure that a function isn't scheduled during your stay. Unless you're hoping that seeing a wedding will magically inspire your partner to "pop the question," you might feel like uninvited guests.

Central Coast and Environs

San Simeon

Outdoor Kissing

HEARST CASTLE, San Simeon
(805) 927-2020, (800) 444-4445
$14 admission
Reservations Recommended

Located seven miles north of Cambria, off Highway 1.

Cambria is known for its proximity to the exceedingly opulent and palatial Hearst Castle. The legendary estate of newspaper publisher and magnate William Randolph Hearst includes 165 rooms and 127 acres of gardens, terraces, pools, and walkways. Every inch is a magnificent testimonial to the craftspeople and architect who spent 28 years building the hilltop estate Hearst called "La Cuesta Encantada" ("the enchanted hill" in Spanish). Daily tours take approximately two hours; each of the four daytime tours and one evening tour covers a different part of the property. Though kissing might be considered inappropriate during your tour, the castle is unquestionably fascinating and worth your while. The fantasies that will be ignited by your glimpse of this real-life Xanadu will last a lifetime.

Romantic Warning: Our only hesitation in recommending a tour of Hearst Castle is that you are bused to the estate with about 50 other visitors. An audiotape accompanies your 5-mile, 12-minute, cramped ride up the hill, and then your large group is herded through the castle. Considering the number of people who tour Hearst Castle each year (approximately 750,000), the state does a wonderful job of getting groups in and out, but the experience is not even close to intimate.

Cambria

The small town of Cambria straddles Highway 1 near the midpoint of the Central Coast, just 230 miles south of San Francisco and 230 miles north of Los Angeles. Perhaps it is the distance from these two major cities that has kept everything here so pristine and underdeveloped. You won't find urban sprawl in this part of the world (at least not yet). Charming Cambria is perhaps the last refuge of its kind along the coastal waters of Southern California.

Red-tailed hawks soar above endless stretches of rolling golden hills dotted with grazing cattle and sprawling oak trees. Along the coast, sea lions bask on rocky outcroppings in the afternoon sun, and gray whales pass by on their biannual migration. Browse through the weathered wood-frame stores and art galleries that line the quiet, small-town streets, or take advantage of Cambria's handful of romantic restaurants and charming inns.

Romantic Warning: We can't say enough about Cambria, but in spite of (or perhaps because of) all these words of praise, don't be surprised if you find yourselves among crowds of tourists during high season. The area can be intensely busy April through October, though it still draws far fewer visitors than Pismo Beach and Santa Barbara, located a little farther south along the coast, or Carmel and Monterey to the north. Cambria is far too small to accommodate extremely large numbers of tourists, so the most romantic time here is still off-season (November through March).

Also, a note about **MOONSTONE BEACH DRIVE**, a small stretch of road bordered on one side by the magnificent ocean and on the other by a row of tightly packed inns, motels, and bed and breakfasts. Although the accommodations here offer the best combination of location and quality, the thoroughfare can be extremely busy. It's not the least bit private or secluded, so you may find the overall kissing potential of the area diminished a notch or two during the peak season.

Hotel/Bed and Breakfast Kissing

BLUE DOLPHIN INN, Cambria
6470 Moonstone Beach Drive
(805) 927-3300
Inexpensive to Very Expensive

SAND PEBBLES INN, Cambria
6252 Moonstone Beach Drive
(805) 927-5600
Inexpensive to Very Expensive

One of the best ways to take advantage of the graceful shoreline of Cambria is to stay at either the Blue Dolphin or the Sand Pebbles, two picture-perfect inns located across the street from the blue waters of the Pacific. Blue Dolphin Inn holds 18 rooms, while the Sand Pebbles Inn has 23. The designer of these almost identical inns included every detail necessary for a soothing, leisurely getaway. Every room features canopied beds, cozy breakfast nooks, and wall-to-wall country floral prints and stripes in various tones. In addition, the rooms have been graced with all the amenities you would expect to find in a small hotel, such as mini-refrigerators stocked with mineral water, TVs and VCRs (discreetly hidden from view in pine armoires), and small private baths. The real finds are the rooms with large whirlpool tubs, gas fireplaces, sweeping ocean views, and garden patios. Breakfast, a simple continental selection of fresh pastries and fruit, is served buffet-style in the lower-level breakfast area and can be taken back to your room. Tea and cookies are also set out each afternoon.

THE BLUE WHALE INN, Cambria
6736 Moonstone Beach Drive
(805) 927-4647
Expensive to Very Expensive
Minimum stay requirement on weekends

Every detail of this contemporary Cape Cod–style bed and breakfast tends to matters of the heart. Expansive floor-to-ceiling windows make the living room a fabulous place from which to survey the panoramic ocean view. Relax, watch for whales (a telescope is provided), and savor the setting sun while enjoying the complimentary wine, cheese, and appetizers served here each evening.

The inn's six guest rooms are set behind the front reception area. Each room is a tranquil, lavish mini-suite where lovers can spend private time together surrounded by elegant comforts: canopied four-poster beds, country-style fabrics, handsome armoires, gas-log fireplaces, comfy love seats, and soaking tubs. The rooms have their own entrances for maximum privacy, and small bottles of champagne are provided on special occasions. High ceilings, white shutters, and muted color schemes give each room an airy ambience without compromising an ounce of coziness. Due to the layout of the rooms, partial ocean views are visible beyond the parking lot, but the best views are found in Rooms 2, 3, and 4. Breakfast is served in the front common area beside those wonderful water-facing windows; begin your day with delectables such as gingerbread pancakes with lemon sauce, orange-pecan French toast, and fresh pastries.

FOG CATCHER INN, Cambria
6400 Moonstone Beach Drive
(805) 927-1400, (800) 425-4121
http://www.cambria-online.com/fogcatcherinn

Inexpensive to Very Expensive
Minimum stay requirement on weekends

With its 60 rooms, large parking lot, and centrally located swimming pool, the Fog Catcher Inn is vaguely reminiscent of a motel. Fortunately, the otherwise ho-hum ambience is offset by the well-kept grounds, the spacious rooms, the proximity to the ocean, and the charming peach stucco exterior trimmed with weathered wood. Although the rooms tend to be more standard than anything else, they are endowed with pastel floral wallpaper, drapes, and bedspreads; high ceilings; dark green carpets; and knotty pine and wicker furniture. There are also small kitchen nooks and stone fireplaces for evening cuddling. While some of the rooms at the back of the inn lack ocean views, their distance from the road and the lushness of the surrounding greenery provide ample seclusion and privacy.

Complimentary breakfast is served in a large cafeteria-like room that is more utilitarian than romantic. If intimate surroundings are a priority, we suggest heading to one of Cambria's charming local cafes or coffee shops for breakfast.

THE J. PATRICK HOUSE, Cambria
2990 Burton Drive
(805) 927-3812, (800) 341-5258
http://www.jpatrickhouse.com
Moderate to Very Expensive
Minimum stay requirement on weekends and holidays

Located in a residential neighborhood along a sloping hillside, this rustic bed and breakfast is unlike anything else you'll find in Cambria. The main house is an authentic log cabin where you can surrender to the cozy ambience by the warmth of a crackling fire. In the early evening, sample wine and hors d'oeuvres in an adjacent glass-enclosed porch overlooking a small, pretty yard. Guests vie for the Clare Room (the only suite located in the main house), so make your reservation early if you want to enjoy the best room here. Secluded upstairs, its country elegance is enhanced by lovely antiques, a fireplace, and beautiful wood walls and floors.

A trellis draped with passionflowers and jasmine covers a walkway leading to the seven remaining guest rooms, located in a separate cottage behind the house. Each room has a wood-burning fireplace, private bath, and built-in window seat. Country touches such as homemade wreaths and handmade patterned bedspreads accent the comfortable rooms. Along with these affable touches, however, you'll find mismatched contemporary and antique furnishings as well as slightly worn carpeting.

In-room massage (for one or two) is available upon request. Conclude your stay with a delicious continental breakfast of fresh fruit, yogurt, breads, muffins, and homemade granola, served in the main house.

OLALLIEBERRY INN, Cambria
2476 Main Street
(805) 927-3222, (888) 927-3222
http://www.olallieberry.com
Inexpensive to Expensive
Minimum stay requirement on weekends

Located within walking distance of downtown Cambria, the Olallieberry Inn has nine distinctive rooms. Six are located in the main house, while the other three are in a separate cottage at the back of the property. A lovely backyard overlooks the Santa Rosa Creek, which flows behind the main house. Most of the rooms have gas fireplaces as well as floral wallpapers and quilts, lace curtains, dried flower arrangements, and antiques, lending the rooms a Victorian sensibility. Two rooms in the cottage have private balconies with serene views of the creek. For romantic purposes, it is important to note that three rooms have detached bathrooms (not the most conducive to privacy), so you will want to request one of the rooms that has an attached bathroom with a claw-foot or sunken tub. In the morning, a full breakfast consisting of stuffed French toast or fresh-fruit crêpes is served downstairs in the main house.

SQUIBB HOUSE, Cambria
4063 Burton Drive
(805) 927-9600
http://www.cambria-online.com/thesquibbhouseandshopnextdoor
Moderate to Expensive
Minimum stay requirement on weekends

Situated in the heart of Cambria, the Squibb House provides easy access to the town's shops and galleries. A short red brick walkway leads you to the door of this country-Victorian bed and breakfast, which is partially obscured from the road by foliage and trees. All five rooms have hardwood floors accented with rugs, beautiful wooden armoires handcrafted by the owner, wicker chairs, dried floral arrangements, down comforters covered by handmade patterned bedspreads, and gas-fired stoves (not the rooms' best asset). Tall windows allow the sunshine to stream in, warming each room with ample light. Several porches equipped with wicker and rocking chairs provide a setting for quiet evening intimacy, as does the brick courtyard located behind the house. In the morning, you can enjoy an extended continental breakfast served in the elegant parlor, which is decorated with plush, beautifully upholstered dark wood furniture, or you can have your breakfast delivered to the privacy of your room.

Romantic Suggestion: If you're interested in wine tasting or just need a few items for an afternoon picnic, visit the gift shop across the street: FERMENTATIONS, 4056 Burton Drive, (805) 927-7141. The fee for tasting is $2 per person.

Restaurant Kissing

HARMONY PASTA FACTORY, Cambria
1316 Tamson Drive
(805) 927-5882
Inexpensive to Moderate
Lunch Monday-Saturday; Dinner Daily; Sunday Brunch

Don't let this restaurant's location in a commercialized shopping center dissuade you from dining here. Because the Harmony Pasta Factory is situated on the third floor, nearly every table in the formal, country-style dining room has a lovely view of Cambria's rolling hills. Linen-cloaked tables are arranged with privacy in mind and topped with candles and flowers. The restaurant's green-and-lavender color scheme is embellished by a local artist's floral stencil designs adorning the walls. It's difficult to decide among all the tasty pasta offerings on the menu, but we recommend the chicken ravioli and the Italian orange cream linguine.

IAN'S, Cambria
2150 Center Street
(805) 927-8649
Moderate
Dinner Daily

A change of pace from Cambria's other casual eateries, this formal, contemporary restaurant provides a lovely setting for a romantic dinner for two. The bright and colorful exterior of the building is hard to miss. Once inside, however, you will find a subtle, sophisticated atmosphere. Wall sconces and candlelight lend a soft sensuality to the otherwise modest interior. Interesting local artwork adorn the walls, and white linen–covered tables topped with long-stemmed red roses are spread throughout the room. The menu offers a variety of classic dishes—from pasta and pizzas to grilled salmon and rack of lamb. The kitchen is sure to please, and the service is gracious without being intrusive.

ROBIN'S, Cambria
4095 Burton Drive
(805) 927-5007
Inexpensive
Lunch Monday-Saturday; Dinner Daily

From the outside, Robin's looks like a congenial country home surrounded by trees, foliage, and thick vines. Fortunately, the inside is just as appealing. Wood tables, a river-rock fireplace, stained glass windows, and attractive wreaths of dried brush accentuate the dining room's carefree and casual attitude. A natural-minded gourmet menu adds to the eclectic allure, with such entrées as Indonesian-style soycake stir-fried with onions, garlic, and chiles, and whole-wheat burritos filled with cheese and black beans. If you choose to sit outside on the glassed-in deck, which is embraced by meandering trumpet vines, your warm words of love will be augmented by the well-spaced heat lamps and softly glowing lanterns.

THE SEA CHEST OYSTER BAR, Cambria
6216 Moonstone Beach Drive
(805) 927-4514
http://seachestoysterbar.com
Moderate; No Credit Cards
Call for seasonal hours.

Ask anyone in Cambria for a dinner recommendation and you're likely to be sent to this endearing spot, located across the street from the ocean. The Sea Chest's delicious fresh seafood, friendly service, and eclectic decor (including a ceiling plastered with business cards) create a cozy charm that is impossible to resist. Hanging green and white lanterns illuminate the restaurant's cabin-like interior. Each table is topped with a small potted plant, a white paper tablecloth, and a collection of crayons. Find a table for two in a corner and enjoy generous portions of lobster, scampi, and succulent oysters served with garlic bread and a fresh green salad. Besides serving fantastic dinners, the Sea Chest also has the best oyster bar in the area.

THE SOW'S EAR CAFÉ, Cambria
2248 Main Street
(805) 927-4865
Moderate
Dinner Daily

It's hard to mix elegant and casual without doing too much of one and not enough of the other, but the cozy Sow's Ear Café pulls it off beautifully.

This romantic dining spot has a dark-wood interior, a massive brick fireplace, fresh flowers on every table, and enough pig paraphernalia to fill a barn. Fresh bread begins each meal, followed by something from the hearty, country-inspired menu—say, fresh salmon baked in parchment with herbs and wine, or chicken-fried steak with savory gravy. Locals and regular visitors to Cambria agree that this charming cafe has the best gourmet cuisine in town, and equally satisfying service.

THE TEA COZY, Cambria
4286 Bridge Street
(805) 927-8765
Inexpensive
Lunch and Afternoon Tea Wednesday-Sunday

It doesn't get much cozier than this authentically British corner of the Central Coast. Follow the short brick walkway, past a rose-covered arbor and overgrown foliage draping along a white picket fence, to the front steps of this charming historic home. Inside, decorative china adorns the numerous tables arranged in the snug but casual dining rooms, done up Old English–style and highlighted with hardwood floors, antiques, hanging antique plates, and photos of the beloved "Queen Mum." A little gift shop is set off to one side so you can take home a taste of England. Imported groceries, gifts, antiques, and royal memorabilia make for fun keepsakes. For your immediate needs, lunch choices include a ploughman's sandwich of Stilton cheese on a crusty roll with pickled onions, plus Cornish pasties and sausage rolls. Best of all, indulge in a Royal Tea for two: scones, double Devon cream, preserves, cakes, finger sandwiches, and, of course, a pot of tea. The warm sunshine streaming through the windows is the only giveaway that you are in California, not England.

Outdoor Kissing

SANTA ROSA CREEK ROAD, Cambria

From Main Street (Business Highway 1), turn east onto Santa Rosa Creek Road.

For a closer look at Cambria's gorgeous countryside, follow this winding byway for 17 miles through verdant farmland and velvet rolling hills. Before you depart on this exquisite, utterly secluded drive, consider stopping at ROBIN'S (see Restaurant Kissing) to pick up picnic items from the deli. A wide variety of pasta and vegetable salads, healthy sandwiches, and freshly baked goods are available. You can also stop along the way at LINN'S FRUIT BIN, (805) 927-1499, located five miles east of Cambria on Santa Rosa

Creek Road, where you can purchase your dessert—homemade pie—and possibly some other country goodies.

Paso Robles

Touring the Central Coast via Highway 1 allows you to enjoy coastal panoramas for miles and miles. There is no doubt that this is the best route for spectacular vistas of California's coastline. Still, you may want to consider veering off the seaside highway for another very special area: the Wine Country surrounding the rural inland community of Paso Robles. Vineyards, horse farms, and almond orchards cover the rolling acres of oak-lined hills here, creating a bucolic scene that could calm even the most anxious city nerves. A large handful of small wineries offer tours and tastings, while the local bed and breakfasts give you an opportunity to stay overnight and slow your pace to that of the country life around you.

Hotel/Bed and Breakfast Kissing

THE ARBOR INN, Paso Robles
2130 Arbor Road
(805) 227-4673
Moderate to Very Expensive

Specifically designed as guest lodging, this newly built country inn is well suited for wine lovers (and lovers in general). The inn is owned by Hope Farms Winery, just across the street, so selected vintage wines and hors d'oeuvres are shared in the main-floor Great Room every evening. The inn and its nine guest rooms are decorated in formal English style with polished mahogany furniture and nicely tailored fabrics, but expansive windows and high ceilings help keep the atmosphere bright and airy.

The private guest rooms are spread out on the first and second floors, and the exclusive Cabernet Suite is on the top level. This decadent unit is decorated in black, gold, and ivory with elegant furnishings. For the ultimate in comfort, there is a cast-iron bedframe on the king-size bed, a six-foot bathtub, a multiheaded shower, and a wraparound patio. All of the rooms have gas fireplaces, private balconies, televisions, and phones. Although the other rooms are not as large as the suite, they are exceedingly comfortable, with plush down comforters, crisp floral linens, four-poster or sleigh king- or queen-size beds, and handsome antiques.

For breakfast, you are given the option of either a continental or a full breakfast. Those who want a hearty start to the day can choose from two egg dishes (an omelet or Mexican scrambled eggs) and two sweeter options

(French toast or pancakes). After this, you can probably skip lunch and just spend your afternoon touring the countryside.

JUST INN, Paso Robles   ❧ ❧ ❧ ❧
11680 Chimney Rock Road, at the Justin Vineyards and Winery
(805) 238-6932, (800) 726-0049
Very Expensive
Minimum stay requirement on weekends

Originally designed as overnight accommodations for visiting wine industry executives, the two private suites at Just Inn are perfectly suited for romantic getaways. An English garden fronts the contemporary two-story home, and 72 acres of vineyards stretch as far as the eye can see. Wine tasting is offered to the public in the Italianate terra-cotta-tiled foyer, but the suites are at the rear of the house, shielded from any possible intrusion.

In the spacious guest suites, a combination of French Country and Italian influences creates an atmosphere that is both stylish and cozy. Earth-toned glazed walls, vaulted ceilings with exposed beams, antiqued pine furnishings, and wrought iron touches lend rusticity while polished hardwood floors, plush upholstered chairs, marble baths with two-person spa tubs, and corner fireplaces add comfortable elegance. A charming mural is painted above the queen-size bed in the separate bedroom, and down comforters and feather beds ensure a good night's rest. Your wine decanter is refilled nightly, and fresh floral bouquets help enhance the mood. For relaxing melodies, the sitting room features a stereo with classical CDs hidden in a pine armoire.

A full gourmet breakfast is served at one large table in the tasting room, or you may ask to have it delivered to your suite. Each room has a balcony (the Tuscany Room has two) where you can sip fresh-squeezed orange juice and admire the acres of symmetrical grapevines. The only potential drawback is that the machinery behind the house is noisy at times (remember, this is a working winery). Eventually, the owners hope to construct a separate facility so guests won't be bothered by any noises other than the chirping of birds, the babble of the resident ducks, and an occasional croak from the bullfrog who lives in the small pond beside the house. Enjoy Just Inn's country escape while you can—life should always be this carefree.

Romantic Suggestion: Just Inn serves gourmet four-course French dinners by reservation only. The cost is $50 per person, but each heavenly bite is worth the expense, plus you have the convenience of not having to drive anywhere. If you care to indulge in one of Just Inn's fabulous vintages with your meal, your suite is just steps away.

Outdoor Kissing

WINE TASTING

For general information about wineries in the Paso Robles area, contact the Paso Robles Vintners and Growers Association at P.O. Box 324, Paso Robles, CA 93447, or call (805) 239-8463.

Affectionately known as "California's *other* wine country," the Paso Robles area has been gaining more attention for its wine every year. Winery-hopping here may not be as convenient as it is in the Napa and Sonoma Valleys, but the fact that the wineries are spread out helps maintain an easy-going country atmosphere (something that is long lost in Napa and Sonoma). There are more than 25 wineries around Paso Robles, but if you have only a limited amount of time, stick to the wineries on the west side of Highway 101. For the most part, we found that these smaller establishments had the most charm and warmth to offer.

BONNY DOON, at Sycamore Farms on Highway 46 West, Paso Robles, (805) 239-5614, is an unusual winery because of its setting on the Sycamore Natural Herb Farm. A charming tasting room is combined with the Herb Farm's gift shop, so the U-shaped tasting bar is trimmed with dried bunches of herbs, potted plants, seeds, and unique gift items. After sipping and shopping, visitors are invited to peruse the well-marked gardens. $2 per glass tasting fee.

CASTORO CELLARS, 1315 North Bethel Road, Templeton, (805) 238-0725, is a small, family-owned winery with something for everyone. There is an antique-filled tasting room, a lovely countryside picnic area, a cute gift shop, and several farm animals—the winery says they're for the kids, but we say they're for anyone who likes animals. Free tasting (for up to three wines).

JUSTIN VINEYARDS AND WINERY, 11680 Chimney Rock Road, Paso Robles, (805) 238-6932, (800) 726-0049, has an elegant European terra-cotta-tiled tasting room. After sampling the fine wines and satisfying your taste buds, wander through the beautifully maintained English garden to smell the fragrant roses. If you are partial to this peaceful setting, you may want to stay here all day and all night. This is a totally viable option if a room is available—Justin Vineyards runs a lovely bed and breakfast called **JUST INN** (see Hotel/Bed and Breakfast Kissing). Free tasting.

LIVE OAK VINEYARDS, 1480 North Bethel Road, Templeton, (805) 227-4766, is true to its name. Charming picnic facilities are set beneath ancient oak trees and beside acres of vineyards. The tasting room is housed in a former one-room schoolhouse that is more than 100 years old. $2.50 per glass tasting fee.

MASTANTUONO, 2720 Oak View Road, Templeton, (805) 238-0676, just off Highway 46, features an inviting gazebo behind the Tudor-style winery. A rustic, Italianate tasting room awaits inside. Free tasting.

SYLVESTER WINERY, 5115 Buena Vista Drive, Paso Robles, (805) 227-4000, looks merely functional and not particularly inviting from the outside, but don't be fooled by the utilitarian exterior. The unique tasting room has the best gourmet cheeses and deli treats in town, so if a picnic is on your romantic agenda, be sure to stop here first. Free tasting.

TOBIN JAMES CELLARS, 8950 Union Road, Paso Robles, (805) 239-2204, is on the east side of Highway 101, unlike the other wineries we have mentioned. Wine Country meets the Wild West in the 100-year-old saloon turned tasting room, which is filled with cowboy paraphernalia. A fun (and unique) time is sure to be had here. Free tasting.

Harmony

You couldn't find a better name for this small country town that takes up less space than a city block and has a population of only 18 people. A handful of art galleries, pottery and gift shops, and a small wedding chapel created from a massive wine barrel make for an unusual country excursion (and an exceptionally unusual place to say "I do"). Be sure to visit the fascinating glass-blowing workshop, PHOENIX STUDIOS, (805) 927-4248, on the town's only street, where you might find a bit of Harmony to take home with you—the artists here produce some beautiful pieces.

Baywood Park

Hotel/Bed and Breakfast Kissing

BAYWOOD INN BED AND BREAKFAST, Baywood Park
1370 Second Street
(805) 528-8888
Inexpensive to Expensive

You may be skeptical the first time you lay eyes on this bed and breakfast. The building used to be a professional center, and the business-office look is still prominent; however, the undeniable treasures inside will more than alleviate any lingering doubt. Each of the 15 theme rooms is an explosion of style and romance, with views of south Morrow Bay. All of them provide an overnight escape to various romantic destinations. Where else can you spend one night in Manhattan, with fresh modern colors and a high-tech split-level layout; the next night in Santa Fe, under a high wood-beamed ceiling with a clean Southwest look; and the next in Appalachia, in a rustic hunting cabin with a romantic river-rock fireplace? And that's only three rooms! Other room styles include California Beach, Queen Victoria, Americana, and Quimper; all are tastefully executed and designed with the romantic traveler in mind.

Every possible need is foreseen, and each room is equipped with a wood-burning fireplace, queen-size bed, sitting area, microwave oven and refrigerator, television, telephone, and private bath. Wine and cheese are served on the mezzanine overlooking the tranquil bay across the parking lot and street, and a full breakfast is delivered to your room. A night in one of these rooms may inspire you to move to the part of the world that your room depicts, or at least plan a vacation there.

San Luis Obispo

Pronounced "San Loo-is Obispo," this busy community has the feel of a sprawling suburb, unlike the pastoral towns just north and south of here. While this may not be wholly advantageous, it does afford you a good assortment of lodging options to choose from.

Hotel/Bed and Breakfast Kissing

APPLE FARM INN, San Luis Obispo
2015 Monterey Street
(805) 544-2040, (800) 374-3705
Inexpensive to Very Expensive

Don't let the location of this inn, set on the edge of San Luis Obispo's business district, deter you from venturing inside. Although the inn is run like a hotel and the 103 rooms do have some hotel-like characteristics, they also have enough country charm to make them kiss-worthy. Some rooms have canopies over king- or queen-size beds, and the decor includes traditional country floral wallpaper and matching linens, gas-log fireplaces, private baths, and TVs hidden in attractive armoires. Sparkling cider and chocolate kisses are part of the welcoming package, and complimentary beverages can be delivered to your room. Continental breakfast is included and can also be delivered to your room by prearrangement. If you want the convenience of staying in town and you like the amenities found in hotels, but you are looking for country hospitality, then you will enjoy the Apple Farm Inn.

GARDEN STREET INN, San Luis Obispo
1212 Garden Street
(805) 545-9802
http://www.fix.net/~garden
Inexpensive to Very Expensive

Several orange trees brighten the exterior of this handsome Victorian inn, conveniently located on a side street within walking distance of downtown. The word that perhaps best describes the inn is nostalgic; from the upright grand piano in the library to the windup gramophone in the breakfast room, everything here has historical significance. You'll feel as if you've taken a step back in time when you walk through the door.

Each of the 13 guest rooms has a unique theme, such as "Field of Dreams" (Kevin Costner has been invited to stay here) or "The Lovers" (named after Picasso's famous painting and embellished with a gorgeous canopy bed and a Jacuzzi tub). Six guest rooms have Jacuzzi tubs (the remaining rooms have short claw-foot tubs), and five have fireplaces; all are beautifully appointed with refurbished antiques, reproduction radios with cassettes, queen- or king-size beds, and lovely wall coverings.

Evening wine and hors d'oeuvres are served downstairs in the comfortable library warmed by a large fireplace. In the morning, you can enjoy the generous homemade breakfast, which is brought to your individual table in a dining room surrounded by stained glass.

SYCAMORE MINERAL SPRINGS
RESORT, San Luis Obispo
1215 Avila Beach Drive
(805) 595-7302, (800) 234-5831
Moderate to Very Expensive

Nestled among oak trees in the peaceful countryside, this cream-colored, Mission-style resort is graced with an abundance of lush greenery and flowers. Natural mineral water hot tubs sit on a nearby hillside (see Outdoor Kissing), and the romantic **GARDENS OF AVILA RESTAURANT** (see Restaurant Kissing) is adjacent to the reception area. Although the resort has 50 rooms, we recommend only the 24 recently renovated, more contemporary guest suites. Dark green carpet, mahogany wood furnishings, gold-framed artwork, and a marble gas fireplace create an air of elegance in the sitting room of each suite. A big-screen TV and wet bar are also provided for your enjoyment. Relax on the comfy floral couch in front of the glowing fire, or daydream from the cozy window seat (though many just overlook the parking lot). In the bedroom, a queen-size four-poster bed covered with a paisley quilt is inviting. Each bathroom has a double-headed shower, and there is a large hot tub on a small private balcony.

Although the remaining 26 guest rooms do not share the same level of elegance as the suites, they still feature hot tubs on private decks. Unfortunately, thin walls, standard hotel layouts and bathrooms, and worn decor prevent us from recommending these rooms. At the time this book went to press, however, plans were being made to renovate them. We hope that the outdated decor and plain atmosphere in these guest rooms will be spruced up to match the rest of this attractive property.

Restaurant Kissing

GARDENS OF AVILA RESTAURANT, San Luis Obispo
1215 Avila Beach Drive, at the Sycamore Mineral Springs Resort
(805) 595-7365, (800) 234-5831
Moderate to Expensive
Breakfast, Lunch, and Dinner Daily

Romance is the focus at this contemporary restaurant, set on a wooded hillside as part of the **SYCAMORE MINERAL SPRINGS RESORT** (see Hotel/Bed and Breakfast Kissing). As a prelude to dinner, guests often start with a glass of wine near the glowing fireplace in the small, cozy lounge, which features an immense mahogany bar. In the restaurant dining room, towering palm plants frame a handful of tables topped with white linen tablecloths and brightly colored napkins. A cathedral ceiling with a massive wrought-iron chandelier and beautiful hanging ferns complete this picture, while tall windows allow a view of a rock wall and landscaped garden outside. The eclectic menu features a little of everything: firecracker chicken potstickers; shrimp pizza with sun-dried tomatoes, pesto, mozzarella, and goat cheese; prime rib; and grilled blackened swordfish topped with sautéed rock shrimp, cilantro, green onion, and tequila lime butter sauce. A rather strange mix of contemporary soft rock and jazz music accompanies your meal, but the friendly and efficient service and delicious food more than make up for it.

Outdoor Kissing

SYCAMORE MINERAL SPRINGS, San Luis Obispo
1215 Avila Beach Drive, at the Sycamore Mineral Springs Resort
(805) 595-7302, (800) 234-5831
$10-$12.50 an hour per person
Open 24 hours a day

Sycamore Mineral Springs is a mecca for vacationers with tired, city-weary muscles or achy backs. Climb the steep, winding footpath to one of the large redwood hot tubs that dot the terraced hillside, shrouded in brush and oak trees. Here you can reserve a tub for yourselves and soak to your hearts' content. In this peaceful forest setting, you will become as revitalized, relaxed, and connected with nature as you've ever dreamed possible. Well, almost. Although the brochure says the tubs are "secluded," do not expect to be unseen by other hot-tub lovers here. Although the tubs are enclosed by wood partitions on each side, it is easy to see into them when standing farther up the hillside. After dark, however, visibility is limited and lack of privacy is no longer as much of an issue (each tub comes equipped with lights to turn on or off). Be sure to ask for a spot that doesn't overlook the busy road below, and remember to bring your own robe (none are provided) for the sometimes chilly walk to and from the hot tubs.

Shell Beach and Pismo Beach

Although Shell Beach and Pismo Beach are suburbs of San Luis Obispo, the pace in these seaside communities is much slower than that in the neighboring town. Unfortunately, the only lodging options here are large hotels. We found only a few establishments that are worth your romantic consideration.

Hotel/Bed and Breakfast Kissing

THE SEAVENTURE RESORT, Pismo Beach
100 Ocean View Avenue
(805) 773-4994, (800) 662-5545
http://www.travelweb.com
Moderate to Unbelievably Expensive

Pounding waves, beautiful sunrises, scintillating sunsets, and the sheer majesty of the ocean provide the perfect setting for a romantic interlude. What better way is there to end (or start) the day than by taking a refreshing stroll along a sandy strip of beach? SeaVenture Resort is a beachside inn that offers easy access to the romantic Central California coastline. There are 50 somewhat nice hotel-style rooms at the SeaVenture, along with some standard hotel-style services such as mini-bars, televisions, room service, and a massage center. Fortunately, 43 of the rooms feature gas fireplaces and private balconies with hot tubs. Expect a very casual, contemporary beach-house feel, with hunter green carpet and painted walls, halogen lamps, floral bedspreads, white furniture, and wicker accents. In the morning, a light continental breakfast basket is delivered to your door at the hour of your choice. Enjoy pastries in bed as you watch the sun rise over the ocean.

The SeaVenture offers a year-round "Romantic Enchantment" package that includes an oceanfront room with a private balcony and spa, a restaurant voucher, roses, and a bottle of champagne. As with most hotels, the rates for this package are lower in the off-season, when you can also take advantage of the lack of crowds and enjoy your romance to the fullest.

Restaurant Kissing

PEZZULO'S BEACH HOUSE, Shell Beach
2665 Shell Beach Road
(805) 773-5618
Moderate
Dinner Daily

Don't forgo this small Italian eatery just because it's located in a shopping village. The view may not be noteworthy, but Pezzulo's authentic Italian cuisine and ambience are not to be missed. Green and white fabrics, large plants, little white lights framing the windows, and colorful watercolors depicting California beach scenes create a warm, welcoming interior. Service is prompt and friendly, portions are beyond generous, and the skilled kitchen staff puts heart and soul into such dishes as the pasta with peas, shallots, and prosciutto, and the special mixture of shellfish served in tomato sauce over linguine. We doubt that you will have room left for dessert, but if you do, try the tiramisu—this delectable dish is worth ordering only when you know it is made from a traditional recipe, and Pezzulo's version is sure to please.

Santa Maria

Outdoor Kissing

FOXEN CANYON DRIVE, Santa Maria

From Highway 101 south, exit onto Highway 154 south heading to Los Olivos. Turn right onto Foxen Canyon Drive. From Highway 101 north, head north on Highway 154 near Santa Barbara and continue past the town of Los Olivos. Turn left onto Foxen Canyon Drive.

Hold onto your stomachs and keep your eyes on the road—this rural country drive is not only winding, it's chock-full of breathtaking farmland that stretches as far as the eye can see. Lush green meadows are dotted with horses and cattle, quaint ranch fences divide the sprawling properties, and gnarled old oak trees seem to take on a life of their own. The road leads to seven wineries, and each one has something special to offer. Turn right at the T in the road (about halfway down) and conclude your drive at the **RANCHO SISQUOC WINERY** (reviewed below). This is a great drive for some loving conversation, and the delightful scenery is about the best you'll find anywhere.

WINE TOURING IN THE SANTA YNEZ VALLEY

From Highway 101 near Santa Barbara, head north on Highway 154 to Highway 246 and turn left. The first winery you will come to is the Gainey Winery, near the town of Santa Ynez.

The Southern California resurgence of enology is as promising as it is intriguing. The majestic Santa Ynez Mountains and valleys are home to a fair number of wineries that are vigorously trying to compete with their Northern California cousins. If you've toured the Napa and Sonoma Valleys, the size of these vineyards could be disappointing. After all, this rich, verdant land, kissed by the sun and perfectly cooled by ocean breezes, has lain fallow until just recently. If you have a penchant for tasting young wines, then a day trip through this select countryside is definitely worth the time and trouble. What can that do for your amorous dispositions? If the scenery doesn't evoke heightened emotions, a picnic at one of these beautiful, inspiring wineries will.

The most visually stirring wineries in the area are **BYRON VINEYARDS**, 5230 Tepusquet Road, Santa Maria, (805) 937-7288; **GAINEY VINEYARD**, 3950 East Highway 246, Santa Ynez, (805) 688-0558; **RANCHO SISQUOC WINERY**, 6600 Foxen Canyon Road, Santa Maria, (805) 934-4332; **SANFORD WINERY**, 7250 Santa Rosa Road, Buellton, (805) 688-3300, (800) 426-9463 in California; and **ZACA MESA**, 6905 Foxen Canyon Road, Los Olivos, (805) 688-3310, (800) 350-7972. These wineries, nestled in picturesque settings embraced by the mountains, are blessed with penetrating views. They have lovely outdoor seating where some potent afternoon memories can be fomented.

Los Olivos

Flanked by abundant vineyards and the rugged Santa Ynez Mountains, the small town of Los Olivos could easily be missed if you weren't looking for it. The town center consists of only a few blocks, but there are a surprising number of good little restaurants and small shops to keep you busy (at least for a while). What will not be busy, though, is the atmosphere of the town. With a population of only 900, the small-community charm of Los Olivos is not at all endangered.

Hotel/Bed and Breakfast Kissing

LOS OLIVOS GRAND HOTEL, Los Olivos
2860 Grand Avenue
(805) 688-7788, (800) 446-2455
Very Expensive to Unbelievably Expensive
Minimum stay requirement on weekends

In the heart of tiny Los Olivos and the Santa Ynez Valley is the luxurious, stately Los Olivos Grand Hotel. From the looks of the modest town, you would expect the lodging here to be rustic and countrified, but there is absolutely nothing rough around the edges at this hotel. Everything from the furnishings to the service displays polish and sophistication. Ten of the spacious country-style guest rooms are located in the main house, and the 11 others are across the street in a building called the West Wing. Attractive detailing such as beamed ceilings, fireplaces, down comforters, and hand-painted tiles create a country-Victorian atmosphere that is sure to please. Five of the rooms have Jacuzzi tubs, and there is a swimming pool and an outdoor Jacuzzi tub for all to enjoy.

Wine and hors d'oeuvres are served in the handsome main-floor bar each afternoon, chocolates are left on your pillows at turndown time, and a full breakfast is presented in the hotel's lobby every morning. The only disappointment we encountered was that the breakfast of scrambled eggs, fried potatoes, and bacon strips was not kept adequately warm, and the rather standard breakfast fare did not fit with the otherwise wonderfully elegant surroundings and service. The hotel's restaurant, **REMINGTON'S** (see Restaurant Kissing), is a different story altogether; you can count on Remington's for a completely satisfying lunch or dinner in a more formal setting.

Restaurant Kissing

MATTEI'S TAVERN, Los Olivos
Highway 154
(805) 688-4820
Moderate to Expensive
Lunch Friday-Sunday; Dinner Daily

Set just off the highway and nestled in the quiet town of Los Olivos, this rustic, exceptionally quaint white frame building looks like anything but a tavern. Built in the late 1800s, Mattei's Tavern was a private residence and hostelry for many years. The story of how it came to be a tavern is fairly involved, but if you would like to get a feel for the home's history, ask for a flyer describing Mattei's colorful past.

Today, this place offers much that is aesthetically suitable for an early-evening interlude. Wisteria drapes over a trellis-covered outdoor patio, and sunlight streams through the windows of the enclosed garden room, where white wicker furniture is arranged. A second, more authentically Victorian-style dining room has wood floors, antique furnishings, a massive stone fireplace, lace-shaded windows, and inviting, well-spaced tables. The food is country-fresh American—not fancy, just very good—and the service is warm and welcoming.

REMINGTON'S, Los Olivos
2860 Grand Avenue, at the Los Olivos Grand Hotel
(805) 688-7788
Expensive to Unbelievably Expensive
Lunch Monday-Friday; Dinner Daily; Brunch Saturday-Sunday

After a day of touring the Santa Ynez Wine Country, Remington's provides an idyllic place for a romantic repast. The formality of the dining room may seem out of place at first, but candles flickering at every table and dimly lit wall sconces will quickly set the mood. Warm pink tones create a sense of intimacy and complement the antiques and fresh flowers placed around the plush dining room. The eclectic menu is a potpourri of cuisines, with an emphasis on Californian and touches of Cajun and Thai. We recommend the blackened halibut with lemon-orange mustard marmalade and the stuffed filet mignon in bourbon creme with wild mushrooms.

Ballard

Most people are tempted to stay in the Santa Barbara area when visiting this part of the Central Coast. Do yourselves a favor and consider this less crowded, far more tranquil town. A few days here will help you rediscover what the words "serene" and "calm" really mean.

Hotel/Bed and Breakfast Kissing

THE BALLARD INN, Ballard
2436 Baseline Avenue
(805) 688-7770, (800) 638-2466
Expensive to Very Expensive
Minimum stay requirement on weekends

You couldn't find a more stunning place for a leisurely escape than this charming inn, set in the midst of the rolling valleys and vineyards of the Santa Ynez Valley. A white picket fence frames the sprawling contemporary farmhouse, and an old-fashioned veranda adorns the front of the building. A large wood-burning fireplace warms the gracious reception area and the main-floor dining room, **CAFÉ CHARDONNAY** (see Restaurant Kissing). A grand oak staircase leads to the authentic Americana guest rooms that range in style from Western to country-elegant to grandmotherly. Affectionate, handsome details abound in all 15 guest rooms, including stained glass lamps, antiques, polished hardwood floors, exquisite handmade quilts, cozy down comforters, and comfortable sitting areas. Seven of the rooms also have wood-burning fireplaces to snuggle beside.

Downstairs, the expansive living room, warmed by yet another fireplace, is the site of a generous, delectable afternoon wine tasting, complete with hot and cold hors d'oeuvres that may include quiche, chicken skewers, and crab dip. In the morning, enjoy a formal gourmet breakfast at a linen-covered table for two in the charming dining room. The tantalizing menu includes such choices as eggs Benedict with a perfect hollandaise sauce; a Danish omelet with Jack cheese, sausage, and mushrooms; or a feather-light waffle with real maple syrup. With a morning start like this, your day in the country is bound to be good.

Restaurant Kissing

THE BALLARD STORE RESTAURANT AND BAR, Ballard
2449 Baseline Avenue
(805) 688-5319
Moderate to Expensive
Dinner Wednesday-Sunday; Sunday Brunch

Colorful flower boxes trim the windows of the charming Ballard Store, and a white picket fence frames the building. Here, in what feels close to the middle of nowhere, you'll find a well-known restaurant serving a remarkable array of international dishes that are beautifully prepared. The countrified ambience is simple and the dining room caters to many families and large groups, so sounds of conversation and laughter from neighboring tables can be intrusive. But the real focus here is the food. Most evenings the menu includes a prix fixe dinner (an unbelievably affordable $20.95 per person) that may offer artichoke hearts baked with garlic butter and cheese, a rich bouillabaisse swimming with fresh seafood, and decadent desserts.

Romantic Suggestion: Gourmet picnic baskets can also be ordered in advance for a perfect afternoon outing. The price is $15 per basket, and the minimum order is two baskets. There are various picnic options to choose from; selections include fresh fruit and cheeses, half of a roasted chicken, French bread, and chocolate-chestnut mousse; or pâté and crackers, prawns stuffed with cheese and cocktail sauce, home-cured olives, and pound cake with raspberries. Except for beverages and something to sit on, the Ballard Store provides everything you will need—the only difficulty will be leaving the goody-filled basket alone until you reach the picnic site.

CAFÉ CHARDONNAY, Ballard
2436 Baseline Avenue, at The Ballard Inn
(805) 688-7770, (800) 638-2466
Moderate to Expensive
Dinner Wednesday-Sunday

Located on the first floor of **THE BALLARD INN** (see Hotel/Bed and Breakfast Kissing), this charming little restaurant serves up regional favorites in an elegant country atmosphere. A massive oak mantel and green marble fireplace mark the focal point, and burgundy-covered tables with fresh flower bouquets are placed around the room. As the name suggests, the wine list offers about 20 chardonnays, but other varietals are also available. The grilled salmon in local chardonnay-caper sauce is a must-try, but if you are looking for something richer, consider the roasted chicken with herbs, mushrooms, and pan juices or the roasted pork chop in Dijon sauce.

Solvang

It's one thing for a town to pay homage to its founding fathers, but Solvang goes a bit overboard. The Danish motif of every storefront is clichéd and all-pervasive; there must be more than 200 businesses here thriving on busloads of tourists caught up in Nordic mania. Despite our feelings that Solvang does not inspire kissing, it must be inspiring something, because the town is thriving. Perhaps the relatively new outlet mall has something to do with it.

Hotel/Bed and Breakfast Kissing

THE ALISAL GUEST RANCH, Solvang
1054 Alisal Road
(805) 688-6411, (800) 425-4725
http://www.alisal.com
Unbelievably Expensive
(price includes breakfast and dinner)
Minimum stay requirement

Nestled in the quiet Santa Ynez Valley, the Alisal encompasses an awe-inspiring 10,000 acres of wilderness and ranchland, which are yours to enjoy as a guest here. Memories of summer camp will come rushing back when you see the list of activities. Every imaginable diversion is available: golf, tennis, lawn games, horseback rides, moonlight dinner excursions to a private lake, fishing, windsurfing, sailing, hayrides, and outdoor barbecues, to mention only a few. (For romantic purposes, a sunset ride should be foremost on your list, but be aware that horseback riding, golf, and tennis involve additional charges unless you have booked a package that includes these activities.)

The guest units are spread out over the property in rambler-style ranch cottages. The 73 homey rooms vary in size, but we found the executive studios the most pleasantly appointed. Southwestern decor with terra-cotta tiles, whitewashed wood paneling, and pastel prints dress up the rooms, and each one has a king-size bed, a wood-burning fireplace, and an outside patio. As for the other units, the studio rooms and two-room suites have dated furniture and are done in darker color schemes, which make them feel a bit dowdy. Still, wood-burning fireplaces and small refrigerators are found in every room, and if you are here to take advantage of all the ranch activities, you probably won't spend a lot of time in your room. An outdoor pool and Jacuzzi tub are surrounded by well-cared-for grounds and ancient sycamores (*alisal*, in Spanish) that gently bow in the wind.

Part of life at the Alisal are the meals (breakfast and dinner) that are included with your stay. A generous breakfast buffet is presented each morning, or menu selections can be ordered à la carte; hearty Western-style and traditional American dishes are offered for dinner. In addition, four reasonably priced restaurants are open for lunch (not included in the price of your room). Breakfast and dinner are both served in the Ranch Room, the Alisal's frontier-inspired main dining hall, which has a brick fireplace, plaid carpeting, red tablecloths, and lanterns at every table. Dinner is a much more formal affair than everything else at the ranch—men are asked to wear jackets and women to "dress appropriately."

Once you have settled into life at the Alisal, you will have a whole new appreciation for the concept of "home on the range." The easygoing atmosphere and slower pace found here is something you could easily get used to.

Romantic Warning: Families flock to the Alisal during spring break, winter vacation, and summer recess. If possible, try to time your visit for when the kids are in school.

Santa Barbara

Santa Barbara has been widely praised. Words such as "idyllic," "heavenly," "flawless," and "irresistible" crop up regularly, and more than one travel expert has referred to it as California's own Shangri-la. Those who have visited this oceanside mecca know that these superlatives are not far from the truth. Against all odds, Santa Barbara has remained small enough to be picturesque and yet is large enough to please most urban sophisticates. It combines the wealthy influence of Los Angeles' upper echelon with the nonchalant, lackadaisical attitude of the young and those who think it's still 1968. In the elegant haute-couture boutiques, the funky hangout-type cafes, and the crowded boulevards along the beach, you can observe the coexistence of very different lifestyles. Regardless of where you fit in the lifestyle spectrum, you will find almost every building, park, promenade, and view to be radiant, desirable, and unbelievably romantic. Satisfy your own curiosity by taking the time and effort to discover this place for yourselves. Yes, it gets crowded. The exodus from Los Angeles northward on weekends can be, to say the least, arresting. But once you arrive and settle down, the masses will seem to disperse, and all you will notice are the blue waters of the Pacific, the undulating profile of the Santa Ynez Mountains, and the carefree sounds of your own laughter and joy.

Romantic Suggestion: Santa Barbara has something for everyone: wineries, hikes, whale watching, tennis, bicycling, flea markets, antique shops, museums, windsurfing, scuba diving, island excursions, and sightseeing attractions. To become more familiar with all the physical and aesthetic opportunities available, stop at the **VISITOR INFORMATION CENTER**, located at the corner of Cabrillo Boulevard and Santa Barbara Street, (805) 965-3021.

Romantic Note: One of the primary reasons to visit the Santa Barbara area is to spend hours luxuriating at the beach, basking in the sun's glory and feeling the sand slide beneath your toes. To avoid the crowds who also want to wallow in this Pacific Coast beauty and warmth, drive north from town on Highway 101 and look for the handful of signs that point the way to off-the-beaten-path beaches. To reach **MESA LANE BEACH**, follow Cliff Street to Mesa Lane, where it dead-ends at the beach. **GAVIOTA BEACH** is located off Highway 101, a few miles south of Gaviota. **REFUGIO STATE BEACH** is in Goleta, just off Highway 101. You won't be entirely alone, and during July and August nothing out here is really a secret, but these beaches won't be quite as intensely populated as the oceanfront walk along Cabrillo Boulevard in the heart of Santa Barbara.

Hotel/Bed and Breakfast Kissing

BATH STREET INN, Santa Barbara
1720 Bath Street
(805) 682-9680, (800) 549-2284 (in California),
(800) 341-2284 (in the U.S.)
Moderate to Expensive
Minimum stay requirement on weekends

Built as a 50th wedding anniversary present for the original owner's wife, the Bath Street Inn has a history of romance. Nestled on a residential palm-lined street near the heart of downtown Santa Barbara, the inn actually consists of two buildings: a modest Queen Anne Victorian home and a small cottage tucked behind. A manicured lawn and flower gardens grace the exterior, and a porch bedecked with chairs and potted flowers welcomes you. In the main house, a wood-burning fireplace warms the cozy antique-filled parlor. All of the eight countrified guest rooms are affectionately homey, with touches such as gabled ceilings and floral wallpapers. Country decor is found in each bright and sunny room throughout the inn, along with a phone, television, and private bathroom (although some rooms have only showers); five rooms have Jacuzzi tubs for two. Several rooms also have gas fireplaces and offer views of the ocean or the spectacular Santa Ynez Mountains. A scrumptious full breakfast of scones and cheese-and-egg frittata, blueberry pancakes, or peach-and-cheese French toast is served in the small dining room of the main house. Weather permiting, you can enjoy your morning repast beneath the blossoming wisteria embracing a citrus tree on the outside brick courtyard.

CHESHIRE CAT INN, Santa Barbara
36 West Valerio Street
(805) 569-1610
http://www.cheshirecat.com
Expensive to Very Expensive
Minimum stay requirement on weekends

We're not exaggerating—every room at this bed and breakfast is charming, intriguingly romantic, beautifully decorated, and filled to the brim with heart-tugging ambience. The colors and furnishings throughout the Cheshire Cat can only be described as creative. Each of the 14 suites has either a queen- or king-size bed, English antiques, a private bath, large windows, and beautiful Laura Ashley wall coverings. Special amenities in some rooms include fireplaces, private patios, high ceilings, attractive sitting rooms, and large, wood-framed beveled windows that let the sun stream in. In three of the most desirable rooms, you can "soak" up the romance in a "heart-stopping" Jacuzzi tub.

In keeping with the inn's name, all of the room labels are extracted from *Alice in Wonderland*. Don't let that cute quirk worry you; it is the only eccentric nuance here. Everything else is Victorian elegance and plush comfort. For example, the burgundy-and-gold Queen of Hearts Room has a private flower-filled patio and a two-person whirlpool tub set in a large bay window overlooking the gardens. Tweedle Dum, one of the two rooms located in the adjacent Coach House, is a deluxe two-room suite that also has a two-person Jacuzzi tub.

If the weather cooperates, an expanded continental breakfast is served at pink-lined tables on the tiled garden patio, where tables are bordered by flowers and a white-trellised gazebo. Otherwise, the morning meal is presented in the Victorian dining room, at one large table.

Romantic Note: Don't expect hands-on attention from the innkeepers; this is not that kind of bed and breakfast. You are pretty much on your own at the Cheshire Cat, which can be preferable for those looking for privacy. One small warning, though: the inn's location near the heart of Santa Barbara means that traffic noise is apparent at busy times of the day.

EL ENCANTO, Santa Barbara
1900 Lausen Road
(805) 687-5000, (800) 346-7039
Very Expensive to Unbelievably Expensive
Minimum stay requirement on weekends

As you drive up the winding road through the tree-covered residential hills of Santa Barbara, you will leave the accelerated pace of the city behind. El Encanto literally means "the enchanted," and the setting is just that. This venerable network of Spanish Colonial cottages and villas overlooks a dazzling Mediterranean-like landscape of glistening blue ocean, sparkling cityscape, and forested mountains.

In its heyday, El Encanto attracted Hollywood stars such as Clark Gable, Hedy Lamarr, and Carole Lombard, to name a few. It is no wonder that the ten acres of lush gardens and charming bungalows were once a playground for the rich and famous. Today, however, that glamorous image has faded somewhat, and many of the 84 units are in need of renovation. Thankfully, each one is still extremely private, but if you aren't careful, you could end up with a poorly lit room decorated with mismatched furniture dating back to the 1970s and a bathroom that is desperately in need of new wallpaper. Some rooms have been recently refurbished, though, and these are the only ones worth your romantic consideration. These sunny units have light color schemes, wicker and Shaker-style furnishings, and white shutters.

Meals are not included with your stay, but the elegant on-site restaurant is open for breakfast, lunch, and dinner daily (see Restaurant Kissing).

FOUR SEASONS BILTMORE, Santa Barbara
1260 Channel Drive
(805) 969-2261, (800) 332-3442
http://www.fshr.com
Unbelievably Expensive
Minimum stay requirement on weekends

The Four Seasons Biltmore is a four-star hotel with an eight-star mentality. It effortlessly lives up to its reputation of superb style and genteel, gracious service. Everything about this palatial resort is gilt-edged, grand, and efficient. The burnished white adobe resort with red-tiled roofs is harbored next to the ocean and surrounded by beautifully landscaped gardens. Once a preeminent oceanside estate, it was left practically intact when it was refurbished to its present stature.

The baronial Spanish-tiled lobby area is just the luxurious beginning of your stay here. Though many of the guest suites are fairly traditional and hotel-like (with fairly stiff rates), most of them also have private balconies or patios that overlook the ocean, mountains, and gardens. Several suites should have their own price category called "Beyond Belief"; these are decorated in beyond-belief fashion with arched windows, Spanish tiles, and opulent appointments.

The Four Seasons Biltmore isn't exactly intimate and may be best suited for conventions and business meetings. But then again, if your expense account can handle the dent and your tastes run toward exclusive surroundings and lavish detailing, you'll find it to be unsurpassed in the entire Santa Barbara area.

The Biltmore is also well known for its more casual restaurants, which include **THE PATIO** (Expensive), set in a lovely garden, and **LA SALA LOUNGE** (Moderate to Expensive), which has stunning ocean views. If you're looking for a more formal affair, however, we whole-heartedly recommend the elegant **LA MARINA** (see Restaurant Kissing).

Romantic Note: A private waterfront nightclub, health club, and Olympic-size pool complex are across the street from the Biltmore. If you are a guest at the hotel, you have full membership privileges during your stay. In all of our traveling and research, this is one of the most exceptional hotel amenities we have discovered.

THE GLENBOROUGH INN, Santa Barbara
1327 Bath Street
(805) 966-0589, (800) 962-0589
http://www.silcom.com/~glenboro
Inexpensive to Very Expensive
Minimum stay requirement on weekends

A beautifully tended yard with fragrant rosebushes frames this Crafts-man-style house, located on a tree-lined residential street within blocks of downtown. There are five rooms in the main house and six more in two adjacent historic cottages. Each light and airy guest room is charmingly deco-rated with mismatched antique furnishings, floral prints, and dark wood accents. Various rooms have canopy beds, lace curtains, fireplaces, and daybeds; most (but not all) of the rooms have private baths, and two have Jacuzzi tubs. Our favorite room is the Nouveau Suite, which has its own private entrance, a garden setting, and a private redwood deck and patio. All guests have access to a private hot tub, and the outside garden is a wonderful setting for wine and hors d'oeuvres in the evening. Extra touches such as romantic dinners for two delivered to your room (by request only), and a full hot breakfast delivered to your door in the morning help make this simple country inn a romantic haven for two.

THE MARY MAY INN, Santa Barbara
111 West Valerio Street
(805) 569-3398
http://www.silcom.com/~ricky/mary.htm
Expensive to Very Expensive
Minimum stay requirement on weekends

Take a trip back in time at The Mary May Inn. This European-style bed and breakfast is made up of two historic homes near downtown Santa Bar-bara. One building, a stately blue Colonial Federal, overflows with elaborate French furnishings and effects from the palaces of Versailles and Trianon. The imperial decor is a bit on the flamboyant (almost garish) side, but if pomp and circumstance are what your hearts desire, you'll love this place. Just across the street, an 1880 Queen Anne Victorian holds four more rooms, which are decorated in a more subtle French country style.

The eight rooms in the Colonial Federal are decorated with regal ap-pointments and furnishings. Ornate canopied beds are draped in yards of satin, and small crystal chandeliers reflect prismatic light about the room. Down comforters, tiled bathrooms, fireplaces, and sitting areas are addi-tional comforts. Three of the rooms in the Victorian have standard-size whirlpool tubs, and the fourth has an oversized claw-foot tub.

Decadent desserts, another rich benefit of staying here, are served each evening. In the morning, generous breakfasts are presented to all guests in the Colonial Federal's dining room or on the outdoor patio. This gourmet morning meal is one of the best you'll find anywhere.

Romantic Warning: The Mary May Inn's location near the heart of downtown Santa Barbara is convenient, but the street can be very busy (and noisy) during rush hour.

OLIVE HOUSE INN, Santa Barbara
1604 Olive Street
(805) 962-4902, (800) 786-6422
Moderate to Very Expensive
Minimum stay requirement on weekends and holiday weekends

This rather oddly shaped Craftsman-style manor, set in a quiet residential neighborhood, is about as homey as they come. Each of the six rooms is appointed with mismatched contemporary furnishings, a cozy queen- or king-size bed with a down comforter, a view of the city or the surrounding mountains, and a private bath with shower. (Only one room has a private bath that is detached.) Hunter green carpet, floral wallpaper, and dark wood furnishings throughout add to the comfortable appeal. Two of the rooms also feature outdoor hot tubs on private decks, making them highly desirable choices. In the morning, a full breakfast is served family-style in the large dining room.

THE PARSONAGE, Santa Barbara
1600 Olive Street
(805) 962-9336, (800) 775-0352
Moderate to Very Expensive
Minimum stay requirement on weekends

Although there is nothing extravagant about The Parsonage, you couldn't ask for a more comfortable home away from home. Originally built as a parsonage for a nearby church in 1892, this small Queen Anne Victorian has been affectionately restored. The five guest rooms and one suite are comfortable, even though the appointments are a bit mismatched. All of the rooms have a collection of fascinating antiques, including an unusual Chinese rug in the Rosebud Room and a gorgeous antique king-size bed in the Las Flores Room. Our favorite is the Honeymoon Suite, which entices couples with a bedroom, solarium, and windows that overlook the city, mountains, and distant ocean. Wine and hors d'oeuvres are presented in the afternoon, and a full gourmet breakfast is served either on a sundeck over-looking the surrounding neighborhood or inside in the formal dining room.

SECRET GARDEN INN AND COTTAGES, Santa Barbara
1908 Bath Street
(805) 687-2300, (800) 676-1622
http://www.secretgarden.com
Inexpensive to Expensive
Minimum stay requirement on weekends

It's no wonder this bed and breakfast is named Secret Garden—the flower-covered grounds are absolutely gorgeous, with brick pathways meandering between the buildings. Two guest rooms are in the main house, four rooms are in a backyard bungalow, two more are in the little house next door, and there is one self-enclosed private cottage. Don't worry if this layout sounds chaotic—it's not. The emphasis here is on rest and relaxation with a flair for country living. Although the rooms could use some sprucing up, each one is decorated with an interesting assortment of antiques and secondhand fur-nishings, and accented with appealing details. Hummingbird is the only room that includes a Jacuzzi tub on its own private deck. Wood Thrush, the private little cottage, is the largest unit, with a king-size bed, claw-foot tub, and beach-house atmosphere. New carpet and some replacement linens would do a world of good for the Secret Garden Inn, but until then, this is still an adequate kissing locale.

Every evening, wine and hors d'oeuvres are followed by a late-night sam-pling of sweets and apple cider in the main living room. Breakfast is often served on the garden patio under generous shade trees. The service here is gracious, and the overall attitude is serene.

SIMPSON HOUSE INN, Santa Barbara
121 East Arrellaga
(805) 963-7067, (800) 676-1280
http://www.simpsonhouseinn.com
Expensive to Unbelievably Expensive
Minimum stay requirement on weekends and holidays
Recommended Wedding Site

Lodgings like the Simpson House Inn make us question our four-lip rating system—this exalted inn goes above and beyond our romantic expec-tations and deserves at least ten kisses. Shielded from its downtown Santa Barbara location by formidable sandstone walls, this stately bed and break-fast is camouflaged by tall hedges and a wrought-iron gateway. The stunningly renovated Victorian mansion sits atop a one-acre knoll of manicured lawns and flowering gardens. Petite English cottages hold more units behind the house, and sprawling oaks and blossoming magnolias dot the grounds with country refinement.

It's no surprise that the Simpson House is consistently named one of the best bed and breakfasts in Southern California in all types of polls—who would argue? Each of the 14 guest rooms is elegantly secluded, and all are lavishly enhanced with varying combinations of teak floors, white wicker furniture, English lace, antiques, Oriental rugs, down comforters, fireplaces, and French doors that open onto private sitting areas. Enjoy the murmurs of the courtyard fountains from the garden cottages and barn suites, all of which are sensationally private and exquisitely outfitted with canopied feather beds and lovely antiques.

A sumptuous breakfast and evening wine and hors d'oeuvres are served on the vine-laced veranda overlooking the gardens. The only difficult part of staying at the Simpson House Inn is the fact that you'll eventually have to leave and return home. Fortunately, you will leave with a new appreciation for the finer things in life—including each other.

TIFFANY INN, Santa Barbara
1323 De La Vina Street
(805) 963-2283, (800) 999-5672
Expensive to Very Expensive
Minimum stay requirement on weekends

Flowers and trees partially shield this green-trimmed gray Victorian inn from the street, and lovely clay-potted begonias brighten the porch steps. As the innkeeper took us on a tour of this lavishly renovated mansion, we sighed at each turn. Each of the seven cozy rooms is attractive and inviting, with antique furnishings, queen-size beds, and Tiffany-style stained glass lamps. One has a canopied brass bed, a wood-burning fireplace, a tiled sunken Jacuzzi tub, and a separate sitting area. Amenities vary from room to room, but they include private terraces, wood-burning fireplaces, down comforters, Jacuzzi tubs, TVs and VCRs, and engaging views of the surrounding trees and greenery. All of the rooms have private baths, and all have marvelous garden or mountain views. A full breakfast is served either inside at the dining room table or outside on the tree-encircled veranda overlooking the garden. Wooden benches in a brick courtyard offer the opportunity to relax and enjoy the flower-scented atmosphere. An evening at this ultra-relaxing inn will definitely rejuvenate both of you.

THE UPHAM, Santa Barbara
1404 De La Vina Street
(805) 962-0058, (800) 727-0876
Moderate to Unbelievably Expensive
Minimum stay requirement on weekends

A manicured lawn and a large palm tree accent the exterior of the Upham, a stately Victorian hotel with the intimate ambience of a bed and breakfast. From the moment we entered the cozy lobby, we knew we were in for a treat. A comfortable two-person couch is arranged in front of a glowing fireplace, and sunlight spills into a small adjacent glass-enclosed sitting room.

There are 50 guest rooms and suites located in eight different buildings on this attractive property. The real finds here are the 14 cottage-style guest rooms, set along a path that meanders through flower gardens and verdant lawns. Each simple country room has a private entrance, a large four-poster bed, mahogany antiques, and a small nondescript bath. Some rooms have private porches, secluded patios, and gas fireplaces; the Master Suite features a wet bar, a Jacuzzi tub, and a private yard with a swinging hammock.

In the morning, an extended continental breakfast is served in the lobby or on the lovely garden veranda; wine and cheese are also offered here in the late afternoon and evening. You might want to try lunch or dinner at LOUIE'S (Moderate to Expensive), a bright and airy restaurant adjacent to the hotel which specializes in seafood and pastas

VILLA ROSA INN, Santa Barbara
15 Chapala Street
(805) 966-0851
Moderate to Very Expensive
Minimum stay requirement

Stroll down the busy street across from Santa Barbara's beachfront and you will find many unromantic, not to mention tacky, motels. Keep walking, and don't stop until you come to Villa Rosa. Once you enter this two-story Mission-style hotel with its stucco walls and red-tiled roof, you will immediately understand what makes Villa Rosa different from its neighbors. The hotel's attention to detail and overflowing friendliness let you know you've found a lovely seaside refuge.

All 18 rooms have contemporary Spanish-influenced furnishings and are generously sized. The stylish Southwest decor is simple and elegant, with neutral tones, exposed rough wood, ivory walls, dark plantation shutters, and private tiled bathrooms. Four rooms have fireplaces; some have a view of the water, but most view the street. Outside on the main floor, a plant-filled, nicely maintained courtyard surrounds a swimming pool.

Continental breakfast and wine and hors d'oeuvres are served in the gracious lobby. To illustrate what a wonderful artist's refuge Villa Rosa is, the inn's unique brochure says, "Henri Matisse never slept here, but if he'd been given the chance, he would have." Given the chance, you should too.

Restaurant Kissing

BLUE AGAVE, Santa Barbara
20 East Cota Street
(805) 899-4694
Moderate to Expensive
Dinner Daily

A smattering of dark wood tables and cozy booths fills the interior of this petite restaurant. The restaurant's intimate atmosphere is created by large fresh flower arrangements, yellow and rose sponge-painted walls, and windows draped with deep maroon velvet and gauze curtains. Small lamps illuminate each table, and a crystal chandelier glimmers in the soft light. The casual Mexican-influenced menu is eclectic and bound to satisfy any taste; there's an assortment of burgers, seafood, and pastas, as well as an astounding array of alcoholic beverages and bottled waters.

BLUE SHARK BISTRO, Santa Barbara
21 West Victoria Street
(805) 564-7100
Moderate
Lunch Monday-Saturday; Dinner Daily

Sunlight streams through the paned windows of this historic building into the stylish yet comfortable Blue Shark Bistro. Two cheerful dining rooms are accented with hardwood floors, hand-painted flowers along arched doorways, and fresh flowers at each white linen–covered table. Votive candles at every table and a fireplace in one dining room add an amorous flair, and the food (Californian with a spicy edge) will warm the senses.

Menu options include calamari fried with pesto and lemon, or filet of beef with horseradish sauce and roasted potatoes. The menu also offers a variety of homemade pastas, fresh seafood, and other creative dishes.

BRIGITTE'S, Santa Barbara
1325 State Street
(805) 966-9676

Inexpensive to Moderate
Lunch Monday-Saturday; Dinner Daily

Brigitte's is an extremely attractive, casual bistro that serves some of the freshest and most ingeniously prepared lunches and dinners in Santa Barbara. What makes this place a standout? We think it's the chic decor in basic black and white, and a menu devoted to a blend of European and California cuisine. An open bar with a marble counter is situated along one side of the restaurant, and an adjacent deli and bakery are attached to the bistro. Tables in the dining room are packed too closely for privacy, and there is nothing to soften the general "noisy cafe" sounds of this crowded restaurant; window tables offer the most opportunities for intimacy, but the foot and street traffic outside is still a romantic minus. If you're looking for a stylish ambience paired with excellent cuisine, Brigitte's is the place to be, so long as privacy is not a priority.

CHAD'S RESTAURANT, Santa Barbara
625 Chapala Street
(805) 568-1876
Moderate to Expensive
Dinner Daily

If you're looking for a romantic, upbeat dinner spot, you couldn't pick a better place. This refurbished, brightly colored historic Victorian home provides the perfect blend of pizzazz and elegance for an amorous encounter. Cozy two-person tables are covered with royal blue and white linens, and accented with small glass oil lamps and fresh flowers. Tables are arranged (sometimes a little too closely) throughout the house's original living and dining rooms. Sconces on terra-cotta-colored walls provide soft lighting, and a fire crackles in the antique marble-and-wood hearth that separates the two dining areas. Contemporary piano music accompanies your meal, taking your mind off the noisy, almost distracting, open bar. Although this popular restaurant is fairly crowded and the friendly service is a bit on the slow side, you can't go wrong with anything on the classic American menu. To get the most for your money, consider the Cajun sampler for two, a generous assortment of appetizers and seafood items. And don't forget dessert—the bananas Foster is exquisite.

CITRONELLE, Santa Barbara
901 East Cabrillo Boulevard, at the Santa Barbara Inn
(805) 963-0111, (800) 831-0431
Expensive to Very Expensive

Reservations Recommended
Breakfast, Lunch, and Dinner Daily; Sunday Brunch

Reservations at Citronelle are hard to come by on weekends, and we can see why. Ocean views from the wraparound bay windows are nothing less than dazzling. The upbeat dining room's casual ambience is crowded but comfortable, enhanced with attractive artwork, wicker chairs, and hardwood floors. We can't say enough about the tantalizing international cuisine the kitchen turns out consistently: the presentations are beautiful, and every taste is a bite of heaven. Porcupine shrimp with celery remoulade is a favorite, and the Japanese-style Norwegian salmon is wonderfully creative. The only disappointment here is the inexperienced staff; fortunately, the food, view, and ambience excuse all.

Romantic Note: Unfortunately, we cannot rave about the inn where Citronelle is located as much as we have about the restaurant itself. The near-waterfront location is a plus, but the rooms are merely hotel-standard.

DOWNEY'S, Santa Barbara
1305 State Street
(805) 966-5006
Expensive to Very Expensive
Dinner Tuesday-Sunday

Everything about this upscale streetside cafe is first-class. Large watercolors brighten the small, casually elegant dining room, and fresh floral arrangements adorn a handful of tables covered with peach and white linens. The menu changes nightly, but the California-style cuisine is always superb. Some of our favorites include the fresh local crab appetizer, served with papaya and lime-ginger dressing, pine nuts, and basil; braised pork loin with apricots and thyme; and fresh halibut in citrus-basil sauce. This restaurant's downtown theater-district location makes dinner and a show a convenient option; but even if you have already purchased your tickets, we know you won't be eager to rush out of Downey's—be sure to plan your evening accordingly so you can linger over a dessert.

Romantic Alternative: Right near Downey's is a sweet Italian eatery called **GISELLA'S**, 1311 State Street, (805) 963-8219 (Moderate to Expensive). A lot of tables are packed into the small dining room, but the lights are dimmed to a warm, intimate glow, and candles add to the ambience. Gisella's isn't fancy, but if you can't get a reservation at Downey's, this little spot is worth checking out.

EL ENCANTO RESTAURANT, Santa Barbara
1900 Lausen Road
(805) 687-5000, (800) 346-7039
Expensive to Very Expensive
Breakfast, Lunch, and Dinner Daily; Sunday Brunch

El Encanto Restaurant is indisputably one of the best places in Santa Barbara to watch the sun set, which immediately qualifies it as a Best Place to Kiss. Whether you choose to sit outside on the terrace or inside the sophisticated dining room, the stunning view will momentarily distract your attention from your lover's conversation. Meanwhile, your taste buds will be experiencing gourmet euphoria. The menu emphasizes California cuisine, and you can choose from an array of beautifully prepared fresh seafood, savory pastas, and delectable meats. And don't forget to leave room for dessert: El Encanto's homemade pastries and ice creams are the perfect finale to an enchanting evening.

Romantic Note: Breakfast and lunch here are casual affairs, but dinner is more formal: jackets are requested.

LA CAPANNINA, Santa Barbara
302 West Montecito Street
(805) 962-6366
Moderate to Expensive
Dinner Daily

Sip some Chianti, hold hands across the table, close your eyes, and smell the authentic aromas coming from the kitchen—you just might think you've been transported to Italy. This small restaurant is turning out some of the most genuine and hearty Italian favorites we have ever tasted (at least in California). The two dining rooms are appointed in an art deco style, with cushioned pink chairs in one area and black ones in the other. White lights adorn the walls, and candles flicker at every white linen–covered table. To enhance your meal, a pianist plays soothing melodies every night.

LA MARINA, Santa Barbara
1260 Channel Drive, at the Four Seasons Biltmore
(805) 969-2261
Expensive to Unbelievably Expensive
Dinner Daily

La Marina's sophistication and style are unparalleled in Santa Barbara, but that is not surprising—this restaurant is part of the **FOUR SEASONS BILTMORE** (see Hotel/Bed and Breakfast Kissing). Is there anything about the Four Seasons that isn't superlative? The sumptuous dining room is both rustic and elegant: exposed wood beams and a taupe-and-cream color scheme accent the stately overstuffed sofas, massive chandeliers, opulent antiques, and exotic flower arrangements. As you would expect, the fresh seafood and ever-changing nightly specials are impeccably presented and utterly delicious.

OYSTERS, Santa Barbara
9 West Victoria Street
(805) 962-9888
Inexpensive to Moderate
Lunch Thursday-Saturday; Dinner Tuesday-Sunday

Oysters might be an aphrodisiac, but that is not the only reason we are sending you here. Though the provocative menu happens to include oysters (and they're as fresh as can be), other seafood and pasta dishes are available and are just as good. This small restaurant is an intimate, sweet spot for lunch or dinner, but the lunch crowd is mostly made up of businesspeople. The inside dining room is semicasual, with an open kitchen, blush-colored walls, and neutral artwork. If you can ignore the busy street nearby, the outdoor patio is especially charming in fine weather.

An extensive fresh sheet changes daily, but all of the seafood is good. Try the cheese ravioli with pesto boiled shrimp and tomato-cream sauce or the pan-roasted tuna with cracked pepper, garlic, and red wine. Desserts such as homemade pie with whipped cream, and apple crisp with brown sugar–almond topping, are sure to leave you satisfied.

WINE CASK, Santa Barbara
813 Anacapa Street
(805) 966-9463, (800) 436-9463
http://www.winecask.com
Expensive
Breakfast Saturday-Sunday; Lunch and Dinner Daily

As the name implies, this sleek, sophisticated restaurant is the place to go for an extensive wine list. Set in a slate courtyard and surrounded by small shops, the Wine Cask also offers delectable fresh food prepared by an adept kitchen staff. Inside, modern artwork covers the walls, and wood-beamed ceilings are intricately etched in gold. A casual wine bar is set off to one side of the dining room, and each table is individually spotlighted from above, giving the room a stately atmosphere.

Classic dishes such as filet mignon grace the menu, but you may also be interested in the horseradish-and-herb-crusted salmon or the roasted duck breast with shiitake mushroom ragout. Presentation is lovely and the knowledgeable, professional wait staff can help you select a fine wine to accompany your meal.

Romantic Note: The restaurant is connected to a large wine shop, and the two establishments work together to put on special wine-tasting/dining events. These state-of-the-art evenings include champagne, hors d'oeuvres, lively conversation, and fun. Connoisseurs and novices alike can discover fine vintages in a cordial, polished atmosphere.

Outdoor Kissing

CHANNEL ISLANDS NATIONAL PARK
Island Packers Company
1867 Spinnaker Drive
(805) 642-1393
Prices start at $21 per person

To reach Island Packers Company, take Route 101 to Ventura. Just south of Ventura, take the Victoria Avenue exit south. Follow Victoria to Olivas Park Drive and turn west. Olivas Park Drive eventually becomes Spinnaker Drive.

The Channel Islands are an ecological preserve of enormous magnitude and productivity: a wilderness spectacle overflowing with perilous cliffs, windswept grasslands, and profoundly remote hiking trails with unparalleled vistas. You are almost certain to stumble upon rock-clad inlets, steep bluffs that lead to white sandy beaches, and tide pools with a miraculous amount of marine life. These waters are a prime destination for those who wish to explore nature's vast range of aquatic creations. From the smallest sea anemones to Pacific gray whales and everything in between, the wonders you see will overwhelm and delight you.

Island Packers is one of several tour companies that lead boating excursions to the Channel Islands, which lie 10 to 70 miles off the coast from Ventura. Choose a tour package that includes a sedate cruise to a tranquil island inlet for serene nature walks, or select one featuring phenomenal snorkeling and swimming in the clear Pacific waters. Some destinations along this wilderness chain are not for delicate individuals who are attached to their car phones and coiffed hairdos. A trek out here is for those with adventure in their hearts and a willingness to leave civilization far behind. By some standards, these volcanic islands might not seem to be a haven for romantic encounters. But once you embark upon a boat voyage to these ancient marine terraces, the exhilaration of the resplendent, immaculate territory that rises before you will make you feel nothing less than rapturous.

Romantic Note: Two of the islands have campsites where the only amenities available, including water, are the ones you pack in yourself.

WHALE WATCHING, Santa Barbara
Captain Don's, (805) 969-5217
Double Dolphin Cruises, (805) 962-2826
Whale Watching on the Condor, (805) 963-3564
Prices start at $24 per person

Several companies in the Santa Barbara area can take you on boat tours to witness the seasonal migration of the humpback, minke, blue, and California gray whales. Do not miss the opportunity to share this splendid adventure with someone you love. These magnificent creatures have an immense lesson to share with humans, a lesson that can be understood only when you see them for yourselves. Don't close your eyes if you do actually kiss on this trip—you might miss an extraordinary breach, wherein the whales propel their massive bodies entirely out of the water.

Montecito

Hotel/Bed and Breakfast Kissing

SAN YSIDRO RANCH, Montecito
900 San Ysidro Lane
(805) 969-5046, (800) 368-6788
http://www.sanysidroranch.com
Unbelievably Expensive
Minimum stay requirement on weekends

Located in the foothills above Montecito, San Ysidro Ranch provides cozy but spacious cottages scattered over well-landscaped gardens and grounds. This is a well-known getaway for the rich and famous, and the high prices are skewed to that clientele, but many feel it's worth the expense. Each unit offers an attractive interior, Frette linens, a goose-down comforter, a TV and VCR, an outdoor terrace, and a wood-burning stove or fireplace. Many of the larger rooms and suites have private outdoor hot tubs.

The best feature of San Ysidro Ranch, though, is the 540 wooded canyon acres that surround the resort. Here you'll find tennis courts, stables, an outdoor pool enclosed by trees, and miles of hiking and bridle trails. This is premium kissing territory. Two devoted souls can be as reclusive here as they choose.

Romantic Note: Parents can put their kids in a complimentary all-day camp during the summer months, and there are special accommodations for pets.

Restaurant Kissing

STONEHOUSE RESTAURANT, Montecito
900 San Ysidro Lane, at the San Ysidro Ranch
(805) 969-4100, (800) 368-6788
Very Expensive to Unbelievably Expensive
Breakfast, Lunch, and Dinner Daily; Sunday Brunch

A landmark in the area, the Stonehouse Restaurant is almost worth the hour-and-a-half scenic drive from Los Angeles just to enjoy the beautiful country setting. The outdoor terrace, sunroom, and lovely garden below all have striking views of the property. Inside, well-worn Oriental rugs adorn the wooden floor, the comfortable chairs all have rattan seats with cushions, and each table is covered with a linen cloth and graced by a single rose in a bud vase. Classical music completes the mood. Sunday brunch is the best bargain at $30 for three courses (bargain is a relative term here). The gourmet dinners are pricey, with such entrées as Maine lobster with foie gras and Colorado lamb with dim sum and eggplant compote. The service is flawless (the wait staff makes you feel like a celebrity, no matter who you are), and the food is some of the best we've had.

Summerland

Hotel/Bed and Breakfast Kissing

INN ON SUMMER HILL, Summerland
2520 Lillie Avenue
(805) 969-9998, (800) 845-5566
Expensive to Very Expensive
Minimum stay requirement on weekends and holidays

If it weren't for the busy highway running adjacent to this New England–style bed and breakfast, we would have given it four lips without a second thought. There is nothing the Inn on Summer Hill hasn't done to make this a thoroughly enchanting place to stay. All of the inn's 16 rooms are luxurious mini-suites, replete with gorgeous fabrics and color schemes, fireplaces, canopy beds covered with goose-down comforters, TVs and VCRs, Jacuzzi tubs, and spectacular views of the ocean (you just have to look past the highway). Continental breakfast is served family-style in the cozy country-style kitchen, and refreshments are served every afternoon in the lovely common area.

Romantic Alternative: If the Inn on Summer Hill is booked (which is likely), consider the nearby SUMMERLAND INN, 2161 Ortega Hill Road, (805) 969-5225 (Inexpensive to Expensive), also located next to the highway. The traffic noise is more noticeable here; still, the 11 country rooms in this Colonial-style house are pleasantly outfitted with quaint folk art, antique four-poster beds, and striking handsome quilts. Some rooms even have fireplaces and ocean views (but again, you have to look across the highway).

Ojai

Centuries ago, when the Chumash Native Americans discovered this paradise they named it Ojai, meaning "the nest," to describe how the mountains cradle the valley. This scenic wonderland, northwest of Los Angeles, is still enjoyed by the many visitors who take leisurely walks, ride horses past majestic sycamore and oak trees, and enjoy the mineral hot springs. Each evening, the setting sun bathes the Topa Topa Mountains to the east in a special glow known as the "pink moment."

Romantic Suggestion: Drive to nearby **MEDITATION MOUNT**, which has superb views of the sunset from a quiet promontory overlooking the valley. (The road branches off Ojai Avenue through a residential area; have your hotel direct you.) Another option is signing up with **PINK MOMENT JEEP TOURS**, (805) 646-2903 ($46 per person) for a three-and-a-half-hour jeep ride that uses every bit of its four-wheel drive to climb up the steep hills in Los Padres National Forest to get a close-up view of the Topa Topa Bluffs.

Hotel/Bed and Breakfast Kissing

OJAI VALLEY INN, Ojai
Country Club Road
(805) 646-5511, (800) 422-6524
http://www.ojairesort.com
Very Expensive
Minimum stay requirement on weekends

The Ojai Valley Inn is a "best-kept secret" that should be shared. Situated in a spectacular rural setting, it is a true break from urban life. The inn dates back to the early 1920s, and the property boasts over 5,000 trees, including many eucalyptus and oaks that are at least 250 years old. Well-tended flower gardens are everywhere, and the scent of honeysuckle lingers in the air.

Welcomed by a very attentive staff, you enter an adobe hacienda with beamed ceilings, tiled floors, fireplaces of native stone, and furnishings in earth tones. The 200 rooms follow the same theme and have private terraces facing the golf course and surrounding valley; some have wood-burning fireplaces as well. The spacious bathrooms are well stocked, and his-and-her bathrobes are provided so you can slip down to the fitness center for a steam and sauna.

If you like active vacations, pack your clubs and/or racquets and spend time on the world-class golf course and tennis courts, which boast a first-rate clubhouse. More rugged types can opt for guided hikes and horseback riding. If you prefer to stay closer to home, lounge by the pools, enjoy a walk around the beautiful property, or take advantage of the complimentary bicycles.

Special romantic packages, including "Romantic Honeymoon" and "Bed and Breakfast," give you many options at this marvelous retreat. During the summer months and holidays, interesting supervised activities for kids last the entire day, so you can enjoy your time together without distractions.

Romantic Note: There are two choices for dining at the inn. Enhanced by numerous paintings of Native American artifacts, the formal **VISTA DINING ROOM** (Expensive) serves up good (though not great) continental cuisine by candlelight with a view of the mountains in the background. Our favorite is the newly renovated **OAK GRILL & TERRACE** (see Restaurant Kissing), which is ideal for an intimate, relaxed dinner on warm evenings.

Romantic Alternative: If you're looking for something less expensive, the **OJAI MANOR HOTEL**, 210 East Matilija Street, (805) 646-0961 (Inexpensive to Moderate) is a charming bed and breakfast in the middle of town. The only drawback is that the six guest rooms share the three bathrooms.

Restaurant Kissing

L'AUBERGE, Ojai
314 El Paseo
(805) 646-2288
Moderate to Expensive
Lunch Saturday-Sunday; Dinner Daily

Massive oak trees and splendid mountain views must have seduced the romantic who, in 1910, decided to build a rambling mansion in the Ojai Valley. Seventy years later, the Franssen family moved into this spectacular site and soon opened their home to serve country French-Belgian cuisine.

L'Auberge, which means "country inn," provides a relaxed, provincial atmosphere for loving gourmands year-round. During warmer months dining on the terrace is preferred, with views of the Topa Topa mountain range in the distance and shade provided by latticework. When the temperature drops, the dining room offers a cozy setting for an intimate meal, with traditional country furnishings and paintings, and tables covered with white lace tablecloths. As you sit by the light and warmth of a stone fireplace, enjoy classic

French dishes such as *coq au vin* or the fresh fish of the day. All the desserts are homemade in the kitchen, and dark chocolate mousse is the specialty *de la maison.*

OAK GRILL & TERRACE, Ojai
Country Club Road, at the Ojai Valley Inn
(805) 646-5511
Moderate
Lunch and Dinner Daily; Sunday Brunch

Completely remodeled since our last visit, this wonderful restaurant now earns a high recommendation for its romantic setting and ambience. Heavy wrought-iron tables and chairs on the lattice-covered terrace face an un-spoiled view of the golf course, backdropped by the distant mountains. Emphasizing the best local foods and wines, the casual fare includes delicious choices such as hearts of romaine tossed with warm grilled chicken, olives, feta cheese, and pinot noir vinaigrette; and local swordfish with toasted couscous, portobello mushrooms, and basil. And best of all, the prices are very reasonable for the first-class menu and service.

THE RANCH HOUSE RESTAURANT, Ojai
South Lomita Avenue, just off Tico Road
(805) 646-2360
Expensive
Dinner Wednesday-Sunday; Sunday Brunch

Off the beaten track, a few miles from town, is where you'll discover one of the loveliest restaurants in Southern California. "Garden setting" barely begins to describe the lush, inviting grounds. Well-concealed paths beckon you to take an intimate walk among the trees, and well-placed benches invite you to sit and enjoy a glass of wine and each other. When you're ready to dine, ask for one of the many tables on the outdoor terrace, which faces a rose garden on one side and a koi pond encircled by tall bamboo on the other. Soft classical music blends with the sounds of a nearby waterfall to put you fully at ease.

Then the hard part begins: trying to decide which of the many gourmet dishes strikes your fancy. The menu changes frequently, depending on what is in season, and local fruits and vegetables are picked fresh each day. Herbs are grown on the premises, and are featured in a variety of dishes. Boneless breast of chicken stuffed with a wild rice and cranberry dressing with wild boar sausage, and fresh swordfish grilled with lemon thyme butter and served with mango salsa are just two of the nightly sensations. Over 600 imported and domestic wines are on the extensive, award-winning wine list; order a bottle and drink a toast to your idyllic evening.

WHEELER HOT SPRINGS, Ojai
16825 Maricopa Highway
(805) 646-8131, (800) 9-WHEELER
Inexpensive to Moderate
Reservations Recommended
Lunch Thursday-Friday; Dinner Thursday-Sunday;
Brunch Saturday-Sunday

This down-to-earth resort is a day-use spa that offers naturally hot mineral baths, skin-care and massage services, and fine dining in the hand-built, rustic wood cabins. The focus of your trip should be the baths ($10 per half hour per person). After changing into bathing suits (or you can go *au naturel*), you and your beloved will be escorted to a private redwood hot-tub room equipped with a skylight, hydrojets, and an adjoining cold bath. The staff leaves fresh flowers and ice water in each room and rings delicate chimes when your time is up.

After the pampering of your choice, stop by the elegant restaurant for cozy creekside dining. The restaurant, for all the spa's earthy appeal, is fine dining at its best. The award-winning cuisine emphasizes French and Italian cooking. Offerings usually include several appetizers, soups, salads, pastas, risottos, and eight or more entrées, including meat, poultry, seafood, and vegetarian dishes. A drink in the adjoining 100-year-old tavern is a nice way to start dinner (on cooler nights, grab a seat by the fireplace). Weekend brunch features a wide range of choices, from eggs Benedict to healthy whole-wheat scones and fresh fruit. Champagne and fresh-squeezed organic orange juice are truly refreshing after a half hour in a hot mineral bath.

Romantic Note: Wheeler Hot Springs offers several package deals: the two best are a hot tub and brunch for two on Saturdays for $48, and dinner and baths for two on Thursdays, Fridays, and Sundays for $72. Call for other specials when making reservations.

Romantic Warning: We have received feedback from some of our readers that they weren't comfortable with the style of massage they received. Depending on how sensitive you are to the quality of your massage, you may be better off just enjoying the baths.

Death Valley

A sojourn in Death Valley is an amazing break from modern civilization. It's one of the few places on earth where the terrain is evocative of the moon's barren landscape. Yet the range of colors and topography are strikingly beautiful, from the snowcapped mountains to the contoured sand dunes on the desert floor. Death Valley is one of the hottest places on earth; temperatures soar above 120 degrees in summertime, which can stifle any romantic inclinations. For that reason, it's best to go at cooler times during the fall or in spring, when desert wildflowers are in bloom.

Two scenic highlights are **ZABRISKIE POINT** and **BADWATER**. Zabriskie Point is conveniently located five miles southeast of Furnace Creek (off State Route 190); it provides a close-up view of golden-hued rock formations that were formed when ancient lake beds pushed upward and were eroded over time by wind and water. Badwater is famous for being one of the lowest spots reachable by car, 279 feet *below* sea level, and is a short, scenic drive from Furnace Creek. (Badwater is located 18 miles south of Furnace Creek off Badwater Road.)

Romantic Note: Death Valley is approximately a five-and-a-half-hour drive northeast of Los Angeles. Keep in mind that you're traveling through desert, so there are long stretches between gas stations and rest areas.

Hotel/Bed and Breakfast Kissing

FURNACE CREEK INN, Death Valley
Highway 190
(619) 786-2345
Very Expensive to Unbelievably Expensive

Besides the breathtaking landscape, Furnace Creek Inn is the main reason a trip to Death Valley can be a romantic and memorable experience. When you come across this world-class resort, after driving through arid desert for more than two hours, it's hard to believe you're not seeing a mirage. This oasis receives plenty of water from a natural spring, so it's surrounded by lush vegetation, including palm trees, flower beds, and a garden with cobblestone walking paths.

Originally built in the 1920s for guests of the Borax Company, the inn features a mission-style theme that has remained through many additions and renovations. The 65 rooms, charmingly decorated in subdued earth tones, have comfortable chairs, small refrigerators, and televisions; a few even have fireplaces. Although the bathrooms are small, they have been attractively spruced up with brass fixtures and decorative tile. Bathrobes are provided and are especially appreciated after a dip in the spring-fed pool. If you request one of the rooms with a terrace overlooking the garden, you can sit in the late afternoon sun and enjoy the view while sipping an aperitif. The deck off the first floor (below the lobby) is open to all guests and also has a good vantage point.

Furnace Creek Inn is an ideal getaway, because there are no distractions. You really are in the middle of nowhere. However, there are tennis courts on the property, golfing and horseback riding are available a few miles away, and the concierge can arrange a guided walking tour for a nominal fee. You can also order a boxed picnic lunch and strike out on your own to take in the many natural wonders (the front desk provides maps and driving routes). Or you may choose to have a massage and spend a lazy day at the pool.

Romantic Note: There are two restaurants on the property. FURNACE CREEK DINING ROOM (Expensive), off the lobby, is more formal and expensive. (Jackets are required at dinner.) Both breakfast and dinner are prix fixe and include a number of courses, so this is not the place to go for a light snack. L'OTTIMOS RESTAURANT and the adjoining OASIS LOUNGE are wonderful alternatives for casual, relaxed dining (see Restaurant Kissing).

Romantic Alternative: If the prices at Furance Creek Inn are beyond your budget, nearby FURNACE CREEK RANCH, Highway 190, (619) 786-2345 (Inexpensive to Moderate) offers affordable rooms in a Western-style setting. This complex is like a small city, complete with post office, country store, coffee shop, swimming pool, stables, and a golf course at one end. It caters mostly to large groups, and the rooms are clean and simple but not luxurious, so you can't rely on setting alone to spark your romantic inclinations.

Restaurant Kissing

L'OTTIMOS RESTAURANT, Death Valley
Highway 190, at the Furnace Creek Inn
(619) 786-2345
Moderate to Expensive

After a day of hiking and sightseeing in Death Valley, come to L'Ottimos for a relaxed, intimate evening. Stone walls accent the rustic decor, which is softened by flickering candlelight. Comfortable armchairs and tapestried fabrics add to the cozy atmosphere, and window-side tables overlook the inn's well-kept garden. The Italian menu offers a good selection of reasonably priced salads, pastas, and fish and meat dishes, and the service is very attentive but unobtrusive.

Adjoining L'Ottimos is the **OASIS LOUNGE**, (619) 786-2345 (Moderate), a dark, sexy bar that features torch singers and cheek-to-cheek dancing. The walls are made of embedded native rock and crystals of borax from the nearby mines, and the massive ceiling supports are actual timbers taken from the trestles of the old Death Valley Railroad. Who would have thought we'd find all this elegance and romantic inspiration in the middle of a desert?

" *Every kiss provokes another.* "

Marcel Proust

$\mathcal{L}$os Angeles County
THE BEACH
Malibu

Hotel/Bed and Breakfast Kissing

MALIBU BEACH INN, Malibu
22878 Pacific Coast Highway
(310) 456-6445, (800) 4-MALIBU
Very Expensive to Unbelievably Expensive
Minimum stay requirement on weekends and holidays

One thing you quickly learn as a travel writer is never to rely on the information you read in a hotel or bed-and-breakfast brochure. We wouldn't call the information misleading, but most of it is embellished and evasive. Still, every rule has its exceptions. The brochure for this inn says: "Inviting interiors are a Malibu Beach Inn trademark.... Each room is designed to create the feeling of being in one's own private cottage on the beach.... Each room has a private balcony that provides unparalleled views from Point Dume to Palos Verdes, perfect for watching an ever-changing ocean filled with sailboats, surfers, dolphins, and sunsets." It may sound like hyperbole, but it is all true, and there is more. All 47 rooms are attractive, with wood-beamed ceilings, tiled fireplaces, hand-painted tile bathrooms (a few with spa tubs), and sliding glass doors that open to the nearby surf.

A complimentary breakfast is served in the tiled oceanfront lobby that adjoins a lovely outdoor terrace. There aren't any restaurants on the premises, but there are many nearby and the inn offers 24-hour room service with a light menu. Shaded beach chairs are provided so you can while away the day at nearby Surfside Beach.

MALIBU COUNTRY INN, Malibu
6506 Westward Beach Road
(310) 457-9622, (800) FUN-N-SURF
Expensive
Minimum stay requirement on holidays

This bed and breakfast is situated just off the main highway, high on a bluff overlooking the Malibu countryside. Its location, close to the beaches and mountains of Malibu, is superior. All 16 rooms are decent and sweetly decorated in a floral motif with wicker furniture. Our favorites are Room 17, with a view and a fireplace, and Room 16, with a large private deck and full ocean view. The restaurant serves casual lunches, which you can enjoy on an outdoor patio with a view of the ocean in the distance. One of the highlights of the Malibu Country Inn is the heated pool, which is surrounded by palm trees and flowers.

Restaurant Kissing

BEAU RIVAGE, Malibu
26025 West Pacific Coast Highway
(310) 456-5733
Expensive to Very Expensive
Dinner Daily; Sunday Brunch

If you're longing for an affectionate rendezvous, head to this charming restaurant and share a Mediterranean-style meal on the flower-filled patio. Although Beau Rivage is located across the street from the sea, the sunny dining room offers sweeping views of the ocean's tidal comings and goings. Such an atmosphere is sure to delight tired hearts in need of an escape from the usual. Tempting specials are out of the ordinary. Try the risotto with shrimp, clams, and mussels, or the medallion of venison with red wine–poached pear and watercress mashed potatoes. Beau Rivage is particularly provocative for a Sunday brunch or early dinner. Take your time; this is leisurely continental dining at its romantic best.

GEOFFREY'S MALIBU, Malibu
27400 Pacific Coast Highway
(310) 457-1519
Expensive to Very Expensive
Lunch and Dinner Daily; Brunch Saturday-Sunday

There is something sybaritic about sitting atop an oceanside cliff, with nothing to do but watch the resplendent blue horizon, appreciate the person you're with, and give your orders to a waiter who will attend to your every need. Geoffrey's offers all that and more. We suggest ordering the brochette of lobster, shrimp, scallops, ahi, and swordfish with mustard-tarragon sauce, and for a delectable dessert, try the chilled lemon soufflé. We would call the food "Malibu fare"; the management calls it an eclectic, cross-cultural experience. Regardless, ask to sit at an outside table tucked between palm trees, where the ocean mist will caress your face as the two of you savor whatever the moment brings.

Outdoor Kissing

PARADISE COVE, Malibu
28128 Pacific Coast Highway, next to Sand Castle Restaurant
$15 parking fee

From Malibu, take Pacific Coast Highway north past Pepperdine University to Paradise Cove Road. Turn left toward the ocean and follow the signs.

Paradise Cove is a small, private beach framed by cliffs on both sides. It's a great hideaway when you want to avoid crowds and curl up with a bottle of wine on the beach (public beaches do not allow alcohol). You'll also find showers, barbecue pits, and picnic tables.

Romantic Note: Nearby **SAND CASTLE RESTAURANT** shares the same parking lot, but you don't have to pay the $15 parking fee if you're going to dine. Its atmosphere is more casual beach than intimate elegance, but the price is right if you want to grab a quick bite.

POINT DUME BEACH, Malibu

From Malibu, head north on the Pacific Coast Highway to Westward Beach Road. Turn left and follow the road to its end at the parking lot below Point Dume. From the southern end of the parking lot, head out across the sand and look for the well-marked trail on the left.

Point Dume Beach is one of the most delightful beaches this area has to offer. The shore is surrounded by golden palisades and dotted with overflowing tide pools, and the surf is far less populated than at better-known Zuma Beach to the north. The only reason for the small numbers here is the remoteness of the area; access to this locale requires some degree of surefootedness and the desire to walk about a mile. Point Dume is not so remote that you will be the only ones around, but your privacy needs should be fulfilled here. On a clear day you can see large portions of the rugged coastline, as well as Catalina Island floating in the middle of a calm, measureless blue realm. Be patient enough to wait for sunset, when the sky will stage a stunning performance for just the two of you. The evening air can become chilly at the beach, so bring a sweater or a cover-up if you plan to watch the sunset.

Romantic Bonus: Whale-watching season begins in late December and continues through late March. Point Dume Beach is a great place to seek out gray whales and to spend time alone outdoors.

Topanga Canyon

Restaurant Kissing

INN OF THE SEVENTH RAY, Topanga Canyon
128 Old Topanga Canyon Road
(310) 455-1311
Moderate
Breakfast Saturday-Sunday; Lunch and Dinner Daily

Inn of the Seventh Ray is one of those rare places where the physical setting and interior ambience are in perfect harmony; the restaurant simply seems to merge with the countryside. Set next to a flowing creek a fair distance from the road, the building looks like a grand old church from the 19th century. Inside you'll find an eclectic collection of rustic rooms with wood-framed windows. Each dining room has a vaulted wood-beamed ceiling and a brick fireplace that fills the area with golden warmth. A large outdoor seating area next to the creek looks out over the valley. Tall lamp heaters next to each table warm the cool night air when the temperature drops past the comfort zone.

The inn serves gourmet health food that is simply delicious. The menu itself reads like a passionate love sonnet. You can easily slip into a mood that complements such a dining experience. Although many vegetarian specialties are served—including freshly baked breads and organic produce, wines, and herbs—meat dishes like lamb, chicken, and steak are also available.

Romantic Note: The road to the inn cuts through an area of Topanga Canyon that you wouldn't think of as enchanting; however, once you arrive, no other word could be more appropriate.

Outdoor Kissing

TOPANGA CANYON
Topanga State Park
20825 Entrada Road
(310) 455-2465
$5 parking fee

From the Pacific Coast Highway, head north on Route 27 (Topanga Canyon Boulevard) four and a half miles to Entrada Road. Turn right onto Entrada Road and follow it to the park entrance.

Under most circumstances, statistical-type information is not the least bit romantic. It's great if you're a surveyor, but it's not a basis for snuggling or affection. For example, knowing that Topanga State Park has 9,000 acres of terrain ranging from 200 feet to 2,400 feet above sea level, won't necessarily do a thing for you. How about if we told you that this park is the second-largest urban park in the nation? What might prove more enticing is knowing that acre after acre of this chaparral-covered wildland has been colored by multihued winter grasses and adorned with perennial flora and foliage. Now that has meaning! You can almost feel the ground move beneath your feet as you see the crest of a hill looming before you. As you stand at the top and the ocean reveals itself between interwoven hills, the only sound you'll hear is your lungs regaining their composure. The hiking here is ideal and more than worth a day trip away from the city.

The number of spectacular canyon hikes in the mountains surrounding the Los Angeles area is too great to outline properly in this type of book. Realistically, not everyone who wants romance has a pair of hiking boots or, for that matter, legs that can handle the job. Still, those who do can climb, walk, or saunter to their hearts' content throughout the backwoods of L.A. Part of this area is **COLD CREEK CANYON PRESERVE**, a paradise of splashing creeks, plummeting waterfalls, and, depending on the season, one of the most spectacular arrays of flora and fauna to be seen anywhere.

Romantic Note: Don't forget to put $5 in the parking meter, and place the parking pass on your dashboard. It won't be very romantic if you return to find a parking ticket on your windshield.

Calabasas

Restaurant Kissing

SADDLE PEAK LODGE, Calabasas
419 Cold Canyon Road
(818) 222-3888
Expensive
Dinner Wednesday-Sunday; Sunday Brunch

If you have had enough of beach life and are ready for something completely different, drive a short distance east from Malibu to Saddle Peak Lodge. You'll feel that you've traveled to another world. Whoever designed this rambling wood hideaway must have grown up mesmerized by *Bonanza*. The building itself is a huge sprawling log cabin that ascends four stories along a rocky point in the middle of nowhere. Inside, there are imposing stone fireplaces, rough-hewn oversize furniture, and interesting Western motifs wherever you turn. If the weather permits, you can sit outside on a stone patio with its own trickling waterfall. Here you can watch the valley succumb to nightfall as you sip warm brandy or a hot cup of coffee.

Meat is the primary culinary emphasis here, including wild game from all over the area. For those who prefer lighter fare, there are some fresh fish offerings, including grilled Lake Superior whitefish on a bed of fresh leaf spinach. This is indeed an isolated place for hearty country dining, where you'll feel far from civilization and closer to the one you're with.

Romantic Note: This remote location has no streetlights, so nighttime isn't just dark, it's *really* dark. Be careful and drive slowly; you could pass by the lodge and never know you'd missed it.

Pacific Palisades

Outdoor Kissing

WILL ROGERS STATE HISTORIC
PARK, Pacific Palisades
1501 Will Rogers State Park Road
(310) 454-8212
$6 parking fee
Open 8:00 A.M. to sunset

From the Los Angeles International Airport, take Interstate 405 north and follow signs to the park.

For those seeking hiking territory close to Los Angeles, this eucalyptus-lined estate is stirring, and the surrounding hills are glorious. The chaparral-covered slopes, dressed in shades of pale green and gold, are criss-crossed by paths that wind up and around to breathtaking vistas of the ocean to the west and the city to the south and east. The museum celebrating Will Rogers' life is interesting, but it won't ignite impetuous conversation or interaction. A wide lawn near the museum is a popular spot for picnic lunches and the polo grounds here host exciting weekend matches. Watching grown men and women maneuver steeds around a field as they chase a small ball with a mallet is not everyone's idea of affection-inspiring activity. However, it is fascinating to witness this elite sport at least once, just to see what it's like.

Santa Monica

Hotel/Bed and Breakfast Kissing

CHANNEL ROAD INN, Santa Monica
219 West Channel Road
(310) 459-1920
http://www.innaccess.com/cha
Moderate to Very Expensive

There are bed and breakfasts ... and then there is the Channel Road Inn. Quality of this caliber is scarce, and when you add to it all the necessary romantic touches, you have one of the most wonderful getaways in Los Angeles. The 14 rooms are beautifully done, with cushy firm beds, lush down comforters, fetching color combinations, and simple but unusual private bathrooms. Large framed windows in every room are draped in billowy fabrics and afford decent ocean views. This cleverly renovated mansion has an elegant, congenial atmosphere, and the earnestness of the innkeepers is felt and seen at every turn. Explore nearby **WILL ROGERS STATE HISTORIC PARK** (see Outdoor Kissing in Pacific Palisades), the Getty Museum, or the Santa Monica Pier; then return to the inn for a soak in the hillside spa—a great finish to a perfect day. Turn-down service includes white robes, homemade cookies, fresh fruit, and flowers.

In the morning, awaken to a tempting array of croissants, breads, muffins, fruits, and baked eggs. Breakfast is served in the lovely dining room or outside on the patio. If breakfast in bed sounds enticing, simply request that it be delivered to your room.

LOEWS SANTA MONICA BEACH HOTEL, Santa Monica
1700 Ocean Avenue
(310) 458-6700, (800) 235-6397
Expensive to Unbelievably Expensive

As you might expect of an oceanfront hotel of this size (350 rooms), the prices are high, the interior is attractive and cavernous, and the service is exemplary, not to mention stuffy. What might surprise you are the cozy guest rooms that are amenable to affection and relaxation. Yes, you'll also find many standard hotel rooms that are little more than passable, but the special rooms (with commensurate price tags) are nicely outfitted with over-size furnishings, thick comforters, and sand-colored fabrics and wall coverings. Regardless of what the concierge might tell you, the most intimate rooms are not the splendid, very expensive one-bedroom suites. Instead, choose one of the ocean-view rooms that are a little larger than standard size and simply gorgeous, with balcony seating for two that is nothing less than spectacular.

Loews has two restaurants; the casual **COAST CAFE** (Expensive) and the more formal **RIVA'S** (Very Expensive) are both very attractive. Although it's not very romantic, the Coast Cafe is bright and contemporary, with a large glass-enclosed deck offering glimpses of the Pacific. Riva's is more elegant, but also more stiff and formal: not necessarily romantic either. However, the food at both restaurants is good, creative, and at times actually brilliant.

Romantic Note: The Sunday brunch buffet at Loews is one of the most cornucopian and luscious in the area. Be warned that after a feast of this dimension, it might be difficult to kiss—or even breathe. The entire lobby is turned over to this extravaganza, which makes for a rather noisy Sunday morning.

SHUTTERS ON THE BEACH, Santa Monica
One Pico Boulevard
(310) 458-0030, (800) 334-9000 (reservations only)
Unbelievably Expensive

Some hotels just ooze sophistication and gracious living, while others dazzle with style and cozy romantic details. Shutters combines both to achieve what is best described as informal luxury. What a find! And what an exorbiant price tag for the ocean-view rooms. The accompanying setting, tasteful furnishings, whirlpool tubs, bright fabrics, sunny rooms, and sliding louvered doors add up to nothing less than an elegant seaside cottage getaway. Well, almost. This is still Santa Monica, there are 198 rooms at the hotel, and **ONE PICO** (see Restaurant Kissing) is *the* place to dine these days, so don't expect remote solitude. But, all in all, this is the best city escape on the water you'll find this close to Los Angeles.

Romantic Note: Downstairs on the beach is Shutters' casual restaurant, **PEDALS** (Moderate). The view is entertaining, the interior attractive, and the menu satisfying.

Restaurant Kissing

CAMELIONS, Santa Monica
246 26th Street
(310) 395-0746
Moderate to Expensive
Lunch and Dinner Tuesday-Sunday

Camelions is an informal restaurant with a rustic feel. After entering through a charming courtyard, you can choose a seat in the garden or opt for a cozy nook inside. The interior's earthy colors, adobe walls, and wood-burning fireplace conspire to create an enchanting setting, and some tables are quite private. Unfortunately, the courtyard is a bit run-down and the service is slow. But once your meal arrives, you'll find no fault with the excellent food. Highlights include the salad of Belgian endive with watercress and pears, the Louisiana crab and wild rice cakes, the gratin of penne pasta with asparagus and fontina cheese, and the grilled swordfish. With a little more attention, this could become one of the gems of the Westside.

MICHAEL'S, Santa Monica
1147 Third Street
(310) 451-0843
Expensive to Very Expensive
Lunch Tuesday-Friday; Dinner Tuesday-Saturday

Although Santa Monica's Third Street often conjures up images of crowded bars and street entertainment, just a block from all the activity is a restaurant that satisfys both the romantic and the gourmet. Rich, butter-toned walls lend a feeling of warmth to the restored private residence. An impressive art collection featuring works by artist David Hockney is displayed throughout the dining area. Instead of intimate dining indoors, we opted to enjoy our meal alfresco on one of the most luscious Mediterranean-style patios in Los Angeles. Soft white candles lit our table, an abundance of fresh flowers surrounded us, and we quickly came to appreciate Michael's concern for pleasing each of the senses.

Food is the ultimate priority here, and the service and presentation only enhance your memorable dining experience. Villeroy & Boch china and Christofle silver create the backdrop for such artfully presented nouvelle cuisine as Atlantic salmon salad with Roma tomato vinaigrette, Shelton Farms grilled chicken with tarragon and *frites*, and 28-day dry-aged New York steak. Every dish is lovingly presented.

If you and your loved one are on a budget, take heart. Tuesday through Thursday, Michael's offers prix fixe lunches and dinners ($26.50 per person for dinner) that include soup or salad, a choice of entrées, and dessert. Any occasion at Michael's is a special one, and you and your partner will leave feeling anxious to return.

ONE PICO, Santa Monica
One Pico Boulevard, at Shutters on the Beach
(310) 587-1717
Expensive
Lunch and Dinner Daily; Brunch Saturday-Sunday

Too few places in Los Angeles realize the potential of the beach as a wonderful backdrop for romantic encounters. With the recent addition of

One Pico, on Santa Monica Beach, this situation is vastly improved. The setting is exquisite. You'll know you're in good hands the moment you enter the circular drive, where a host of valets will greet you. Then stroll through the lobby and slide into your seat. (With luck, you might snag one of the tables near the wall of glass doors facing the ocean.)

A massive fireplace and a large arrangement of exotic flowers are the centerpiece of the dining room. Fresh fish dishes and light pastas are featured on the reasonably priced menu, which includes mushroom ravioli tossed in herbs, roast Chilean sea bass, and grilled veal chop with crisp potato cake. Appetizer portions are so generous that two could easily make a meal. Rockenwagner's famous bakery down the street provides the mouthwatering bread.

Romantic Suggestion: Before claiming your car, take advantage of the locale by taking a leisurely stroll on the beach.

VALENTINO, Santa Monica
3115 Pico Boulevard
(310) 829-4313
Expensive to Very Expensive
Lunch Friday; Dinner Monday-Saturday

Valentino, which is celebrating its 25th anniversary, is beloved by many couples who have celebrated their own special occasions here over the years. The three intimate dining rooms and glass-enclosed patio are awash in earth tones of rust and brown. Everything is comfortable, yet elegant. As you sink into the lovely fabric-covered chairs, you'll be invited to choose a wine from the widely praised list and order from the gourmet Italian menu. Pastas are the house specialty and are consistently done to perfection. Main courses include a selection of fresh fish, veal, and chicken, and desserts are delectable. If this is your first trip, you'll realize why people have been coming back for over two decades.

Venice

Hotel/Bed and Breakfast Kissing

THE VENICE BEACH HOUSE, Venice
15 30th Avenue
(310) 823-1966
Inexpensive to Expensive

There are not many traditional bed and breakfasts close to Los Angeles, but The Venice Beach House is a surprising exception that blends nicely into the oceanfront community that surrounds it. The large blue frame house is one block from the part of Venice Beach that is famous for its hordes of scarcely-clad roller skaters. The interior is simply but comfortably decorated, and most rooms are bright, attractive, and spacious (only five of the nine rooms have private baths). Overall it lacks polish and charm, even though one of the rooms has a Jacuzzi tub and another has a fireplace. Some of the rooms have new furnishings, and plush carpet has been added throughout, which is a welcome improvement. Homey and laid-back, The Venice Beach House is a respectable alternative to hotel accommodations—and the reasonable prices are hard to ignore. If beach property, a relaxing atmosphere, and hearty, full breakfasts are priorities for your heart and soul, then this is a place you could easily curl up in and call home.

Outdoor Kissing

OCEANFRONT WALK, Venice

Take Washington Boulevard east from Marina del Rey to Pacific Avenue and turn south. Continue for ten short blocks to Hurricane Street and park. The beaches are due west for the next two miles.

This isn't the part of Venice you're thinking of, the part you've seen in more movies and TV shows than you can count, where eccentric people stroll or roll by in droves. Actually, it's hard to imagine a beach anywhere in the Los Angeles area that isn't overwhelmed by locals and tourists alike. You can search for a long time to find a stretch of unoccupied shoreline. Just as options seem to be dwindling, here is one area you ought to visit.

Driving west along Washington Boulevard, you might normally plan to turn north along the coast, trying earnestly to avoid Venice Beach. If you turn south instead, onto this street that looks more like an alley, you will be surprised by what you'll find. The area is lined with small condominium-type apartment buildings. The units on the west side of the street border an expansive beach that is everything a beach should be: spacious, white, uncluttered, secluded … and vacant. Ah, the feeling of a gentle beach getaway: the softness of the sun enveloping you in a warm blush; a cushion of sand underneath your blanket; the surf's pulsating, rhythmic splashing onto the shore. Is it any wonder that the right beach with the right someone can provide the ultimate in romance? There are other sections of beach like this elsewhere (particularly down south and farther north), and if the temperature is below Southern California standards most of them will be empty. This location, however, is kissing reliable in almost any kind of weather.

Marina del Rey and Playa del Rey

Hotel/Bed and Breakfast Kissing

THE INN AT PLAYA DEL REY, Playa del Rey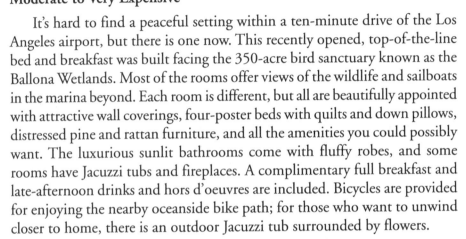
435 Culver Boulevard
(310) 574-1920
http://www.innaccess.com/pdr
Moderate to Very Expensive

It's hard to find a peaceful setting within a ten-minute drive of the Los Angeles airport, but there is one now. This recently opened, top-of-the-line bed and breakfast was built facing the 350-acre bird sanctuary known as the Ballona Wetlands. Most of the rooms offer views of the wildlife and sailboats in the marina beyond. Each room is different, but all are beautifully appointed with attractive wall coverings, four-poster beds with quilts and down pillows, distressed pine and rattan furniture, and all the amenities you could possibly want. The luxurious sunlit bathrooms come with fluffy robes, and some rooms have Jacuzzi tubs and fireplaces. A complimentary full breakfast and late-afternoon drinks and hors d'oeuvres are included. Bicycles are provided for enjoying the nearby oceanside bike path; for those who want to unwind closer to home, there is an outdoor Jacuzzi tub surrounded by flowers.

THE RITZ-CARLTON, Marina del Rey
4375 Admiralty Way
(310) 823-1700, (800) 241-3333
Very Expensive to Unbelievably Expensive

Of all the hotel chains across the country, The Ritz-Carlton is perhaps the most consistent when it comes to style, elegance, quality, and service: you can anticipate careful attention to detail and pampering at every turn. And this branch in Marina del Rey is no exception. Expect to find the distinctions The Ritz-Carlton is known for: rich, stately appointments and amenities, luxurious bathrooms, and conscientious, kid-glove treatment. Although the rooms are basically just very nice hotel rooms, they are comfortable and quite handsome. The hotel also offers tennis courts, a swimming pool, and, of course, a view of the marina.

    Romantic Note: THE DINING ROOM (Expensive) and THE CAFE (Moderate) both provide ultra-expensive, regal dining experiences. THE LOBBY LOUNGE AND TERRACE (Moderate) is a sedate, plush spot for cocktails and high tea.

    Romantic Alternative: THE MARINA DEL REY HOTEL, 13534 Bali Way, Marina del Rey, (310) 301-1000 (Moderate to Expensive) is a very attractive hotel in the heart of the marina; most of the rooms look out over the harbor. The casual atmosphere has hints of elegance, the service is surprisingly good for a hotel of this size, the rooms are fairly spacious, and the above-average hotel furnishings are very comfortable. The real find here is the **CRYSTAL SEAHORSE** (Moderate to Expensive), which serves excellent California cuisine in a serene and elegant harbor-view setting.

Manhattan Beach

Hotel/Bed and Breakfast Kissing

BARNABEY'S HOTEL, Manhattan Beach
3501 Sepulveda Boulevard
(310) 545-8466, (800) 552-5285
Expensive to Very Expensive

Barnabey's is patterned after 19th-century European hotels. Each of the 128 rooms here is individually decorated with antiques, brass lamps, lace curtains, and carved wooden bedsteads. But best of all, the hotel is only a short walk to the beach, and bicycles are available for those who want to go exploring. You may want to avoid the crowds altogether by taking advantage of the indoor pool and spa. A full complimentary breakfast is included, and the **AUBERGE AT BARNABEY'S** (Expensive) serves continental cuisine in an intimate setting.

Palos Verdes Estates

Restaurant Kissing

THE BISTRO OF LUNADA BAY, Palos Verdes Estates
724 Yarmouth Road
(310) 541-3316
Expensive
Dinner Tuesday-Saturday

Although the name has changed from J'Adore to The Bistro of Lunada Bay, we still adore this restaurant. The owner's *tres* French attitude is fully reflected in this out-of-the-way restaurant, located in a small shopping area in Palos Verdes Estates. The menu is outstanding, and the care with which the dinners are prepared is evident in every bite. In addition to traditional French dishes like bouillabaisse and terrine de foie gras, specials may include venison, wild boar, and quail. You'll also find lighter fare, such as angel-hair pasta with Canadian Bay shrimp. Wine tastings are held regularly, and the

Bistro features a five-course prix fixe menu for $40. All the scrumptious desserts are made daily. The Palos Verdes area offers one of the more exquisite drives near the city, and a dinner here would finish your day beautifully.

RIVE GAUCHE, Palos Verdes Estates
320 Tejon Place
(310) 378-0267
Expensive
Lunch Tuesday-Sunday; Dinner Daily

Set in a quaint shopping area just off the main street in Palos Verdes, La Rive Gauche is a popular spot. Locals know that this traditional restaurant is an attractive place for candlelit dinners and leisurely romantic conversation. Occasionally the quality of the traditional French cuisine isn't top-notch, but when it's good, it's very good. The fish is the freshest around, and the sauces are light and flavorful. A pianist plays nightly, and you can request your sentimental favorite to ensure that the evening lives on in your memories.

Outdoor Kissing

MALAGA COVE, Palos Verdes Estates

Palos Verdes is just south of Redondo Beach. If you are traveling on Pacific Coast Highway, turn west onto Palos Verdes Boulevard, which will take you into the hills along the coast. There is plenty of free parking around Malaga Cove. From Interstate 405, exit at Hawthorne Boulevard, take Hawthorne to Palos Verdes Boulevard, and turn west.

The Palos Verdes Peninsula offers a magnificent display of nature: the rugged cliffs are usually dotted with beautiful wildflowers, and waves rushing against the bluffs form foamy whitecaps as they break. Hiking trails meander along the hilly coastline and offer spectacular views of the coast all the way to Malibu. The Malaga Cove trail allows you to walk down a semisteep incline; at the bottom, you'll find some large rocks that provide the perfect place to sit and snuggle. This is a very private and secluded spot to watch the sun set into the Pacific Ocean.

Long Beach

Restaurant Kissing

RAGAZZI, Long Beach
4020 Olympic Plaza
(310) 438-3773

Moderate
Dinner Daily

Located next to the Long Beach pier, Ragazzi offers sumptuous Italian cuisine in an oceanfront bistro setting. Ragazzi was designed to re-create the mood of coastal Italy, so every seat in the place has a view. The outdoor dining area overlooks the beach, and has a huge fire pit and decorative lights. The authentic recipes were collected from Italian cities such as Torino, Bozen, Bologna, Firenza, and Potenza. After dinner, a coastal stroll is only steps away.

THE REEF, Long Beach
880 Harbor Scenic Drive
(310) 435-8013
Moderate to Expensive
Lunch Monday-Saturday; Dinner Daily; Sunday Brunch

There are not many restaurants in the Los Angeles area where you can dine in a French country setting, next to a glowing fireplace, with a spectacular view of the city lights reflecting off the calm water. The Reef is such a place. This restaurant is large but cozy, with overstuffed sofas in the entryway, a downstairs cafe, and an outdoor patio dining area directly overlooking the harbor. Each intimate booth is surrounded by bookshelves, lantern candles, and small antiques. For even more privacy, request a booth upstairs near the back. The limited menu, which emphasizes California-style fish and pasta dishes, is only somewhat reliable, but the atmosphere is really the high point here.

Outdoor Kissing

GONDOLA GETAWAYS, Long Beach
5437 East Ocean Boulevard
(310) 433-9595
$55 an hour for two people
Reservations Required

Gondola Getaways offers old-world boating right in the heart of Long Beach. Authentic Venetian gondolas cruise the narrow canals and waterways of Naples Island, next to the resort area of Belmont Shores. These narrow waterways (pollution-free, by the way) are remarkably secluded and lined by architecturally unique homes and crisscrossed by brick footbridges.

As you arrange yourselves in the gondola, you are handed a warm blanket to snuggle under. A basket of bread, cheeses, and salami is provided, as well as glasses and an ice bucket; it's up to you to bring the beverage of your choice. A gondolier gently guides the boat through the beautiful canals, accompanied by classical music. Nighttime cruises are especially romantic, as the moonlight spreads a golden mantle over the water.

Romantic Note: Reservations are required at least a week in advance. Gondola Getaways is open seven days a week, from 11 A.M. to 11 P.M. Boats that carry larger groups are also available.

Seal Beach

Hotel/Bed and Breakfast Kissing

THE SEAL BEACH INN AND GARDENS, Seal Beach
212 Fifth Street
(310) 493-2416, (800) HIDEAWAY
Expensive to Unbelievably Expensive

Located only a block from the beach, this restored vintage inn resembles an old-world country lodge. The 24 artistic suites and rooms are uniquely decorated with antiques and collectibles, from wrought-iron railings to ancient statuary. Lacy curtains, wall tapestries, and unusual linens are additional demonstrations of the care and attention given to every detail. Outside, the beautiful flowers and plants form a visual feast, and an eight-foot frescoed fountain from Paris stands guard over a lush patio adjacent to the swimming pool. A lavish buffet breakfast is included, and gourmet picnic baskets can be prepared upon request.

WEST LOS ANGELES

Beverly Hills

Hotel/Bed and Breakfast Kissing

THE BEVERLY HILLS HOTEL, Beverly Hills
9641 Sunset Boulevard
(310) 276-2251, (800) 283-8885
Unbelievably Expensive
Recommended Wedding Site

This film-industry landmark, located on 12 acres in the heart of residential Beverly Hills, is famous for being a favorite celebrity hideaway. The Beverly Hills Hotel has recently reopened in grand style after undergoing one of the most extensive restorations in history, to the tune of over $100 million. Such extravagance is relfected in every glorious detail. Each unique guest room has been elegantly appointed with warm colors, patterned fabrics, and original art.

All the rooms feature comfortable sitting areas, walk-in closets, attractive beds with Ralph Lauren linens, and full entertainment centers with TVs, VCRs, and CD players (an extensive video and CD library is available). Many rooms also offer terraces, wood-burning fireplaces, and separate entrances. The spacious baths are done in pink marble and Italian granite, and include a charming hat box filled with deluxe toiletries and terry bathrobes. If you can afford to splurge, choose one of the 21 bungalows scattered throughout the winding gardens. The privacy and luxuriousness of these bungalows make them ideal for a romantic tryst. As you roam the grounds, you'll also discover two tennis courts and a competition-size pool (flanked by private cabanas, lounge chairs, and a cafe for poolside dining). The "Pink Palace" is back and we're glad.

Romantic Note: The world-renowned **POLO LOUNGE** (Expensive), where many Hollywood deals have been cut, serves everything from breakfast through late-night suppers and offers both indoor and outdoor seating. More formal dining is available in the **POLO GRILL** (Very Expensive), and the **FOUNTAIN COFFEE SHOP** (Moderate) is still a favorite for a quick bite. The **SUNSET LOUNGE**, adjacent to the lobby, serves a wonderful traditional afternoon tea (see Restaurant Kissing).

THE BEVERLY HILLS INN, Beverly Hills
125 South Spalding Drive
(310) 278-0303, (800) 463-4466
Expensive to Very Expensive

Located a few blocks from the expensive shops and restaurants in the heart of Beverly Hills, this lovely 52-room inn is much less pricey than other hotels in the neighborhood. And the rates include complimentary parking and a full breakfast. Each room is tastefully decorated in subdued colors and has upholstered chairs, cable television, a mini-bar, and small, pretty bathrooms. The best feature is the outdoor pool surrounded by potted flowers and palms, where you can enjoy a lazy lunch. The intimate **GARDEN HIDE-AWAY ROOM** (Moderate) serves lunch and dinner in a tropical setting and is becoming quite popular with the locals.

THE BEVERLY PRESCOTT HOTEL, Beverly Hills
1224 South Beverwil Drive
(310) 277-2800, (800) 421-3212
Expensive to Very Expensive

As an upscale luxury hotel, the Beverly Prescott is a stunning example of how to wisely use $13.5 million to complete a major renovation. There is no comparison to what it once was as the Beverly Hillcrest; the past is now long forgotten in a blend of oversized furnishings, elegant detailing, and lush fabrics. The lobby is simply splendid, with beautiful pastels adorning the interior and black-and-white lawn furniture displayed on an outdoor court-yard. Each of the 140 sumptuous rooms has a private balcony and a grand bathroom with marble accents and a separate glass shower stall. The suites are romantically preferable because of their spaciousness.

Romantic Note: The Beverly Prescott's restaurant, **THE CHEZ**, (310) 772-2999 (Moderate to Expensive), is newly redecorated in vibrant colors, with cane armchairs and some banquettes. The best tables, however, are out-side by the pool. Breakfast is the most romantic time here, with a more relaxed clientele, but the menu soars for lunch and dinner. Exceptional, eclec-tic taste sensations include tostadas with ahi tuna and chopped salsa, and (for those whose romantic impulses are heightened by an oyster orgy) North-west oysters on the half shell with three sauces.

FOUR SEASONS HOTEL, Beverly Hills
300 South Doheny Drive
(310) 273-2222, (800) 332-3442
http://www.fshr.com
Unbelievably Expensive

Although the Four Seasons is technically across the street from Beverly Hills, it is very much on a par with the other hotels in this exclusive neigh-borhood in terms of stature and ambience. Everything is done right here. We were very impressed with the attentive service, and the regal, tasteful furnishings reflect the richness of European art. Most rooms have French doors, attractive views, and all the luxurious amenities you could ask for. Two highlights are the outdoor terrace and pool area, and the live jazz in the **WINDOWS LOUNGE** every Friday and Saturday evening.

Romantic Note: **GARDENS RESTAURANT** (Very Expensive) is an ideal spot for an intimate formal dinner. Tables are set discreetly apart in a number of small, attractive rooms. The Mediterranean menu is pricey, but features gourmet cuisine like smoked Norwegian salmon on a potato cake and oven-roasted veal chop with fava beans and grilled radicchio. And the desserts are delectable, especially the warm chocolate truffle cake with banana-rum ice cream.

THE PENINSULA HOTEL, Beverly Hills
9882 Little Santa Monica Boulevard
(310) 551-2888, (800) 462-7899
Unbelievably Expensive

Located in the heart of Beverly Hills, this extremely refined, stunning hotel is clearly a bastion for the local and international movers and shakers of the movie industry. Without question, this is the ultimate in deluxe hotel accommodations. Every floor has its own private valet, and each room has its own call button to summon service. Most rooms are designed to favor the pursuit of business, with private fax machines and phones everywhere you look. There is even a Rolls Royce available for complimentary lifts to Rodeo Drive and Century City, or for rent by the hour if you want to go off on a tour of your own. The list of amenities goes on and on. All of the rooms are beautiful, and the bathrooms are appropriately sleek and sexy. However, the most coveted guest locations are the villas with their own private entrances. Garden pathways lead you to these lavish accommodations, which feature private terraces, spas, and fireplaces. Sigh. You can't get much more majestic than this.

Romantic Note: BELVEDERE (Expensive), the hotel's restaurant, would be enchanting for almost any meal, but romance is not foremost on anyone's mind here. The food is exquisite, from the appetizer of Sonoma foie gras in black mushroom aspic to the entrée of baked sole in a herbed brioche crust with chervil butter. But this is a deal-making restaurant, and many a contract is signed after a meal here.

Romantic Suggestion: Even if you aren't a guest at the hotel, consider having afternoon tea in **THE LIVING ROOM** (see Restaurant Kissing).

THE REGENT BEVERLY WILSHIRE, Beverly Hills
9500 Wilshire Boulevard
(310) 275-5200
Unbelievably Expensive

This is one of the sexiest hotels we have ever seen. At most big-name hotels, it's the lobby area or the restaurants that elicit acclaim; the guest rooms tend to be just nice, average hotel rooms. This is not the case at the Regent. Even though the lobby is nice enough and the restaurants serve excellent food, the lush, beautifully appointed guest suites are where you want to be for a weekend with your special companion. You can embrace from here until eternity, or for as long as you can afford the stiff room rates.

These enormous suites have overstuffed sofas and chairs, ultra-thick down comforters, special windows that let the light in but keep the noise out, and tall ceilings. But their most alluring feature may be the sensual bathrooms, which are the size of most ordinary hotel rooms. The marble floor and counters frame a bathtub built for two, a separate glass shower stall built for a small crowd, and a lovely vanity area for *apres*-bath primping. All this comfort, combined with superb service, makes for an extraordinary getaway.

    Romantic Suggestion: Across the street from The Regent Beverly Wilshire is a stretch of shops (including a wonderful branch of Rizzoli's bookstore that serves cappuccino) reminiscent of a European street. **ONE RODEO**, at the corner of Wilshire Boulevard and Rodeo Drive, is a short upward climb and great for romantic strolling. The hill is paved in cobblestones, and the gorgeous Italian-style architecture is surrounded by flowing fountains.

Restaurant Kissing

CHEZ HELENE, Beverly Hills
267 South Beverly Drive
(310) 276-1558
Moderate to Expensive
Lunch Monday-Saturday; Dinner Daily

    Even from the outside, Chez Helene looks like the perfect place for a leisurely, quiet evening or an afternoon of warm conversation and ambrosial dining. The thatched-roof brick home is located on the outskirts of the Rodeo Drive shopping district, surrounded by office buildings and bustling stores. This architectural anomaly holds something very special inside. The casual interior feels friendly and quaint, with wood-beamed ceilings and hardwood floors. If you prefer, you can sit outside in the garden near the fountain. The small menu is authentically French and masterfully prepared (the three-course prix fixe dinner for $28 is a great buy), and the service is congenial and relaxed. Take your time as you whisper sweet nothings, because no one here will hurry you along.

IL CIELO, Beverly Hills
9018 Burton Way
(310) 276-9990
Moderate
Lunch and Dinner Tuesday-Saturday

    Most of the trattorias in Los Angeles are alike: good food, noisy cluttered atmosphere, tables lined up right next to each other, and brusque service that leaves emotions a bit jarred. For socializing that's great; for romance it's intolerable.

Il Cielo is different. First of all, everything served is wonderfully fresh and hearty, and there are some very creative appetizer and pasta combinations. Second, the amorous potential of this place is given an added boost by the vine-cloaked patio in front, embroidered with trellises, flowering plants, and comfortable, intimate seating. Inside, wooden tables, a glowing fireplace, and hand-painted ceilings make the interior as fetching as the exterior. A star-filled summer night would be well spent at this rare, inviting Italian cafe.

THE LIVING ROOM, Beverly Hills
9882 Little Santa Monica Boulevard, at The Peninsula Hotel
(310) 551-2888
Moderate
Breakfast, Lunch, Afternoon Tea, and Dinner Daily

Afternoon tea is such a refined, elegant way to pamper yourselves and indulge in each other's company. The Living Room, in **THE PENINSULA HOTEL** (see Hotel/Bed and Breakfast Kissing), is unsurpassed for this pleasure. A harpist's lyrical melodies soothe and refresh your senses as you sit in plush couches and overstuffed chairs reminiscent of the Victorian era. Beautiful place settings do perfect justice to the unfolding courses. The complete Royal Tea ($23 per person) consists of a glass of champagne, fresh straw-berries and cream, finger sandwiches, scones with jam and Devonshire cream, an assortment of delectable pastries, and, of course, your choice of tea from over a dozen blends. Formal gardens just outside offer an opportunity to walk off some of those newly acquired calories and to steal an embrace.

Romantic Note: On cool winter days, you may want to request the sitting area in front of the fireplace.

SUNSET LOUNGE, Beverly Hills
9641 Sunset Boulevard, in The Beverly Hills Hotel
(310) 276-2251
Moderate
Lunch, Afternoon Tea, and Dinner Daily

Newly renovated and reopened, **THE BEVERLY HILLS HOTEL** (see Hotel/Bed and Breakfast Kissing) is a Los Angeles landmark that harks back to the glamorous days of Hollywood. Afternoon tea is an ideal way to enjoy this rarefied atmosphere, and at a reasonable cost. Located adjacent to the lobby, the Sunset Lounge greets you with the sound of live harp music as you're seated in comfortable salmon-colored velvet chairs. A delicious assortment of tea sandwiches, scones, and fruit tarts and truffles accompanies aromatic teas served in Wedgwood china cups. The service is very attentive but unobtrusive. This is the perfect way to spend a cozy, intimate afternoon in beautiful surroundings.

Bel Air

Hotel/Bed and Breakfast Kissing

HOTEL BEL AIR, Bel Air
701 Stone Canyon Road
(310) 472-1211, (800) 648-4097
Unbelievably Expensive
Recommended Wedding Site

We are not exaggerating when we say the Hotel Bel Air is probably the best place to kiss in the Los Angeles area (if you can afford it). We are not the first (nor the last) starry-eyed romantics to rave about this luxury hotel. From the 11 acres of garden and forest primeval to the plush contemporary interior and overindulgent service, every detail will make you forget that this is a hotel. Instead, you will think you're living in a sumptuous fairy tale.

Each room is stunningly decorated with luxurious furnishings, and many have wood-burning fireplaces, balconies, and private patios. Glass doors draped in soft billowy fabrics frame the private entryways to some of the bungalow-like suites. Even the standard rooms are fairly plush and inviting, and the setting is really the best there is in the entire Los Angeles area. The dining rooms and adjoining bar/piano lounge are formal and handsome, yet they also feel soft and inviting, as if being close and whispering sweet nothings were also part of the menu. Numerous benches are sprinkled throughout the beautifully manicured grounds, and the elegant patio surrounding the outdoor swimming pool is a great spot for lunch. The Bel Air is a four-star experience by most standards; by ours, it's a four-kiss extravaganza.

Romantic Note: The Bel Air is actually more affordable than you might think, at least in comparison to other posh hotels in the area, and it is infinitely more refined and charming. The setting alone is well worth the price. Double-check your holiday budget and consider making your escape to this intoxicating, luxurious place.

Restaurant Kissing

FOUR OAKS RESTAURANT, Bel Air
2181 North Beverly Glen Boulevard
(310) 470-2265

Very Expensive
Lunch Tuesday-Saturday; Dinner Daily; Sunday Brunch

Four Oaks is one of those ambitious, alluring dining productions Los Angeles is famous for. What makes this particular epicurean cafe an ardent spot for lunch or dinner is its Beverly Glen Canyon setting; you'll feel you've left the city far behind. This cottage-like home has been redone to reflect polished country refinement, and is surrounded by oak and eucalyptus trees. The fairly petite rooms flow naturally, one into the other, though the tables are a tad too close for kissing comfort. Weather permitting, the outdoor patios are exceptionally lovely sites for dining. But what else would you expect in Bel Air? The food is a five-star celebration, from the smoked salmon cake with crisp potato to a four-course vegetarian "excursion" with all natural products, and the setting can't be beat.

Westwood

Restaurant Kissing

DI STEFANO'S, Westwood
1076 Gayley Avenue
(310) 208-5117
Inexpensive
Lunch and Dinner Daily

Westwood Village is UCLA territory, filled with bustling students and crowded movie houses. Amid this noisy, youthful atmosphere is a restaurant at odds with its surroundings. Hidden in the middle of Gayley Avenue, Di Stephanos is a family-owned restaurant that serves reasonably priced traditional northern Italian food. Sinatra love songs and '40s jazz establish a romantic ambience. Each of the eight cozy booths is surrounded by antique etched mirrors. A large wooden cupboard and flowered wallpaper give the room a genial atmosphere, while the candelabras and antique ceiling fan provide a touch of elegance.

PRIMI, Westwood
10543 West Pico Boulevard
(310) 475-9335
Expensive
Lunch Monday-Friday; Dinner Monday-Saturday

Primi is one stunning restaurant. The casual dining room includes a long black lacquered bar and views of the slick, open kitchen. Glowing candles on the linen-covered tables illuminate a sultry, romantic garden area. Dinner here is a delectable Italian experience: Primi is renowned for gourmet pasta dishes, such as the porcini mushroom ravioli and the black garganelli with grilled scallops and bacon.

Century City

Restaurant Kissing

LUNARIA, Century City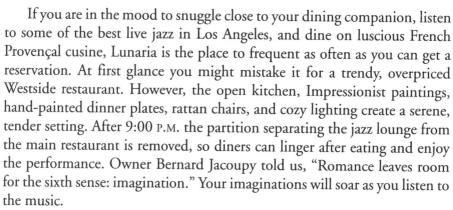
10351 Santa Monica Boulevard
(310) 282-8870
Expensive
Lunch and Dinner Tuesday-Saturday

If you are in the mood to snuggle close to your dining companion, listen to some of the best live jazz in Los Angeles, and dine on luscious French Provençal cuisine, Lunaria is the place to frequent as often as you can get a reservation. At first glance you might mistake it for a trendy, overpriced Westside restaurant. However, the open kitchen, Impressionist paintings, hand-painted dinner plates, rattan chairs, and cozy lighting create a serene, tender setting. After 9:00 P.M. the partition separating the jazz lounge from the main restaurant is removed, so diners can linger after eating and enjoy the performance. Owner Bernard Jacoupy told us, "Romance leaves room for the sixth sense: imagination." Your imaginations will soar as you listen to the music.

Romantic Note: If dinner at Lunaria is beyond your budget, a good alternative is to go for dessert. While enjoying the wonderful French delicacies, you will be able to view the stage. Or you can reserve a table in the jazz lounge ($5 per person per show) and order a snack there.

HOLLYWOOD AREA

West Hollywood

Hotel/Bed and Breakfast Kissing

THE ARGYLE, West Hollywood
8358 Sunset Boulevard
(213) 654-7100
Very Expensive to Unbelievably Expensive

Both inside and out, The Argyle is exceedingly elite and authentically art deco. If you are not an aficionado of the '20s, you could find the interior a bit much, to say the least. If you are an art deco buff, you will find that the guest suites reflect the same attention to elegance and detail as the public areas, but with a more sensual appeal. Sleigh beds, black-and-white tile baths, soaking tubs, intricate moldings, and shadowy lighting from sconces and recessed ceiling lights create a deluxe setting. There are 44 one-bedroom suites and 19 so-called standard rooms. The suites are preferable, but only because of space; all the other heart-stirring details are the same.

Romantic Note: The Argyle's restaurant, **FENIX** (Expensive), is too business-oriented for intimate dining, but breakfast or lunch on the terrace overlooking the city and the lap pool can be a soothing experience, once everyone puts away their cellular phones. All is forgiven when you begin what can be described as a dining production. Start your meal with the clam and mussel chowder or the rosti potato with golden caviar. The entrées are also impressive; our black cod roasted with fennel and spinach was delectable. Perhaps the only thing more tempting is the dessert selection. If you can ignore the business types, a rendezvous here can be nearly magical.

CHATEAU MARMONT, West Hollywood
8221 Sunset Boulevard
(213) 656-1010, (800) 242-8328
Very Expensive to Unbelievably Expensive
Minimum stay requirement on holidays

Chateau Marmont has been a legendary Hollywood hideaway since 1929. In fact, the management values privacy so much it didn't want us to include the hotel in this guidebook. We felt differently. The romantic possibilities are just too enticing to ignore. The building is modeled after a Loire Valley castle, and the sumptuous furnishings, wood-paneled walls, and beautiful throw rugs transport you to that elegant locale. A few bedrooms have garden views; the suites and bungalows feature full kitchens and dining rooms, and some have direct access to the outdoor pool. Who knows—you could end up in the same room Clark Gable shared with a paramour in times past.

Romantic Note: A small, intimate dining room (Expensive) serves breakfast, lunch, and dinner.

LE MONTROSE, West Hollywood
900 Hammond Street
(310) 855-1115, (800) 776-0666
http://www.travel2000.com
Expensive to Unbelievably Expensive

From the outside Le Montrose looks like an urbane, residential apartment building. Inside, it is an attractive, well-run hotel with amenities that make it one of the better places to stay in greater Los Angeles. Each of the spacious rooms features a gas-burning fireplace, settee, and tile bathroom with a large glass-enclosed shower. Up on the roof you'll find a wonderful swimming pool and a whirlpool spa with sweeping, unobstructed views of the entire area. The rooftop tennis court enjoys the same vista.

Romantic Note: A charming, petite restaurant on the main floor (Expensive) serves relaxing breakfasts and intimate lunches and dinners for guests only. The food is surprisingly good, but the atmosphere and privacy are even better.

WYNDHAM BEL AGE, West Hollywood
1020 North San Vicente Boulevard
(310) 854-1111
Expensive to Unbelievably Expensive

The Bel Age tries very hard to be a formal luxury hotel, and in some regards it succeeds, but essentially it is a very nice, slightly pretentious hotel. The lobby and hallways are decorated with interesting pieces of original artwork. From the rooftop sculpture garden and pool, which feature panoramic vistas of the city below, to the vine-trellised courtyard filled with massive, modern wood carvings, there is much to appreciate in addition to the accommodations. This is an "all suite" hotel, and some accommodations are more like apartments than hotel rooms. In smaller rooms, the bedroom area is separated from the living room by a raised platform edged with a wrought-iron banister. All of the rooms are attractively appointed with marble bathrooms and soft lighting. We have to admit that, in spite of everything, we were delighted with the Bel Age for the conveniences and the style.

Romantic Suggestion: If a culinary *tour de force* is part of your romantic itinerary, you would do well to have dinner at the Bel Age's DIAGHILEV, (310) 358-7780 (Expensive). This ultraexpensive, ultraposh dining room serves a unique blend of French and Russian cuisine that is sheer perfection. Soft classical music, deftly played on a harp and grand piano, creates a softly sentimental atmosphere for the entire evening. But the food is the true seduction here, so be prepared.

The more casual BRASSERIE RESTAURANT (Moderate) is a pleasant place to meet for breakfast before exploring the city or to enjoy live jazz on weekend evenings.

Restaurant Kissing

CAFE LA BOHÈME, West Hollywood
8400 Santa Monica Boulevard
(213) 848-2360
Expensive
Lunch Monday-Friday; Dinner Daily

The Italian Renaissance meets the Addams family at this slightly peculiar, yet distinctive restaurant. In many ways Cafe La Bohème is the epitome of romantic dining: the massive stone fireplace, towering wood-beamed ceiling, balcony seating, and handsome crimson-draped wood booths create a magnificent setting. Striking crystal chandeliers and immense windows add elegance and light. But the bizarre wall sconces, the strange statue at the entrance, and the almost gloomy Gothic feeling leave you wondering exactly who let this designer out of the house.

While you speculate about your evocative surroundings, dishes such as grilled pesto salmon with a wonderful citrus sauce or sliced duck breast with plum wine-ginger sauce easily bring the subject back to matters of the heart. After the main course has been fully savored, you can pull the drapes closed and relish the cappuccino mousse cake with hot fudge sauce or baked bananas in phyllo with butter pecan ice cream—topped by a kiss or two, of course.

DAR MAGHREB, West Hollywood
7651 Sunset Boulevard
(213) 876-7651
Expensive
Dinner Daily

At first glance, this place may seem a bit too commercial and popular to be truly romantic, but something unbelievable happens once you wander into this traditional Moroccan restaurant. More special occasions are celebrated here than almost anyplace else in the city. The inside is adorned with tiled mosaics and fountains. The aura is so enticing your skepticism will melt away and no one else in the restaurant will matter but the two of you.

The seven-course prix fixe dinner is a great deal at $30 per person. Feast on exotic food (eaten with your fingers), sink back into satiny pillows, and let the seductive music soothe your senses. While the belly dancers perform, allow yourselves to be pampered in a style once reserved for sheiks and caliphs.

EL COMPADRE, West Hollywood
7408 Sunset Boulevard
(213) 874-7924

Moderate
Lunch and Dinner Daily

Tucked away in the midst of Sunset Strip is a Mexican restaurant that practically transports you to a resort village south of the border. A piano-guitar combo performs Spanish ballads (they were playing "Amor" when we walked in), and enclosed booths swathed in dark shades and dim lighting invite couples to sit close and snuggle.

On a warm day, the frothy margaritas hit the spot, and the flavorful dishes are very tempting. The appetizer sampler of fresh jumbo shrimp, quesadillas, miniature tacos, and pork is excellent and inexpensive. If you're not already a fan of authentic Mexican restaurants, this one will persuade you to reconsider.

GEORGIA, West Hollywood
7250 Melrose Avenue
(213) 933-8420
Expensive
Dinner Daily

Georgia's sultry atmosphere is very conducive to an intimate evening. A lush outdoor patio leads into a Caribbean-style dining room. Soft lighting from gold leaf-shaped sconces reflects off the wine red walls. Comfortable chairs with rattan seats match the dark plantation shutters on the windows, and sexy jazz plays lightly in the background. The mood can't be beat, and Southern cooking has never been more seductive. Start your evening with a Savannah (champagne with fresh peach nectar) or a Georgia peach daiquiri. Corn muffins with butter and a small pitcher of pure cane sugar syrup give you something to nibble on while perusing the menu. The emphasis here is on traditional down-home Southern cuisine, such as fried chicken, catfish, and smothered pork chops. (In the best interests of your heart, all fried foods are prepared in 100-percent cholesterol-free canola oil.) Our favorites are the house-smoked barbecued ribs with creamy garlic coleslaw, and the broiled salmon with honey-mustard glaze, fried green tomatoes, roasted new potatoes, and okra *maque choux*.

L'ORANGERIE, West Hollywood
903 North La Cienega Boulevard
(310) 652-9770
Very Expensive
Dinner Tuesday-Sunday

Los Angeles has a love affair with French restaurants. The sheer number of these lavish dining rooms is mind-boggling. At first glance, the task of making a decision among them may seem overwhelming. But to devotees of haute cuisine and haute socializing, only a few elite selections are worth contemplating. The process is even further simplified for those who are more concerned about each other than with the other people who may be there. If intimacy, quiet conversation, words of love, and lingering gazes are important to you, you will soon narrow the field to L'Orangerie, one of those rare, popular places that are the essence of romantic French dining.

The interior is reminiscent of a Loire Valley chateau: the room is highlighted by tile floors, lofty ceilings, abundant foliage, arched doorways, and Louis XIV furnishings; classical music plays in the background. The kitchen more than lives up to this splendor. The menu is intriguing and the dishes are skillfully and artistically prepared. If you find food seductive, be prepared to swoon at every course. Then, for a perfect finale, adjourn to the sexy bar area for an after-dinner drink while listening to the live piano music.

LE CHARDONNAY, West Hollywood
8284 Melrose Avenue
(213) 655-8880
Expensive to Very Expensive
Lunch Tuesday-Friday; Dinner Tuesday-Saturday

Le Chardonnay is what a brasserie dining experience should be: charming, refined, casual, and very cosmopolitan. In Paris a brasserie can be all those things and your wallet will not necessarily feel the impact; that is not true here. Nevertheless, at Le Chardonnay you can enjoy an afternoon or evening that is as relaxed as it is savory and congenial. The interior is a radiant combination of brass moldings, hand-painted tiles, carved wood detailing, mirrored walls, and an exposed cast-iron oven that sends flickers of firelight dancing across the glassy polished interior. The seating here is discreet, with tables and banquettes well spaced for intimate dining, and the service is polite. House specialties like rotisserie chicken and Sonoma duck *foie gras* sautéed with sweet apples are excellent; for dessert, the dark chocolate soufflé with vanilla ice cream is phenomenal, especially when shared.

Mid-Wilshire

Restaurant Kissing

ATLAS BAR & GRILL, Mid-Wilshire
3760 Wilshire Boulevard
(213) 380-8400

Moderate
Lunch Monday-Friday; Dinner Monday-Saturday

Billed as "a modern-age supper club," Atlas is one of the few places where you can enjoy live jazz while dining by candlelight. Request one of the banquettes along the back wall for the most privacy, and be prepared for dim lighting (all the better to sneak in a kiss or two). The eclectic menu features delicious dishes at reasonable prices. Texas chili, seared ahi tuna over spring mixed greens, penne pasta with grilled breast of chicken, and grilled sea bass Veracruz are our favorites. You may be tempted to take a spin on the dance floor before sharing one of the tantalizing desserts.

Romantic Warning: A few times a month, Atlas hosts private parties that start around 10:30 P.M. If you're having dinner when this occurs, be forewarned that the noise level rises and furniture is moved away before your very eyes. Also, some of the featured musical groups are more romantic than others. Your best bet is to call ahead and see what is scheduled.

Outdoor Kissing

FRIDAY NIGHT JAZZ, Mid-Wilshire
Los Angeles County Museum of Art
5905 Wilshire Boulevard
(213) 857-6000
Jazz Concert: Free; Museum Cafe: Inexpensive
Open Tuesday-Sunday; Dinner Friday

Every Friday evening year-round, from 5:30 P.M. to 8:30 P.M., the Los Angeles County Museum of Art showcases L.A.'s finest jazz artists in free outdoor concerts. In summer, the balmy nights and late-setting sun provide the perfect backdrop for sensuous tunes. You can call to receive the monthly calendar of groups scheduled to appear. The museum shop and galleries are open until 9:00 P.M., and drinks and a light supper are available from the museum cafe.

Hollywood

Restaurant Kissing

CAFE DES ARTISTES, Hollywood
1534 North McCadden Place
(213) 461-6889
Moderate to Expensive
Lunch Tuesday-Friday; Dinner Tuesday-Sunday; Sunday Brunch

In a city known for its slick, chic interiors, Cafe des Artistes is like a breath of fresh air for those in search of easygoing, rustic, yet genteel dining. The rough-hewn country interior is modest and lovely, with only a handful of tables in the dining area. The shady patio seating is cloistered beneath abundant foliage that nevertheless permits the warmth of the sun to shine through. You will find the same atmosphere and the same delectable French Provençal menu selections (ranging from filet mignon to lamb stew) at both lunch and dinner. And the Sunday brunch is one of the most relaxing in town.

CITRUS, Hollywood
6703 Melrose Avenue
(213) 857-0034
Expensive
Lunch Monday-Friday; Dinner Monday-Saturday

Citrus' popularity with the entertainment industry precedes this review and influences it just a bit. With a different crowd, Citrus might have received three lips from us. We find that high-powered meetings and tender romantic interludes are best when served separately. However, the food and the setting make this restaurant something of an oasis for both palate and heart. The restaurant is replete with tall potted plants, large tropical floral arrangements, and wood and canvas umbrellas interspersed among well-spaced tables. Overhead a towering tent-like ceiling creates a unique outdoor country atmosphere.

The inventive dishes here are best described as light French with a California twist. Baby salmon with potato garlic purée, mini goat cheese ravioli with pesto sauce, and Brie in phyllo with frisee salad are all delicious. Chocolate lovers can indulge with the chocolate-hazelnut bar with vanilla sauce, chocolate sorbet, or chocolate-pear cheesecake mousse. Top your meal off with a sweet kiss.

MUSE, Hollywood
7360 Beverly Boulevard
(213) 934-4400
Expensive
Dinner Tuesday-Saturday

Dark and masculine, modern and stark, Muse caters to our desire for unadorned intrigue and a clandestine rendezvous. High white walls showcase a rotating display of art and are framed by wooden beams above and a polished concrete floor below. Try to get a booth at the back to maximize your privacy.

An eclectic menu of Asian and California-style dishes begins with appetizers such as Chinese dumplings, egg rolls, and ravioli with porcini mushrooms. In addition to traditional entrées such as rack of lamb and filet mignon, you can order red Norwegian salmon on garlic-seared spinach with papaya salsa, wild rice, and grilled vegetables.

Since a large part of the romantic appeal is the dark atmosphere, it's best to go for dinner. You can take advantage of the dim lighting and feast on each other to your hearts' content.

OFF VINE, Hollywood
6263 Leland Way
(213) 962-1900
Moderate
Lunch Monday-Friday; Dinner Daily; Sunday Brunch

From the moment we stepped out of the car, the delicious scent of lilacs and the beauty of blooming flowers told us we were definitely "Off Vine" and about to enter a romantic oasis. Just beyond the threshold carved out of bougainvillea, a small outdoor patio and open porch provide a welcome spot for Sunday brunches, weekday lunches, and dinner beneath the stars. Inside the converted two-story house, you get the impression you're in an artist's beach cottage at the turn of the century. The whitewashed walls are punctuated with original artworks (all for sale), and big, open windows look out to the flower beds and allow the sun to stream in.

The style of the cuisine matches the atmosphere. You can choose from a variety of creative pastas and daily seafood specials. Make sure you order the house specialty, chocolate soufflé, for a decadent finale at this one-of-a-kind Hollywood hideaway.

Romantic Warning: Old homes with hardwood floors are charming, but don't make for good acoustics. The patio area is a beautiful way to avoid the noise.

PATINA, Hollywood
5955 Melrose Avenue
(213) 467-1108
Expensive to Unbelievably Expensive
Lunch Tuesday; Dinner Daily

Joachim Splichal is arguably the best chef in Los Angeles (which is not a romantic argument, but truly a delicious one that no one loses), and Patina is the perfect showcase for his talents. Begin your evening with an aperitif in one of the booths adjacent the elegant bar. Now you're ready for the feast to follow.

The two small dining rooms are beautifully appointed, comfortable, and understated. Gourmet French cuisine is the main attraction here, and it is served with impeccable grace. You'll be tempted by corn blinis with fennel-marinated salmon, wild mushroom risotto with baby artichokes, Maine lobster à la Thai, gratin of lamb with garlic mashed potatoes, and many other unusual dishes. And the adventure doesn't stop there. The most popular dessert is the caramelized banana tart with chocolate and banana sorbet. Since many men (and more than a few women) readily confess that the way to their heart is through their stomach, the seduction is well on its way.

YAMASHIRO'S, Hollywood
1999 North Sycamore Avenue
(213) 466-5125
Expensive
Dinner Daily

Yamashiro's (meaning "mountain palace") is perched on a hill overlooking most of the city. In addition to enjoying the breathtaking panoramas, you can meander around the eight acres of sculptured Japanese gardens. Sushi is the house specialty, but there are many other choices, and the service is very attentive. A glass-enclosed bar area offers one of the best vantage points, and is a great place to rendezvous for drinks. This is an impressive place to spend an unhurried evening above the night lights of Los Angeles.

Outdoor Kissing

WATTLES PARK, Hollywood

From La Brea Avenue turn north onto Hollywood Boulevard, then west onto Curson. The park is at the intersection of Curson and Franklin.

The Los Angeles area is blessed with dozens of parks, but not all provide a refuge for those who want to appreciate the outdoor life in a composed setting. This one does. When you first encounter the fenced boundaries of the park, you'll wonder if you made a mistake in reading the directions, but don't worry—you really are here. Half of this park is a cooperative garden, with a hodgepodge of crops and plants (not exactly a place you want to go traipsing through). The other half includes a cloistered array of palm trees, stone benches, and a thriving fish pond. At the far end of the grounds is a stone-edged path that coils up an amber-colored hillside. The hilltop view opens onto the canyon below. Wattles Park is a pocket of green where you are likely to find yourselves with no distractions except the sound of your own voices.

Romantic Note: Another park option is the southern tip of GRIFFITH PARK, located at the corner of Los Feliz and Western Avenue, as you head north on Fern Dell Drive into the park. Here wooden bridges cross flowing streams cascading over rocks, and thick foliage shades you wherever you go. This special forest refuge may prove to be just the secluded outdoor spot you are seeking.

Downtown Los Angeles

Hotel/Bed and Breakfast Kissing

THE REGAL BILTMORE HOTEL, Los Angeles
506 South Grand Avenue
(213) 612-1575, (800) 245-8673
Very Expensive to Unbelievably Expensive

The Biltmore Hotel is as grand as any palace in Europe. Built in 1923 and renovated in the 1980s to re-create the original aura of Renaissance Italy, this landmark is filled with towering ceilings, arched doorways, and painted murals that are a feast for the eyes. The 683 rooms are all elegantly furnished and include all the amenities. In addition to a full-service art deco spa and health club, guests can enjoy the use of an indoor Roman-style swimming pool. This hotel's only drawback, perhaps, is its location in the heart of downtown Los Angeles. To some people, staying in downtown Los Angeles is equivalent to a vacation in the midst of urban blight. Yet for those who can conquer their big-city apprehensions, a weekend here could seem like a holiday in an island utopia. And weekend rates for couples are greatly reduced for deluxe accommodations. Even if you only tour its immense gilded halls and stop briefly to sip a brandy in the lobby bar, the Biltmore is well worth the trek downtown.

Romantic Note: The Biltmore's award-winning restaurant will lavish you with outstanding meals. BERNARD'S, (213) 612-1580 (Expensive to Very Expensive) is sensational and thoroughly fascinating; here, dining is an art, and not just a meal. For a lovely afternoon tea, the RENDEZVOUS COURT (Moderate), crowned by a three-story ceiling and surrounded by potted palms and a large fountain, is one of the best spots in town.

Romantic Suggestion: For outstanding live theater and concerts, wander a few blocks to the MUSIC CENTER, 135 North Grand Street, (213) 972-7211.

WYNDHAM CHECKERS HOTEL, Los Angeles
535 South Grand Avenue
(213) 624-0000, (800) 996-3426
Very Expensive to Unbelievably Expensive

Located in central downtown Los Angeles, this small, gracious luxury hotel looks strikingly European on the outside, and that same classic design is reflected in the beautiful lobby and rooms. Luxury suites come with silk canopy beds, fireplaces, intimate sitting rooms, and separate dining areas. Oversized beds, attractive linens and wall coverings, and all the amenities, including a selection of 50 movies, may tempt you to stay in. But Checkers has other lures, including a stunning outdoor rooftop spa and pool, and a romantic walkway between the hotel and the nearby Central Library grounds.

Romantic Note: Rates are reduced on the weekend, and some local transportation is provided.

Romantic Suggestion: After a day spent exploring nearby museums, you can review your outing in **THE LOUNGE** over the formal tea service ($18 per person). In early evening, this is also a good place to nibble on complimentary hors d'oeuvres before enjoying a gourmet dinner at **CHECKERS RESTAURANT** (see Restaurant Kissing).

Restaurant Kissing

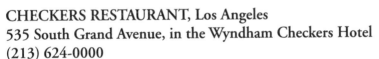

CHECKERS RESTAURANT, Los Angeles
535 South Grand Avenue, in the Wyndham Checkers Hotel
(213) 624-0000
Very Expensive
Breakfast, Lunch, and Dinner Daily

Set in one of downtown's most tasteful hotels, Checkers Restaurant is one of the city's most romantic getaways for both atmosphere and fine dining. The elegant yet comfortable interior is decorated in muted greens and tans. Tables are widely spaced, or you can choose to sit *à deux* in a velour-backed banquette. Many of the dishes on the eclectic California-style menu have an Asian influence, and all are delicious. Cold appetizer favorites include tiger prawns and Pacific yellowtail sashimi; entrées such as grilled beef tenderloin with yams and pecan cake, or New Zealand rack of lamb with rosti potatoes, are succulently sensational.

OTTO'S GRILL & BEER BAR, Los Angeles
135 North Grand Avenue, at the Music Center
(213) 972-7322

Moderate
Lunch and Dinner Tuesday-Sunday

Located on the ground level of the Music Center, this charming restaurant is a convenient place to rendezvous before or after a concert or play. It's necessary to reserve ahead, and we recommend requesting one of the comfortable semicircular booths. Black-and-white photos of old-time stars like Judy Garland and Mary Martin adorn the walls, and there is a beer bar near the front of the restaurant. Our favorite choice for lunch is the tender grilled salmon on assorted lettuces with asparagus and citrus dressing. The Italian-influenced menu also offers many tempting pasta, fish, and steak dishes at reasonable prices.

Romantic Warning: Parking at the Music Center is $7, and there aren't many other parking options in the neighborhood unless you're willing to walk a few blocks.

GLENDALE/PASADENA

Glendale

Restaurant Kissing

FRESCO, Glendale
514 South Brand Boulevard
(818) 247-5541
Moderate
Lunch Monday-Friday; Dinner Monday-Saturday

Located on a major thoroughfare in Glendale, Fresco offers romance seekers a reasonably priced escape at the end of a hectic day. Inside the unassuming stucco structure, the soothing tones of a baby grand piano emanate from a softly lit bar. The white walls are punctuated with columns and archways, reminiscent of a Mediterranean villa, and the floors are awash in plush ocean blue carpeting. Although the dining room tables may be a little too close for intimacy, recessed alcoves with tables for two provide privacy and quiet.

Northern Italian dishes predominate at Fresco, where risotto is the pride of the menu. We enjoyed the risotto *a frutti di mare* and a fresh tomato-based seafood stew. Other specialties include gnocchi with walnut sauce and penne with grilled radicchio and chicken. For a perfect finale, try the dish of fresh strawberries and cream with a crispy meringue topping.

Pasadena

Hotel/Bed and Breakfast Kissing

THE RITZ-CARLTON HUNTINGTON
HOTEL, Pasadena
1401 South Oak Knoll Avenue
(818) 568-3900, (800) 241-3333
Very Expensive to Unbelievably Expensive

As you've probably figured out from previous listings, we think The Ritz-Carlton hotels provide a wonderful environment brimming with romantic possibilities. The Ritz-Carlton Huntington is a prime example of what we mean, with its gracious hospitality, understated yet elegant rooms, and beautiful setting. When you approach this faithfully restored 1907 landmark, you'll get a glimpse of the 23 acres of beautifully manicured gardens and courtyards. Tennis courts and an Olympic-size pool are also on the grounds. By the end of our stay, you'll feel so pampered it will be hard to leave.

Romantic Note: Gourmet cuisine is served in the ornate **GRILL** (Expensive), and the informal **TERRACE CAFE** (Moderate) has popular outdoor seating.

Restaurant Kissing

DICKENSON WEST, Pasadena
181 East Glenarm Street
(818) 799-5252
Expensive
Lunch Tuesday-Friday; Dinner Tuesday-Saturday

Tucked into a small shopping center, Dickenson West is a welcome new addition to the Pasadena scene, and couples are trekking here from all over Los Angeles. They are drawn by the excellent cuisine and serene space. A few tables are placed outdoors, surrounded by potted plants and shaded by umbrellas, but the two small dining rooms are just as intimate and inviting. Original art adorns the walls, and orchids grace the tables.

The tempting four-course prix fixe dinner is a bargain at $37 per person, considering the gourmet entrées included in the price. You can choose from hot buttered oysters with fresh leek ragout to smoked pork tenderloin and potato onion cake with sweet potato turmeric sauce. A chef's-selection cheese course is followed by desserts such as pumpkin crème brûlée and chocolate shortbreads. As you reluctantly depart, you'll realize you've just spent a few hours enjoying each other's company in paradise.

THE RAYMOND RESTAURANT, Pasadena
1250 South Fair Oaks Avenue
(818) 441-3136
Expensive
Lunch Tuesday-Friday; Dinner Tuesday-Sunday;
Brunch Saturday-Sunday

With the coziness of a mountain lodge and the intimacy of a petite cafe, the Raymond Restaurant combines a relaxing ambience with innovative and tasty food. Tucked away from the main road, this converted 1930s bungalow retains a homey feel with its dark wood paneling, varnished pine floors, and small, separate rooms. Our table was one of only four in the room, so we had plenty of privacy. The old-fashioned booths in the front two rooms are probably the best choice for a romantic dinner (you can sit close and cuddle), although there really isn't a bad table in the place. Muted lighting and antique photos of how the property used to look are nice additions to the cozy interior.

Entrées are expensive (about $26 each), but couples on a budget can order from the "Dine Light" menu, which includes soup or salad, a set entrée, dessert, and a glass of the house wine for a fixed price of around $26. This is a wonderful deal and a great way to enjoy this delightful hideaway without breaking the bank. The menu changes weekly, but usually offers veal, beef, chicken, and seafood dishes. During the day or on a warm evening, enjoy the colorfully landscaped outdoor patios.

Outdoor Kissing

ANGELES NATIONAL FOREST

Take Interstate 210 north of Los Angeles to the Angeles Crest Highway; follow the highway through the Angeles National Forest.

The Angeles Crest Highway follows a dramatic path into the heart of the Angeles National Forest. As you follow its tendril-like course, each bend in the road exposes an abrupt change in the perspective and dynamics of the landscape. One curve may reveal a deep ravine framed by perilous mountain peaks, while another manifests a procession of massive golden hills weaving their way to eternity. Imagine the fervor you'll feel in the midst of these constant scenic transformations. Your oohs and aahs will be echoed by the smiling person sitting next to you.

Did you remember to bring a basket of goodies? Mountain picnics have a flavor all their own; the combination of altitude (Charlton Flats is 5,300 feet straight up from sea level), fresh air, lofty pinery, and stupendous views whet the appetite and the heart. Charlton Flats offers all that, and privacy too. Even during the weekend, this area receives few visitors.

THE HUNTINGTON LIBRARY AND BOTANICAL GARDENS, Pasadena

1151 Oxford Road
(818) 405-2141
$7.50 admission
Open Tuesday-Sunday

Unless you happen to be in love with a bookworm, you would never think of going to a library for a lovers' tryst. On the other hand, the Huntington's 150 acres hold magnificently sculpted gardens and woods that are enticingly romantic. The landscape architects and horticultural geniuses who created this wonderland fulfilled their deepest floral fantasies every inch of the way. The meadows, glens, and groves are lavishly decorated with foliage and plant life. The rose garden, Zen garden, Japanese garden, and jungle garden are works of art that defy description. Ask someone special to accompany you hand in hand through these grounds: you'll surely find a corner of Eden you can call your own.

Romantic Note: Avoid visiting the library on weekends unless you want to share this wonderland with hordes of families.

Romantic Option: High tea is served in the **ROSE GARDEN TEA ROOM**, (818) 683-8131 ($11 per person) and reservations are a must. This is a perfectly British experience through and through. Civilized finger sandwiches, including cream cheese and mango chutney or black caviar with egg and scallions, accompany walnut tortes, scones, and chocolate tartlets. What an utterly enchanting addition to a splendid day at the gardens.

Romantic Suggestion: JULIENNE, 2649 Mission Street, San Marino, (818) 441-2299 (Moderate) is a quaint little French cafe that is probably one of the finest in the area. The food is exquisite, the aromas are heavenly, and the lovely interior features tile floors, windows shaded with lace, and wall mirrors draped in forest green. A cappuccino with a freshly baked muffin or a thick slice of creamy light quiche can be a lovely finale to a long day spent exploring the gardens at the Huntington Library.

South Pasadena

Hotel/Bed and Breakfast Kissing

THE BISSELL HOUSE
BED AND BREAKFAST, South Pasadena
201 Orange Grove Avenue
(818) 441-3535, (800) 441-3530
Moderate to Expensive
Minimum stay requirement on weekends

Hosts Russell and Leonore Butcher couldn't be more welcoming, and they have made Bissell House a wonderful place to escape to for a perfect weekend. Surrounded by ancient trees and a 40-foot hedge, the historic three-story Victorian mansion holds four lovely guest rooms furnished with antiques and luxurious linens. There are no phones or televisions in the rooms, just an inviting ambience with all the creature comforts, including a spacious luxurious bath. Wine, fruit, and fresh flowers are placed in each room, and complimentary breakfast is served in the mornings.

Romantic Alternative: If your hearts are set on Pasadena and the Bissell House is all booked, try the nearby **ARTISTS' INN**, 1038 Magnolia Street, (818) 799-5668 (Moderate to Expensive). The decor in each of the five guest rooms was inspired by a particular artist or art period.

SAN FERNANDO VALLEY

Chatsworth

Restaurant Kissing

MILLER'S ACORN RANCH, Chatsworth
23360 Lake Manor Drive
(818) 888-2099
Moderate
Lunch Tuesday-Friday; Dinner Tuesday-Sunday

As you drive through the curvy hills on Lake Manor Drive, it is easy to forget that you are in Chatsworth. Barren stretches of land with scattered houses and ranches make you wonder if a restaurant exists along this winding street. Miller's Acorn Ranch is easy to miss, but keep your eyes open, because it is enchanting and well worth a visit. While the exterior resembles a small farmhouse in the middle of vast wilderness, the atmosphere inside is comfortable, warm, and inviting. With no more than 20 tables placed in front of a roaring fireplace, this is one of the coziest spots in the valley. Lace-trimmed windows, antique ceiling lamps, and shelves holding aged relics surround the homey dining room. Outside patio seating is also available. The ranch-style menu includes seafood, ribs, steaks, and pasta dishes.

Woodland Hills

Restaurant Kissing

BRANDYWINE, Woodland Hills
22757 Ventura Boulevard
(818) 225-9114
Expensive
Lunch Monday-Friday; Dinner Monday-Saturday

Brandywine's mouthwatering French menu changes daily. Pastas, exotic meats, and flavorful salads are generally listed and always worth ordering. Our hard-to-find Copper River salmon was beautifully prepared. The small dining room is the essence of intimacy, but try to get one of the enclosed booths along the wall for even more privacy.

Romantic Note: At lunchtime, the entrées are much less expensive (about half the price of dinner) and just as delicious.

VILLA PIACERE, Woodland Hills
22160 Ventura Boulevard
(818) 704-1185
Moderate
Lunch and Dinner Daily; Sunday Brunch

Villa Piacere's nicely landscaped, attractive entrance hints of the pleasures to come. We recommend a table on the popular outdoor terrace, available on a first-come, first-served basis, or you can reserve a table in the wood-paneled dining room near the large fireplace. The menu lists northern Italian dishes such as grilled veal sausage and lobster ravioli, along with with specialties such as Louisiana crab cakes and sautéed Mexican shrimp. You'll probably want to linger over a cappuccino so you can prolong the evening while being serenaded by live guitar music.

Sherman Oaks

Restaurant Kissing

MISTRAL, Sherman Oaks
13422 Ventura Boulevard
(818) 981-6650
Expensive
Lunch Monday-Friday; Dinner Monday-Saturday

For lovers who desire more than a *soupçon* of European romance, Mistral provides both the tastes and sounds of France. You'll hear French being spoken by both the patrons and the staff. Dim lights, dark paneling, ornate chandeliers, and rose-colored mirrors from the 1920s highlight a setting perfect for a stylish interlude. Be sure to grab one of the small tables against the wall, so you and yours can sit side by side and eat cheek to cheek.

A drink at the antique cherry-wood bar is a great way to start your meal. The food is excellent, ranging from grilled steak to seafood to pasta specials such as angel-hair pasta with shrimp and asparagus. Many of the dishes are loaded with garlic and exceptionally well seasoned. This chic and cosmopolitan restaurant is a bit of Paris in Los Angeles, and certainly costs a lot less than airfare for two to France.

Romantic Warning: Noise is a problem when the restaurant is full, so you may prefer going in the middle of the week rather than on a Friday or Saturday night.

Studio City

Restaurant Kissing

PINOT BISTRO, Studio City
12969 Ventura Boulevard
(818) 990-0500
Expensive
Lunch Monday-Friday; Dinner Daily

Master chef Joachim Splichal opened this San Fernando Valley jewel as a less expensive, less formal version of his signature restaurant, **PATINA** (see Restaurant Kissing in Hollywood). And the crowds have been flocking here ever since. Designed to resemble an elegant French bistro, the handsome dark interior, with its wood-paneled walls and candlelit tables, projects an aura conducive to seduction.

The main draw, however, is the enticing cuisine. You might start with the caramelized onion tart with marinated salmon or the cabbage pockets stuffed with Maine lobster. Tempting entrées from the grill include the pinot porterhouse steak with celery root gratin and the grilled chicken breast with a morel mushroom potato torte. There are also flavorful lighter choices from the spa category. Desserts are so decadent, you may want to choose one to savor together.

North Hollywood

Hotel/Bed and Breakfast Kissing

LA MAIDA HOUSE
AND BUNGALOWS, North Hollywood
11150 La Maida Street
(818) 769-3857
Moderate to Very Expensive
Minimum stay requirement

Telling you that North Hollywood isn't romantic is much like telling you that the Pope is Catholic. In fact, if we told you otherwise you'd probably throw away this book. Nevertheless, in the middle of unromantic North Hollywood there is a romantic oasis called La Maida House, the city equivalent of Fantasy Island for loving couples.

When you arrive, pretend that this 7,000-square-foot villa is your own private mansion. Wander through the many different sitting rooms and select your own personal nest. As at most bed and breakfasts, each room is decorated individually, but at La Maida House the 11 rooms have exceptional variations. The Cipresso Suite is softly colored by stained glass windows that overlook the rose garden; the king-size four-poster canopied bed is encircled by oversize wicker furniture. The Giardino Room has its own garden and a stained glass atrium, and the Portico Room has a Jacuzzi tub and a private flower-filled patio. The other rooms are equally beautiful, and the gourmet country breakfasts (no animal products) are tantalizing.

Romantic Note: At your request, the innkeepers will prepare a truly grand four-course dinner, a picnic basket, or a pre-theater supper.

" *With a kiss, let us set out for an unknown world.* "

Alfred de Musset

Catalina Island

Catalina Island is a little taste of Hawaii, located 22 miles from the mainland in the sparkling Pacific Ocean. Fifty-four miles of shoreline encircle this island, and what a shoreline it is! You will discover hidden beaches, rugged cliffs, meandering trails, and abundant marine life (including gray whales during their yearly migration). Most of the enchanting countryside is a deep, lustrous green, and the island is invigorating, sparsely populated, and remarkably smog-free. Ferries from the mainland dock in the port of Avalon, a European-style town replete with seaside restaurants, sidewalk cafes, and charming accommodations.

One of the more becoming aspects of this illustrious port of call is that transient cars are not allowed; the dominant forms of wheeled transportation on the island are golf carts, bikes, and motor scooters. Those of you who feel more married to your automobile than to your mate will find leaving the car behind a welcome change. But bring your walking shoes, because even getting to your hotel room can mean hiking up stairs and down hallways.

The latest figures claim that "a million tourists a year" enjoy this island retreat, so your best bet is to avoid the most crowded times, which are weekends and Tuesdays. Why Tuesdays? you ask. Because every Tuesday two large cruise ships arrive in the morning, and their passengers spend the day in Avalon.

Romantic Note: The best way to get to Catalina is by private yacht, but if you are not endowed with that particular worldly possession, your next best option is a 14-minute helicopter ride (from San Pedro or Long Beach) on **ISLAND EXPRESS HELICOPTER SERVICE**, (310) 510-2525, (800) 2-AVALON ($121 per person round-trip). The helicopters leave every hour, hold up to six passengers, and give you a great view of the wide expanse of ocean and the cliffs of Catalina and Avalon Bay as you approach. Be forewarned that you're allowed only 25 pounds of luggage, and you'll be weighed too. If you prefer to go by water, **CATALINA EXPRESS**, (310) 519-1212, (800) 464-4228 ($36 per person round-trip) is the fastest and easiest mode of transport; unfortunately, it resembles a Greyhound bus on the water—definitely not the most *romantic* experience. Both Island Express and Catalina Express depart from shared terminals in San Pedro or Long Beach, and both offer package deals with Avalon hotels.

SAIL CATALINA, (310) 592-5790 ($48 per person round-trip) is a new boat service that departs in the morning from Huntington Harbor, south of Long Beach, and returns from Catalina midafternoon. This is the nicest boat service, since it seats only 47, and the return trip from Catalina is a peaceful sail (usually the motor is used only on the trip to the Island). The **CATALINA PASSENGER SERVICE**, (714) 673-5245 ($33 per person round-trip) holds 500 passengers and departs from Newport Beach at the Balboa Pavilion. The only service from San Diego at this time is **CATALINA AIRLINES**, (619) 279-4595, (800) 339-0FLY in California ($100 per person round-trip), a small plane that departs from Montgomery Field at 2 P.M. each afternoon and arrives at the Catalina Airport in the Sky in just 30 minutes. Return flights from Catalina leave each afternoon at 3 P.M.

Romantic Suggestion: Because automobiles are scarce on Catalina, the locals use golf carts to get where they want to go. Although the island's shops, restaurants, and spectacular views are all accessible by foot, you might want to rent one for the fun of it and create your own private tour of the city and its surrounding hills. Golf carts run around $30 per hour and can be found at **CATALINA AUTO AND BIKE RENTAL**, (310) 510-1600, and **CARTOPIA**, (310) 510-2493. If this price is too steep for your budget, try **BROWN'S BIKES**, (310) 510-0986. Here you can rent a couple of mountain bikes at $9 per hour for each bike ($20 for all day); or double the fun with a bicycle built for two ($12 per hour or $30 for all day).

Romantic Note: Many of the hotels offer rooms with views, sometimes at the same price as rooms without views, so be sure to ask what is available and put in your request. Also, there are often package deals with the boat and air services and many of the tour operators on the island.

Avalon

Hotel/Bed and Breakfast Kissing

CASA MARIQUITA, Avalon
229 Metropole Avenue
(310) 510-1192, (800) 545-1192
Moderate to Very Expensive
Minimum stay requirement on holidays

Built in 1990, Casa Mariquita is the newest addition to Avalon's array of accommodations. Located one block from the beach, this inviting inn offers simply adorned rooms lining a pretty outdoor tiled walkway. Potted palms and flowers line the walkway leading to your room, with glimpses of the water in the background. If you splurge on the Penthouse Suite, at $250 per night, you can enjoy the benefits of a stocked kitchen and two balconies (one with a full harbor view). Even if the Penthouse is out of the question, all guests will enjoy the complimentary continental breakfast that is served outside on the lovely main patio.

HOTEL METROPOLE, Avalon
205 Crescent Avenue
(310) 510-1884, (310) 300-8528, (800) 541-8528
Expensive to Unbelievably Expensive
Minimum stay requirement on weekends

For romantics who thrive on being where the action is, Hotel Metropole is the place to be. Built only steps from the water, this New Orleans–style hotel is perched above an expansive courtyard brimming with colorful shops and restaurants. Of the hotel's 48 rooms, its spacious suites are by far the most enticing, especially since they have some of the best views of the island's sun-sequined harbor. However, all of the accommodations are spotless and charmingly decorated in a floral motif with framed Impressionist prints on the walls. Many feature Jacuzzi tubs, gas fireplaces, and private balconies with mountain, courtyard, or ocean views.

After a complimentary continental breakfast of freshly baked muffins, orange juice, and gourmet coffees, you can take a dip in the outdoor rooftop Jacuzzi tub, lounge on the sundeck, or go window-shopping in the Metropole marketplace. Ah, so many choices, so little time.

Romantic Suggestion: We highly recommend the Metropole's restaurant, **THE CHANNEL HOUSE** (see Restaurant Kissing), one of the more romantic dining spots on the island.

HOTEL VILLA PORTOFINO, Avalon
111 Crescent Avenue
(310) 510-0555, (800) 34-OCEAN
http://www.catalina.com/vp.html
Moderate to Very Expensive
Minimum stay requirement on weekends seasonally and on holidays

Ideally located across the street from the harbor and a short walk from the Casino Theater and **DESCANSO BEACH CLUB** (see Outdoor Kissing), Hotel Villa Portofino is one of Catalina's top choices for a romantic interlude. Take advantage of the "Suite Deal" offered during low season; this includes an ocean-view suite, round-trip boat transportation, an island tour, and champagne and chocolates for $220 per night. All 34 rooms have charming Mediterranean decor, and continental breakfast is served on the popular sundeck. Beach chairs and plush towels are also provided, and the sand is only a few feet away.

Romantic Suggestion: Enjoy a delicious meal and a romantic atmosphere at **RISTORANTE VILLA PORTOFINO** (see Restaurant Kissing).

HOTEL VISTA DEL MAR, Avalon
417 Crescent Avenue, Third Floor
(310) 510-1452, (800) 601-3836
Moderate to Very Expensive
Minimum stay requirement on weekends and holidays

Everything about the tastefully decorated Hotel Vista Del Mar will remind you that you're on an island retreat, especially the soft ocean-inspired pastels, wicker furniture, and ubiquitous palms. Thirteen rooms face a tropical atrium courtyard with sunlight streaming in from above. All the rooms are comfortable, but we prefer the two beautiful oceanfront suites, each with scintillating views, a wet bar, gas fireplace, and large Jacuzzi tub. The lobby terrace also faces the water, with large open archways that frame the endless Pacific.

THE INN ON MOUNT ADA, Avalon
398 Wrigley Terrace Road
(310) 510-2030
Unbelievably Expensive
(price includes breakfast, lunch, and dinner)
Minimum stay requirement on weekends
Recommended Wedding Site

Romance doesn't get any better than at The Inn on Mount Ada. This luxurious hideaway is the epitome of elegance, relaxation, and pampering in the grand style. The inn was built in 1921 as a mansion for the Wrigley (chewing gum) family and converted into a bed and breakfast in 1985. The Wrigleys once owned most of the island, and they chose this site in the hills above Avalon because it is "where it was determined that the sun first touched Avalon and was last seen as it set over the Catalina hills."

The six beautifully appointed rooms all have sitting areas, queen-size beds, and small but opulent baths. Best of all, they offer spectacular views of the surrounding five-acre garden and the boat-dotted bay below. Guests have the run of the house and are welcome to help themselves to snacks in the kitchen at any time and generally make themselves feel at home in the common areas. There is a large den with TV and VCR, a sunporch, and a large living room with comfortable overstuffed chairs and a baby grand piano. Breakfast, lunch, and dinner are included in the room price and are served in the formal dining room. Also included are complimentary golf carts to travel down the hill to the beachfront less than two miles away.

Romantic Note: If the exorbitant price of staying here is beyond your means but you'd like a taste of the good life, you'll be happy to know that **THE INN ON MOUNT ADA DINING ROOM** (see Restaurant Kissing) has recently opened up to nonguests on a first-come, first-serve reservation basis.

THE OLD TURNER INN, Avalon
232 Catalina Avenue
(310) 510-2236, (800) 410-2236
Expensive to Very Expensive
Minimum stay requirement on weekends and holidays

Located in a charming neighborhood a short walk from the harbor, The Old Turner Inn is housed in a 1927 residence that has been completely renovated into a homey bed and breakfast. All five guest rooms feature antiques, queen- or king-size beds, full private baths, and ceiling fans that circulate the ocean breezes. Four of the rooms hold wood-burning fireplaces, and the two larger rooms on the second floor are adjacent to a glassed-in sitting porch with plenty of radiant sunshine streaming in. Complimentary wine and hors d'oeuvres are served in the evening, and a breakfast buffet is presented each morning.

THE ZANE GREY PUEBLO HOTEL, Avalon
199 Chimes Tower Road
(310) 510-0966, (800) 3-PUEBLO
Inexpensive to Expensive
Minimum stay requirement on weekends and holidays

This Hopi-style pueblo, tucked into the hills above Avalon, was built in 1926 by novelist Zane Grey. It's a bit off the beaten track; luckily, a courtesy taxi will pick you up from the boat dock, because this is a 15- to 20-minute hike from the harbor. There are several advantages to staying here: in addition to the great views, this is the only hotel in Catalina that has a private pool. The 17 rustic rooms offer queen-size beds and private baths with showers, but lack phones and televisions (their absence can be bliss for some, agony to others). The outdoor patio is a wonderful place to share an evening toast on a warm night; on cooler nights, the fireplace in the living room sheds a suitably romantic glow.

Restaurant Kissing

ARMSTRONG'S FISH MARKET AND
SEAFOOD RESTAURANT, Avalon
306 Crescent Avenue
(310) 510-0113
Moderate to Expensive
Lunch and Dinner Daily

If you prefer dressing down to dressing up for dinner, but want to find a place where romance is still on the menu, try Armstrong's. The only prerequisite is that you have a taste for seafood. Armstrong's has the freshest fish around, probably because the owner, Russ Armstrong, used to be a fisherman. Since the restaurant is set right on the water, it also claims the most glorious views. Our favorite seating was on the outside deck, where we could enjoy the sun streaming down and watch swimmers paddling by a few feet away.

Inside you'll dine by candlelight, but that's really the only formality here. Plastic tablecloths, nautical decor, and shorts-clad waiters with sunburned noses lend the room a very comfortable and casual atmosphere. At the end of a long day of sightseeing, it's easy to appreciate such simple pleasures.

CAFE PREGO, Avalon
605 Crescent Avenue
(310) 510-1218
Moderate to Expensive
Call for seasonal hours.

Reminiscent of a neighborhood Italian trattoria, Cafe Prego is one of the coziest dining rooms in Avalon for an intimate evening. Checkered tablecloths brighten the rather dark room, and daily specials are listed on a chalkboard. House specialties include fresh fish caught by local fisherman and Florentine pasta dishes. In keeping with Italian tradition, the featured dessert is gelato, a large scoop of ice cream in a hard chocolate shell, ideal for sharing and feeding each other.

THE CHANNEL HOUSE, Avalon
205 Crescent Avenue, at the Hotel Metropole
(310) 510-1617
Moderate to Expensive
Call for seasonal hours.

While Avalon has quite a few eating establishments, most will simply hand you your meal along with a few paper napkins. Sure, there are some nicer restaurants on the island, but a lot of them are a bit rowdy, bustling with tourists, and not at all suited for romance. The Channel House is a pleasant exception. At lunchtime, the outdoor patio garden facing the Pacific is a wonderful place to enjoy Catalina's temperate weather, along with reasonably priced sandwiches, burgers, salads, and pasta dishes.

The pretty interior has the feel of a Victorian summer home. Even though the cuisine is elegantly European at dinnertime, if you dress casually you will still feel at ease. Friday and Saturday nights are especially romantic, when diners are serenaded with live piano music.

THE INN ON MOUNT ADA DINING ROOM, Avalon
398 Wrigley Road, at The Inn on Mount Ada
(310) 510-2030
Moderate to Expensive
Reservations Required
Breakfast, Lunch, and Dinner Daily

Our favorite romantic lodging on Catalina Island recently opened up its formal dining room to nonguests. The best part is that after enjoying a first-class, prix fixe breakfast, lunch, or dinner, you are welcome to enjoy your coffee or after-dinner drink in the inn's adjacent living room or on the sundeck overlooking the gardens and harbor.

Seating is extremely limited in the dining room, so you must call well in advance to see if tables are available. Breakfast ($7.50 per person) includes continental breakfast plus an egg or French toast dish. A "deli-style" lunch ($15 per person) offers casual fare and includes beer or wine. The three-course dinner (including salad, entrée, and dessert) features a daily special highlighting whatever is fresh on the island and also includes your choice of alcoholic beverage for $40 per person, plus tip. Taking a taxi is the best way to get up the hill. Afterwards, enjoying the view and the walk down makes an ideal romantic finale to this memorable experience.

RISTORANTE VILLA PORTOFINO, Avalon
111 Crescent Avenue, at the Hotel Villa Portofino
(310) 510-0508
http://www.catalina.com/vp.html
Moderate to Expensive
Dinner Daily

Although Ristorante Villa Portofino is a bit more formal than most of the other restaurants on the island, its atmosphere is warmly inviting and romantic. The subdued pastel decor seems to blush under the discreetly recessed lighting, while comfortable upholstered chairs and soft music put diners at ease. The waiter will pamper you with doting service and delicious northern Italian cuisine. If you like fish, you'll surely love the grilled salmon with sautéed asparagus or the large prawns marinated in herbs. Share a kiss or two over a frothy cappuccino, sweetened by an order (or two) of tiramisu: ladyfingers dipped in espresso and topped with rich mascarpone and chocolate.

Outdoor Kissing

DESCANSO BEACH CLUB, Avalon
The Casino Theater
(310) 510-7400

Walk to the end of Crescent Avenue, in the direction of the Casino Theater. Continue past the Casino building, following the signs along the path.

A palm-tree-lined stroll past the Casino Theater leads to a "private" beach club where you can spend the day for only $1.50 (a small service charge added to your food bill). Umbrellas, chairs, and towels are available to rent, and there is a concession for kayaks and water sports. Unlike public beaches, you can drink alcoholic beverages here, and an outdoor beachside bar serves lunch until 5 P.M. on weekdays, and barbecues on Friday, Saturday, and Sunday nights.

Romantic Suggestion: Kayaks are available from **DESCANSO BEACH OCEAN SPORTS**, (310) 510-1226, http://www.catalina.com/CIX.html. Prices for a single kayak rental start at $10 per person per hour and longer, and guided tours are also offered. You may be tempted to lean over and exchange a kiss while gliding along in the water, but be careful—a kiss is not an easy proposition in a kayak (although it is possible).

DISCOVERY TOURS, Avalon
(310) 510-8687

Many locations, including Pleasure Pier and Crescent at Catalina.

Discovery Tours, one of the main tour operators on Catalina, has just about any sightseeing package you could desire. Options include the Avalon Scenic Bus Tour, Seal Rocks Cruise, Glass Bottom Boat, Inland Motor Tour, and the four-and-a-half-hour Sundown Isthmus Cruise.

Romantic Alternative: CATALINA ADVENTURE TOURS, (310) 510-2888, also offers bus tours, glass-bottom boat tours, and a harbor cruise.

THE WRIGLEY MEMORIAL AND
BOTANICAL GARDEN, Avalon

Located at the head of Avalon Canyon, two miles from the beach.

When your heart is set on taking a break from the beach, this 37-acre garden is a soothing respite. Plenty of seclusion can be found amidst the cacti, succulents, and other plants native to the California offshore islands. The Wrigley Memorial honors William Wrigley, Jr., who developed Catalina Island until his death in 1932.

"I have found men who didn't know how to kiss. I've always found time to teach them."

Mae West

Orange County

THE COAST

Newport Beach

Hotel/Bed and Breakfast Kissing

DORYMAN'S OCEANFRONT INN, Newport Beach
2102 West Oceanfront
(714) 675-7300, (800) 634-3303
Very Expensive to Unbelievably Expensive

Doryman's is so enticing you will want to embrace immediately after entering the front door. Everything about this bed and breakfast suggests Victorian affluence, starting with the lovely antique furniture and floral wallpaper. The finishing touches are impeccable, from fine linens on the beds to Italian marble and brass fixtures in the bathrooms. Six of the ten rooms have ocean views and two are luxurious suites with Jacuzzi tubs and spacious sitting rooms. If you can bear to tear yourselves away, you can enjoy sumptuous breakfasts and delightful afternoon teas in the parlor.

FOUR SEASONS HOTEL, Newport Beach
690 Newport Center Drive
(714) 759-0808, (800) 332-3442
http://www.fshr.com
Very Expensive to Unbelievably Expensive

Located across from Fashion Island, a premier shopping destination, this resort is elegant from start to finish. The tasteful, expansive lobby, with a relaxing lounge area and a delightful restaurant, offers plenty of room for conversation, and the attentive staff provides gallant service. Although we would describe the rooms as upscale rather than affectionate, their separate living rooms provide the perfect spot for lounging and snuggling. It's hard not to feel regal and pampered in even the least expensive rooms. The rooms on the higher floors are the most sought-after; they offer panoramic views of the coast and Newport's skyline. Guests have access to a complete spa and exercise facilities, including aerobics classes, a lap pool, a Jacuzzi tub, tennis courts, massage, and steam. Poolside dining is also available.

PORTOFINO BEACH HOTEL, Newport Beach
2306 West Oceanfront
(714) 673-7030
Moderate to Very Expensive
Minimum stay requirement on weekends

If Doryman's is booked, or if you're just looking for a less expensive option, try this comfortable hotel. Facing the water and just a short walk from the sand, Portofino's offers 15 rooms and three villas decorated in earth tones and equipped with queen-size beds. All have marble baths, and some have Jacuzzi tubs and ocean views. A complimentary continental breakfast is served in the attractive sitting room off the lobby. Then all you need to do is step outside to soak up the sun and surf.

Romantic Note: The adjoining restaurant, RENATO (see Restaurant Kissing), also serves meals in the hotel's sitting room. This is a great place to curl up in front of the fireplace on comfortable overstuffed chairs.

Romantic Warning: Portofino's only drawback is its proximity to the parking lot for Newport Pier, which is often bustling with wayward surfers and enthusiastic crowds.

Restaurant Kissing

21 OCEANFRONT, Newport Beach
2100 West Oceanfront
(714) 673-2100
Expensive to Very Expensive
Dinner Daily

As the sun plays out its final performance of the day, melting into the turquoise sea, 21 Oceanfront prepares for its nightly encore. Time and again, couples in search of romance come to this warm and elegant restaurant, expecting brilliant sunsets, attentive service, and fine cuisine. They rarely leave disappointed. Just a few hundred yards from the crashing waves, seafood and pasta are served in a graceful green marble and black-accented interior. You may even want to pack a bag for the night: with the exquisite **DORYMAN'S OCEANFRONT INN** right upstairs (see Hotel/Bed and Breakfast Kissing), you can have everything your hearts need without traveling anywhere else.

AUBERGINE, Newport Beach
508 29th Street
(714) 723-4150

Expensive to Very Expensive
Dinner Tuesday-Saturday

This popular new addition to the Newport scene is beloved by couples for the coziness of its dining room and the gourmet "French-American" cuisine. Formerly a florist's shop, Aubergine has been converted into a sunny clapboard cottage. The 36 seats are fairly close together, so try to get one of the tables next to the French windows overlooking brightly colored flower boxes. No matter where you sit, you can look forward to a delicious meal. Breads are baked every morning, and unusual fresh fish dishes include Mediterranean rouget and New Bedford scallops served with a light potato purée and yellow squash. Gourmets may wish to order from a six-course prix fixe tasting menu; these dinners cost $48 per person. The warm Valrhona chocolate soufflé cake with prune Armagnac ice cream makes a perfect finale to your perfect evening.

DOLCE, Newport Beach
800 West Coast Highway
(714) 631-4334
Moderate to Expensive
Lunch Monday-Friday; Dinner Daily

Dolce brings a touch of Italy to the Newport dining scene. In nice weather the courtyard is the place to be. The entrance is brightened by colorful spring flowers in pots, while a canopy overhead keeps the sun at bay. Comfortable iron chairs with cushions are placed at small tables adjacent to a fire pit in the middle. Smoking is allowed at the bar on the far end, so you may want to request a table on the opposite side if you are not a smoker.

The interior is more formal, with comfortable upholstered chairs that match the maroon carpet, Italian Renaissance prints on the walls, and live music softly playing in the background. An extensive menu offers reasonably priced hot and cold appetizers, an assortment of pasta dishes, and delicious entrées such as fresh fish with herbs, breast of chicken, and veal with prosciutto, mozzarella, and asparagus. Top off your meal with a homemade dessert and a special Dolce after-dinner drink.

PASCAL, Newport Beach
1000 North Bristol Street, in Plaza Newport
(714) 752-0107
Expensive
Lunch Monday-Friday; Dinner Tuesday-Saturday

There are those who suggest that a proper romantic evening on the Pacific Coast must come with an ocean view. Although a view is nice, there is something to be said for an intimate table in cozy surroundings with excellent food, good wine, and waiters who are savvy enough to be there when you need them and scarce when you don't. Pascal is such a place.

Located in a small shopping area, Pascal is a refreshing surprise. Large bouquets of fresh flowers and smaller vases of roses are everywhere you look, and an immense floral mural has been painted onto its white brick wall. Tables are attractively dressed with quilted tablecloths and matching napkins. The decor is country French and so it the food. The owner/chef, Pascal, and his wife came here from France, bringing all their carefully guarded secrets for culinary excellence. Tempting hors d'oeuvres such as herb ravioli in foie gras or marinated salmon with a creamy potato risotto are followed by classic fish and steak dishes. The aroma of garlic perfumes the air, and warm feelings abound. It's not unusual for Pascal to leave the kitchen to introduce himself and make sure you are happy with your meal. While he's visiting your table, you may want to let him know that you are pleased not only with his fine cuisine, but with the romantic bit of France he has transported to Newport Beach.

Romantic Suggestion: Pascal has a wonderful shop next door where you can pick up fine wine, French cheeses, quiches, and pastries for a snack or picnic.

RENATO, Newport Beach
2304 West Oceanfront
(714) 673-8058
Moderate to Expensive
Dinner Daily

Located just off the beach near the **PORTOFINO BEACH HOTEL** (see Hotel/Bed and Breakfast Kissing), Renato offers gourmet Italian cuisine in a charming setting. If your heart is set on an ocean view, request one of the two window-side tables; however, all the tables are intimate and beautifully appointed. Classical music sets the mood, and in keeping with the atmosphere, more formal dress is requested: shorts and baseball caps are not permitted. Traditional pasta selections fill the menu, along with a variety of fish, chicken, and veal dishes. Our favorite is the fettuccine with sweet onions, chicken, mushrooms, and sausage. You may want to finish the evening by indulging in a serving of homemade ice cream, rolled in walnuts and light meringue, and topped with whipped cream and chocolate sauce.

THE RITZ, Newport Beach
880 Newport Center Drive
(714) 720-1800
Expensive to Very Expensive
Lunch Monday-Friday; Dinner Daily

Elegant, opulent, and, yes, even a bit gaudy, is how we would describe this lavish continental restaurant. However, the glitz is what has made The Ritz such a popular spot for romantic dining. People love to come here on special occasions, dressed to the hilt. Bejeweled and bedecked in their finest attire, they eat rich food, sip expensive wine, and enjoy the restaurant's show-stopping presentations.

In one part of the restaurant, dark woods and deep burgundy leather inspire a classically romantic atmosphere; in another room, peach walls, ornate mirrors, and gilded frames create a lighter, more baroque ambience. Meals such as spit-roasted rack of lamb and bouillabaisse with lobster have made this an award-winning restaurant, with attractions for connoisseurs of food and romance alike.

THE VIEW LOUNGE, Newport Beach
900 Newport Center Drive, at the Marriott Hotel
(714) 640-4000
Moderate
Cocktails, Appetizers, and Sushi Daily

Chain hotels like the Marriott or the Sheraton rarely, if ever, meet the romantic standards of this travel series. It's not that these places can't be extravagant and luxurious; it's just that they are often cavernous, loud, and business-oriented, qualities that don't promote affection and cuddling. The View Lounge is an exception.

Picture a sea of shimmering lights and sunset colors that gently fade into a cobalt night dotted by stars and a vibrant moon. That's what awaits you every evening at the lounge. Stretching from Long Beach to Laguna Beach, the spellbinding view may be the best in all of Orange County. The lounge serves cocktails and light hors d'oeuvres, and recently added a sushi bar. Bands playing Top 40 and jazz music perform here nightly. If you prefer dialogue to dancing, come during the sunset happy hour, when a table by the window is a highly coveted spot.

Outdoor Kissing

INSPIRATION POINT, Newport Beach
3100 block of Breakers Drive

From East Pacific Coast Highway, take Marigold south to Breakers Drive.

Yes, there really is an Inspiration Point, and you can bet it's been the inspiration for many a romantic encounter over the years. Too small to be called a park, but more lush than your average lookout, this is a great place to bring a picnic basket and someone you love. With any luck, you'll find the tiny mound of grass overlooking the sparkling sea reserved just for the two of you. But if not, you can enjoy the surrounding splendor from one of the nearby benches or from the terrace just down the hill.

Inspiration Point is the kind of place where people come to write poetry, propose marriage, or even exchange "I do's." Flowers encircle the bluff and grow in colorful patches all the way down the cliffs. Although there isn't a home around here that costs less than a million dollars, wealth comes in many forms. Sharing nature's resplendence with someone you love is worth more than all the rubies in the world.

Romantic Alternatives: Another local spot of inspiration is **KINGS ROAD PARK**, Kings Road at St. Andrews Road, a picturesque park overlooking the shore. Or visit **GALAXY PARK**, Galaxy Drive at Mariners Drive, which provides a beautiful vista of the lagoon and the Newport skyline. The only sounds you're likely to hear around here will be birds singing in the trees and gardeners snipping the bushes of the perfectly manicured estates that surround it.

IRVINE COAST CHARTERS, Newport Beach
3412 Via Oporto, Suite 201, at the Lido Marina Village
(714) 675-4704
Very Expensive to Unbelievably Expensive

If you are anxious to let your love set sail, these are the people to talk to. How about a cruise on a yacht, complete with staff to serve you a gourmet meal by candlelight? Better yet, why not a romantic gondola ride around the bay, followed by a vessel filled with string musicians who will serenade you? Dream it up and this company will make your Love Boat fantasies come true.

Balboa

Hotel/Bed and Breakfast Kissing

BALBOA INN, Balboa
105 Main Street
(714) 675-3412
Moderate to Very Expensive

This picturesque Spanish-style inn is a stone's throw from the Balboa Pier and the glistening sea. Though most of the rooms are pretty standard and in need of some attention, there are a couple of enchanting ocean-view suites that will have your hearts pounding the minute you cross the threshold. Our favorite is the Honeymoon Suite, complete with a gas fireplace and private balcony. From this vantage point, the ocean is so close you can see the waves roll onto the sand, hear the surf lash against the shore, smell the ocean breeze, and taste the salt in the air.

Romantic Warning: On weekend nights, the live bands playing at the popular nightspot across the street can be heard until the wee hours of the morning.

Restaurant Kissing

BASILIC, Balboa Island
217 Marine Avenue
(714) 673-0570
Moderate to Expensive
Dinner Tuesday-Sunday

There are small romantic restaurants, and then there are *really* small romantic restaurants. Basilic is an intriguing example of the latter. Squeezed in between shops on the main drag of Balboa Island, the outside alone is enough to provoke your interest. Its facade is reminiscent of a quaint country cabin. A flower box overflows with colorful blossoms, and reflections from the candlelight inside dance on the beveled edges of the cut-glass windows.

Inside, you may feel a bit claustrophobic. Don't worry, though. Like a miner in a small cavern, you will quickly feel the thrill of knowing you've uncovered a precious jewel. Floral tapestried banquettes line both sides of the room, divided by an aisle. Small tables dressed in pink linens occupy the space, making it intimate, though not very private. Still, the French-inspired food, the candlelight, and the romantic music create the kind of ambience made for whispering sweet nothings.

Romantic Alternative: Just up the street you'll find **AMELIA'S**, 311 Marine Avenue, (714) 673-6580 (Inexpensive to Moderate). This Italian restaurant has been here for more than 30 years, as the mementos covering its walls illustrate. Though these nostalgic touches don't really add to the romance, they don't hinder it either. A corner table, some mouthwatering pasta, and a little Pavarotti playing in the background will surely result in a most memorable evening.

BRITTA'S CAFE, Balboa
205 Main Street
(714) 675-8146
Inexpensive to Moderate
Breakfast, Lunch, and Dinner Daily

After an arduous day of sightseeing, when you're ready for a quiet romantic dinner but don't want to get dressed up, head to Britta's. This is one of the few places where candlelight, shorts, and sandals seem to go together. Just down the street from the Newport Pier and around the corner from the playful **FUN ZONE** (see Outdoor Kissing), this charming little cafe is popular with the suntanned locals.

Here the coffee smells of cinnamon, and fresh flowers adorn every table. Though it's not fancy by any means, Britta's has a sort of underlying refinement. Perhaps it's the walls lined with works by local artists, or the soft classical music that fills the room. It could be the unexpected quality of the food; Britta's is attached to a gourmet kitchen shop and you can quickly tell a pro is at work. The food is simple but lovingly prepared; pasta, meat dishes, and sandwiches make up the bulk of the menu. Don't stop there, though—the dessert tray is calling your names.

Outdoor Kissing

BALBOA ISLAND

Take Jamboree southwest to Marine Street or board the ferry at the Fun Zone in Balboa.

If you'd like to find something fun and romantic to do in the Newport Beach area, consider taking the ferry to Balboa Island. The three-car ferry has been around since the 1920s and transports passengers, animals, and bicycles to the island from the Balboa **FUN ZONE** (reviewed below). As you cross the small channel, you can't help but gape at the incredible estates that line the island. The houses seem like an endless potpourri of gingerbread confections, some Cape Cod–style, others right out of a Hans Christian Andersen storybook. On Marine Street, you'll find an enticing assortment of restaurants and specialty shops to wander through hand in hand. Or slip away to the water's edge to enjoy a picnic and perhaps a kiss or two.

BALBOA PAVILION AND FUN ZONE, Balboa

Take Balboa Boulevard to Main Street and turn left.

The Balboa Fun Zone is perfectly delightful entertainment for anyone who's tired of being an adult. Turn off the fax machine, put down the cellular phone, and walk down the boardwalk that is Balboa's answer to Coney Island. Eat cotton candy to your hearts' delight, take silly pictures in the photo booths, play "keep away" in the bumper cars, and ride the colorful carousel. After dark, a spin on the Ferris wheel will not only afford a spectacular view of the lights along the water, but will also provide a marvelous spot to sneak a few kisses.

Romantic Suggestion: During the day, sightseeing cruises leave the harbor about every half hour. The **PAVILION QUEEN**, (714) 673-5245, a pretty double-deck Mississippi-style riverboat, will float you past the expensive yachts, million-dollar homes, and winding channels that make this area legendary.

Corona del Mar

Restaurant Kissing

FIVE CROWNS, Corona del Mar
3801 East Pacific Coast Highway
(714) 760-0331
Moderate to Expensive
Dinner Daily; Sunday Brunch

This place has tryst written all over it. The dining rooms have cozy corners or banquettes where couples can sit side by side. Villeroy and Boch china, classical music, and long floral curtains contribute to the English formality. In addition, the waitresses are dressed in period costumes, complete with bonnets, aprons, and white stockings. The traditional continental cuisine is quite good and sometimes excellent, and features grilled fish, prime rib, and rotisserie chicken.

ROTHSCHILD, Corona del Mar
2407 East Pacific Coast Highway
(714) 673-3750
Expensive to Very Expensive
Lunch and Dinner Daily; Sunday Brunch

This is the stuff adoring encounters are made of: an intimate setting, beautiful surroundings, and impeccable service. Not only will you feast on some of the best northern Italian cuisine around, but your eyes can feast on handsome European antiques and 19th-century paintings in the three cozy dining rooms. We began our meal with the popular house specialty: toasted artichokes marinated in herbs and white wine. The pastas are made on the premises, and many are served with fresh fish. As you share all of this with the one you love, you may just want to top off your evening with a kiss—a chocolate kiss, made with the finest Belgian chocolate and laced with plump, juicy raspberries.

Outdoor Kissing

SHERMAN LIBRARY AND GARDENS, Corona del Mar
2647 East Pacific Coast Highway
(714) 673-2261
$3 admission

While the Sherman Library is dedicated to the romantic and colorful past of the Pacific Southwest, its expansive sun-drenched gardens promise a different sort of romance and color. Stretching across two acres in the heart of fashionable Corona del Mar, the perfectly manicured grounds invite you to linger over a light lunch shaded by a bower of fuchsias. Stroll through the tropical conservatory bursting with exotic fauna, or snuggle on a bench in a courtyard surrounded by a kaleidoscope of brightly colored flowers. Amidst the trickling fountains and burgeoning blossoms, you can cultivate some pretty special moments here.

Laguna Beach

Hotel/Bed and Breakfast Kissing

THE CARRIAGE HOUSE, Laguna Beach
1322 Catalina Street
(714) 494-8945
http://www.carriagehouse.com
Expensive; No Credit Cards
Minimum stay requirement on weekends and holidays

Most bed and breakfasts have their own charming idiosyncrasies. Given the right touches, nothing is quite as affection-producing as staying in a home where the longings of the heart have been diligently considered. These touches include the aroma of freshly baked pastries first thing in the morning, downy quilts, antique bibelots and finery, and, of course, your own personal bathroom. The Carriage House is a perfect old-fashioned New Orleans–style bed and breakfast that can turn just another weekend out of town into a lasting memory.

Each of the six suites reflects a different part of the world, ranging from the English countryside to the Orient; all have their own sitting rooms and most have kitchens. They face a brick courtyard filled with tropical plants and flowers. You won't find a lot of ocean views at the Carriage House—just comfort, privacy, and pleasure.

CASA LAGUNA INN, Laguna Beach
2510 South Pacific Coast Highway
(714) 494-2996, (800) 233-0449
Moderate to Very Expensive
Minimum stay requirement on weekends and holidays

Built in the 1930s, Casa Laguna's main house and adjoining buildings are a combination of California Mission and Spanish Revival styles. The *casitas*, comprising 19 courtyard or balcony suites, were added in the '40s as word of Laguna Beach's artist colony began to spread.

The inn is settled into a hillside lush with lofty palm trees, tropical plants, and flowers. The grounds also contain winding paths, an aviary, and a small greenhouse. There are several tiled terrace areas to lounge in, but sunsets are best enjoyed from the inn's intriguing bell tower or from the deck above the sparkling pool. It's pretty rare to find a bed and breakfast with a pool, much less one that overlooks the ocean. But then again, Casa Laguna Inn is not your average bed and breakfast.

The rooms are small but endearing, and all are appointed with antique furnishings and private bathrooms. You can tell these rooms were built decades ago because they're neither big nor luxurious. You can choose from a courtyard or ocean-view room, but in our romantic opinion you really should splurge on the Cottage. Here you'll find everything you could want or need for an unforgettable night of romance. Besides providing an incredible view from its private deck, the Cottage also has a fireplace, living room area, and a fully equipped kitchen for nights when you'd prefer to eat in. Breakfast and afternoon tea are on the house.

Romantic Warning: The only reason this charming inn doesn't get a higher rating is because of the constant hum of traffic from the Pacific Coast Highway below. Chances are, though, the only sounds you'll hear will be the patter of your hearts.

EILER'S INN, Laguna Beach
741 South Pacific Coast Highway
(714) 494-3004
Expensive
Minimum stay requirement on weekends

During our research, we were concerned that any oceanside town near Los Angeles would be overrun with people who, like us, were in search of a nearby, sequestered getaway. And it's true: the oceanside towns are stuffed to the gills with seclusion seekers, so one must do some rather creative seeking to get away from the throngs. Eiler's Inn feels removed from the masses, even though it is in the center of Laguna Beach.

The picture-perfect guest house wraps around a slightly disheveled New Orleans–style brick courtyard overgrown with thick plants and punctuated with white wrought-iron tables and chairs. Bed sizes in the 11 rooms vary from double to king-size, but all of the rooms are furnished with antiques and two open onto a sundeck with ocean views. The relaxed atmosphere is enhanced by the hearty breakfast served every morning. With the Pacific Ocean's turbulent surf beckoning at your back door, everything is in order for sparkling private time together.

INN AT LAGUNA BEACH, Laguna Beach
211 North Pacific Coast Highway
(714) 497-9722, (800) 544-4479
http://www.innatlagunabeach.com
Expensive to Unbelievably Expensive

Romance has never been this convenient. The Inn at Laguna Beach is a few steps from the water's edge, and many of the 70 rooms feature ocean-view terraces perfect for enjoying the complimentary continental breakfast or watching the sun set at day's end. The rooms are cloaked in the colors of the sea, with walls embellished by the work of local artists. Amenities include TV/VCRs, clock radios, robes, and microwave ovens. Also, this is the only hotel on the beach that has air-conditioning. A rooftop sundeck and a beachside pool and spa await you, or you can pick up towels, chairs, and shade umbrellas at the front desk and head for the beach.

Romantic Note: Although breakfast is provided, the inn does not offer room service. The staff recommends calling the **GALLOPING GOURMET**, (714) 376-2611, a local catering service supplied by 15 restaurants in the area.

LAGUNA HOUSE, Laguna Beach
541 Catalina Street
(714) 497-9061, (800) 248-7348
Expensive
Minimum stay requirement on weekends and holidays

Laguna House is a welcome retreat from the crowds thronging to the shops and restaurants along Pacific Coast Highway. The "beach cottage" decor features wicker and light wood furniture, and floral fabrics complement the down comforters on the queen-size beds. Only one of the nine suites has an ocean view, but they all face a secluded brick courtyard filled with tropical plants and a fountain. The courtyard also features comfortable outdoor furniture that invites you to curl up together with a book or a glass of wine.

SURF AND SAND HOTEL, Laguna Beach
1555 South Pacific Coast Highway
(714) 497-4477, (800) 524-8621
Expensive to Unbelievably Expensive

A recent $26 million renovation has created a superior oceanside getaway in the heart of Laguna Beach. From the moment the valet takes your car (which is important given the lack of parking in the area), almost everything about your stay will be relaxing and contented. All 156 rooms have ocean views and balconies that overlook the glistening surf. The color scheme is subdued and elegant, a mixture of bleached woods and creamy shades of beige. Plush robes, marble baths, and glass-enclosed showers make lounging here absolutely luxurious. The hotel also offers 1,500 feet of spectacular private beach, a seaside swimming pool, and two great restaurants known as **SPLASHES** and **THE TOWERS** (see Restaurant Kissing).

Restaurant Kissing

THE BEACH HOUSE, Laguna Beach
619 Sleepy Hollow Lane
(714) 494-9707
Breakfast, Lunch, and Dinner Daily; Sunday Brunch

The Beach House is the perfect choice for couples who want a view of the sparkling Pacific, but would rather don shorts than suits. Linen tablecloths, fresh flowers, and candlelight create a cozy mood as couples dine on the fruits of the sea and drink in glorious sunsets. In addition to a broad selection of seafood, the Beach House also features prime rib, steak, lamb, and veal. An early lunch on the sun-drenched patio is a great time to share a coffee-flavored kiss as you reflect on your plans for the day.

CEDAR CREEK INN, Laguna Beach
384 Forest Avenue
(714) 497-8696
Moderate
Lunch Monday-Saturday; Dinner Daily; Sunday Brunch

On warm days, the best tables at the Cedar Creek Inn are those on the recently added outdoor patio; tables here are shaded by umbrellas, and flower boxes and trees circle the patio. On cold nights, lovers sit inside near the enormous stone hearth while a pianist serenades them with romantic melodies. Chicken, salmon, steak, and pasta entrées include soup or salad, and the menu also offers a large selection of sandwiches.

THE COTTAGE, Laguna Beach
308 North Pacific Coast Highway
(714) 494-8980
Moderate
Breakfast, Lunch, and Dinner Daily

The Cottage is right out of a William Buffet painting: a 1914 beach bungalow filled with pastel-clad lovers enjoying breakfast. On any given weekend, you'll find locals and tourists waiting their turn to do brunch here. And why not? The home-style cooking is hearty and inexpensive, and the tables inside are comfortable and cozy. Evenings on the delightful garden patio are quiet and intimate, but there's something about breakfast here that makes it the most romantic meal of the day.

LAS BRISAS, Laguna Beach
361 Cliff Drive
(714) 497-5434
Moderate to Expensive
Breakfast, Lunch, and Dinner Daily

Las Brisas is one of the few restaurants in Laguna Beach with a beguiling ocean vantage point. Sit on the tiled outdoor terrace, where you can order cocktails and appetizers while watching swirling eddies explode over the rocks below. If you desire quiet and privacy, move to the elegant interior, with its semicircular wall of floor-to-ceiling windows facing the Pacific. This more formal setting features wooden chairs, linen tablecloths, and fresh roses. The menu, inspired by the cuisine of the Mexican Riviera, lists fresh seafood specialties. We recommend Mexican favorites such as mesquite-broiled double breast of chicken with tropical fruit salsa, and jalapeño fettuccine with shrimp, scallops, mussels, and crab. When sunset nears, a single path of sunlight graces the water's surface; then, slowly, the collage of color crescendos into nightfall while you ponder where the evening will take you next.

Romantic Warning: This is a very popular spot, so the earlier you arrive the less crowded it will be. In fact, some nights the parking lot fills up and you'll probably have to hike a few blocks.

RENAISSANCE, Laguna Beach
234 Forest Avenue
(714) 497-5282

Moderate to Expensive
Breakfast Seasonally; Lunch and Dinner Daily

The front terrace of this dynamic, ultramodern cafe is where locals like to sit and watch the world go by. Inside, the ambience is very sexy. Most of the tables are for two, and the wooden chairs have exotically designed vinyl seats. A high ceiling allows room for original artwork on the walls, and the concrete floor adds to the bohemian appeal. Live music begins each night around 8 P.M. and features jazz, guitar, and blues. The Renaissance serves interesting California cuisine, like vegetarian baked eggplant or linguine layered with salmon and tiger shrimp. If it weren't for the noise level, we would have gladly given this place a higher lip rating.

THE SORRENTO GRILLE
AND MARTINI BAR, Laguna Beach
370 Glenneyre
(714) 494-8686
Expensive
Dinner Daily

Although the interior of this dining spot is exceedingly elegant, it can get excessively crowded and noisy, making it difficult to carry on a conversation or even hear yourselves think. But during less busy times, this can be a romantic and intimate place; just be sure to request one of the small tables on the balcony or one of the booths on the open mezzanine. Wherever you sit, you're sure to enjoy the provocative Italian cuisine. Begin with the crispy fried oysters or grilled artichokes, followed by entrées such as pasta, blackened rare ahi steak on risotto cake, or grilled filet mignon with potato gratin. The room's textured terra-cotta and beige walls, rustic tile, and bleached woods are merely a backdrop for the floor-to-ceiling windows.

SPLASHES, Laguna Beach
1555 South Pacific Coast Highway, at the Surf and Sand Hotel
(714) 497-4477, (800) 524-8621
Moderate to Expensive
Breakfast, Lunch, and Dinner Daily; Sunday Brunch

Set right on the sandy beach, this light and airy restaurant is enhanced by classical music, a flickering hearth, wall-to-wall ocean views, and the crashing waves just 25 feet away. The menu lists an assortment of contemporary Mediterranean dishes, such as Catalan shrimp and scallops gratinée with tomato-paprika sauce, vegetarian moussaka with a red tomato coulis, and breast of chicken with andouille cornbread stuffing. In addition, the fresh fish entrées are always superb. Choose to sit inside, or dine alfresco on the hotel's palm-shaded terraced patio. Splashes Bar, just a few steps away, enjoys the same decor and splendid vistas.

TI AMO, Laguna Beach
31727 Pacific Coast Highway
(714) 499-5350
Moderate to Expensive
Dinner Daily

Welcome to seduction, Italian-style. The tantalizing smells. The heavenly ocean view. Yes, this is definitely a restaurant after your hearts. The food, like the decor, is inspired by the Italian Renaissance. This means that the house specialty is authentic regional cuisine, made from classical Italian recipes that have been handed down from century to century. For a truly historical menu, you might want to order the gnocchi with veal and wild mushroom ragu; ravioli with snow crab, rock shrimp, and orange fennel sauce; or grilled filet of salmon. Leave some room for ice cream and berries, with a house cappuccino to sip on the side.

All this is served up in a cozy cottage divided into several rooms. Each dining room is warm and intimate. The living room has a cozy hearth, there are two small ocean-view rooms, and a pretty patio features live classical music. As you bask in the golden glow of the sun setting over the ocean, you may realize that you've fallen under the spell of this bewitching restaurant. With a name like Ti Amo, Italian for "I love you," it had to be worthy of whispering such sweet and passionate words.

THE TOWERS RESTAURANT, Laguna Beach
1555 South Pacific Coast Highway, at the Surf and Sand Hotel
(714) 497-4477, (800) 524-8621
Moderate to Expensive
Dinner Daily

The Towers Restaurant is located a dramatic nine stories above the surging sea in the **SURF AND SAND HOTEL** (see Hotel/Bed and Breakfast Kissing). It boasts a view that is nothing short of impressive. In contrast, the interior is worn and dated, with mirrored walls and ceiling; that's too much reflection for anyone. Still, at sunset the view is everything, and nothing else really matters. The menu includes a tempting array of meat and seafood dishes. Try the grilled swordfish, served over wild rice with a carrot-saffron sauce, or the New York steak with green peppercorn sauce and roasted potatoes. Live piano music nightly is more sing-along than serenade, but it is fun, if a bit dated, just like the decor.

Outdoor Kissing

CRESCENT BAY POINT PARK, Laguna Beach

Take the Pacific Coast Highway to Laguna Beach and turn west onto Crescent Bay Drive. A sign points the way to the park.

Located in a quiet, suburban neighborhood, this marvelous oasis arches out over the Pacific Ocean. Multilevel walkways crisscross the park, and cliff-edge belvederes provide fine views. In the evenings, sunset splashes the sky with shades of gold, amber, red, and violet that are astonishing in their intensity. This is the place to throw a blanket onto the ground and linger over "a jug of wine, a loaf of bread—and thou."

Dana Point

Hotel/Bed and Breakfast Kissing

BLUE LANTERN INN, Dana Point
34343 Street of the Blue Lantern
(714) 661-1304
Moderate to Unbelievably Expensive

The Blue Lantern Inn is managed by the Four Sisters Inn Corporation, a group that knows everything there is to know about creating romantic accommodations. The other bed and breakfasts under this management— the White Swan Inn and Petite Auberge in San Francisco, the Green Gables Inn and Gosby House in Pacific Grove, and the Cobblestone Inn in Carmel— are stunning, plush places to get away from it all.

The Blue Lantern is located on a bluff overlooking the incredible California coastline. It holds 29 rooms, each with its own fireplace, Jacuzzi tub, mini-stereo system, fluffy terrycloth robes, sweeping views, and comfortable bed overflowing with pillows. In the morning, stroll onto your own private sundeck and linger over a gourmet breakfast. In the afternoon, sip a cup of tea by the hearth in the library. At night your bed is turned down and chocolates are left next to a teddy bear with a card that reads, "Good-night. Sleep tight. Don't let the bears bite." A little corny for some tastes, but definitely endearing.

MARRIOTT'S LAGUNA CLIFFS RESORT
AT DANA POINT, Dana Point
25135 Park Lantern
(714) 661-5000, (800) 533-9748
Very Expensive

Take an elegant, upscale hotel, mix in a touch of Disney magic, and you've got Marriott's Laguna Cliffs Resort. This Cape Cod–style resort has more than a bit of fairy tale about it. Like a great castle, it is set on a grassy knoll high above the sea, blushing in soft pastels and brimming with bright flowers. So why not live like royalty? Spend a pleasant afternoon splashing in the pool, playing tennis, or enjoying a massage in the health spa. The end to a perfect day, or the beginning of a perfect night, may come when you share a quiet moment on your private seaside terrace and survey the moonlit domain lying before you.

Romantic Note: WATERCOLORS RESTAURANT (Moderate) is open for breakfast, lunch, and dinner; the LANTERN BAY BAR & LOUNGE (Moderate) features entertainment and dancing.

THE RITZ-CARLTON LAGUNA NIGUEL, Dana Point
One Ritz-Carlton Drive
(714) 240-2000, (800) 287-2706
Very Expensive to Unbelievably Expensive
Minimum stay requirement on weekends and holidays

"Luxurious" doesn't begin to describe The Ritz-Carlton: the hotel is lavish, opulent, and very expensive. Actually, how much you spend here is up to you. For example, you can reserve the Presidential Suite ($2,000 per night) or you can just drop by for a drink and sunset viewing at the oceanfront lounge (about $10). The romantic possibilities are endless. The hotel is like a grand white castle perched on an ocean bluff. You can be assured that those who stay here get the royal treatment: service and elegance is what the Ritz does so well. The comfortable and attractive rooms are decorated in pleasant pastels. Those with the best views command the highest tariffs.

Guests have access to tennis courts, crystal-clear swimming pools, a fitness center, golf course, specialty shops, and a beauty salon. But you don't have to be a guest to enjoy the lovely restaurants, or to savor afternoon tea in the library filled with rare antique books. Guests and visitors alike can linger over cocktails in the posh lobby area adorned with silk-lined walls, overstuffed couches, and grand, comfortable chairs. From this vantage point, you can take in rousing ocean views and partake in stimulating conversation.

Romantic Note: THE DINING ROOM (see Restaurant Kissing) more than lives up to its surroundings. It is a kiss-worthy destination for couples ready to splurge on an unforgettable meal.

Restaurant Kissing

THE CHART HOUSE, Dana Point
34442 Street of the Green Lantern
(714) 493-1183
Expensive to Very Expensive
Dinner Daily

Located at the pinnacle of Dana Point, the Chart House enjoys a view that stretches all the way from the harbor to the shore. After spiraling down the staircase to reach the main floor, you'll come upon several circular dining rooms, each embellished by exotic flowers and astonishing ocean vistas. The design is exquisite. Ask to be seated at a booth in the alcoves along the side, rather than in the big dining room, which is noisier. The aroma of fresh seafood adds to the feeling that you've discovered seaside rapture, although the menu also offers plenty of tasty meat and pasta dishes. Afterwards, you may want to enjoy a drink on the outdoor patio to get the full effect of the incredible mountaintop vista. It's absolutely breathtaking.

THE DINING ROOM, Dana Point
One Ritz-Carlton Drive, at The Ritz-Carlton Laguna Niguel
(714) 240-5008
Unbelievably Expensive
Dinner Tuesday-Saturday

An evening at The Dining Room promises to be a lavish culinary fantasy come true. Under glistening chandeliers, you can dine side by side, while the attentive wait staff caters to your every need. Sure, it's wildly expensive and, for most, perfectly impractical, but your taste buds will be eternally grateful. Hmmmm, should you order the five- or the seven-course dinner? Do you want to start with the terrine of layered foie gras or the gratin of spatzle and smoked salmon in a light pesto sauce? Decisions, decisions. After you've finished your last course, don't forget to drop by the hotel's Library Room, which overlooks the ocean, for a snifter of cognac in front of the crackling hearth. A fantasy evening come true just wouldn't be complete without this loving finale.

LUCIANA'S, Dana Point
24312 Del Prado
(714) 661-6500
Moderate to Expensive
Dinner Daily

While it's easy to find restaurants with spectacular ocean views in this area, sometimes a romantic interlude calls for simple comforts with few distractions. At Luciana's you can rediscover the joys of quiet conversation and good food, of holding hands while basking in the glow of candlelight. The interior of this small brick cottage is modest but elegant, a pleasant contrast of dark woods and crisp green linens. Under the high wood-beamed ceiling of the main dining area, you'll find a scattering of tables arranged within pleasant distance of a crackling hearth. A few feet away is another dining area that resembles a library. Wednesday through Saturday nights, Luciana's features live piano music and a singer specializing in seductive Mediterannean songs; guests are serenaded as they dine on sumptuous northern Italian cuisine. While the kitchen specializes in delicious pasta dishes, you can also find a number of fish, veal, and chicken entrées on the menu. Just find a quiet corner or a table by the fire and enjoy yourselves as a heavenly evening unfolds around you.

WIND AND SEA, Dana Point
34699 Golden Lantern, at Dana Point Harbor
(714) 496-6500
Moderate
Lunch and Dinner Daily

If you prefer a casual setting with a harbor view, look no further than Wind and Sea. Nestled at the mouth of the marina, this restaurant boasts close-up views of the passing boats through floor-to-ceiling windows. Splurge on the popular seafood sampler for two or choose from the large selection of steaks, fish, sandwiches, and salads. Comfortable rattan chairs and accents add to the nautical theme. This isn't the most intimate dining experience around, but it feels very authentic and charming.

Outdoor Kissing

HERITAGE PARK, Dana Point

Follow Del Prado (Pacific Coast Highway) to Golden Lantern and head west. Keep going until you come to the park.

As you approach this velvety expanse of lawn, high on a windswept hill, don't be surprised if you find that another couple or two have also come here to drink in the view and create memories as special and enduring as the sparkling sea before them. The park has several tiers with small terraces that are popular for weddings. The top one, encircled by blossoming bougainvillea, is a perfect place to feel the warmth of the sun, hear the whisper of the wind, and watch as the boats come home to the harbor. Only a kiss could make the moment more complete.

LANTERN BAY PARK, Dana Point

Heading toward the ocean on Dana Park Harbor Road, turn right onto Park Lantern and follow it to the top of the hill.

This is one of the most romantic spots in the area, with a breathtaking view of the harbor and the dazzling Pacific Ocean. Memories of any time spent on its turf with someone you love will be richly treasured.

Romantic Alternative: Sandwiched between the Ritz-Carlton and a scattering of exclusive estates is **SALT CREEK BEACH PARK**, a hillside stretch of lawn with a million-dollar view. A popular spot for surfing, it's also a great place to marvel at the splendor around you. Ritz guests can take a garden walkway to the park. Those who come by car can park in the large metered lot off Pacific Coast Highway and meander down to the park.

San Clemente

Hotel/Bed and Breakfast Kissing

CASA TROPICANA, San Clemente
610 Avenida Victoria
(714) 492-1234, (800) 492-1245
http://www.casatropicana.com
Expensive to Unbelievably Expensive
Minimum stay requirement on weekends

This unusual inn, set above the San Clemente Pier, offers a tremendous vista of the sparkling Pacific. Each of the nine guest chambers follows a tropical or jungle theme, from the Bogie-and-Bacall-inspired Key Largo to the romantic Out of Africa, complete with a four-poster bed draped in mosquito netting. Several of the rooms carry the theme a little too far: the ceiling of the Emerald Forest is entirely covered with vines, and the Bali Hai will make you feel like you should be drinking something with an umbrella in it. But maybe there's something to be said for fulfilling those "Me Tarzan, you Jane" fantasies.

Most of the rooms have fireplaces and Jacuzzi bathtubs, and two of the three suites have complete kitchenettes ideal for an extended getaway. If you really want to take a trip to Fantasy Island, consider splurging on the Penthouse. This elaborate suite has its own sundeck and a 180-degree ocean view. It also features a seductive three-way fireplace that is accessible from the master bedroom, adjoining sitting room, and large step-up tub overlooking the sea.

Romantic Warning: If you wish to leave your car at the inn while exploring San Clemente, you can take the train to a nearby stop. The bad news is that this same train passes right by the hotel hourly, disturbing an otherwise peaceful setting.

Restaurant Kissing

THE FISHERMAN'S RESTAURANT & BAR, San Clemente
611 Avenida Victoria
(714) 498-6390
Moderate to Expensive
Breakfast Saturday; Lunch and Dinner Daily; Sunday Brunch

A walk on the San Clemente Pier is a must. And while you're there, why not enjoy the relaxed setting of the Fisherman's Restaurant? Blue-and-white-striped umbrellas, wooden tables, and black-and-white photos of fishermen reeling in their catch enhance the nautical theme. The fresh fish of the day is written on a chalkboard, and the rest of the menu lists a wide variety of oysters, mussels, scampi, salmon, snapper, and many other mouthwatering choices. The lounge/bar area is located across the pier, so its noise doesn't intrude on diners. From either place, you can observe a spectacular sunset almost every night.

Outdoor Kissing

LESLIE PARK, San Clemente
182 Calle de Los Alamos

Take the El Camino Real exit from Interstate 5 and go west. Turn left onto Avenida Valencia and left again onto Calle de Los Alamos.

Pssssst. If you're looking for a tuft of grass, a dazzling view, and a little privacy, we have just the place. But because it is just a pocket park in the midst of an exclusive San Clemente neighborhood, we'd better keep this a little hush-hush. Be forewarned, though: you won't find towering trees, picnic tables, or winding paths here—just two simple benches. But while this tiny hillside meadow takes up the space of just one small house lot, its vista of the ocean is truly immense. So come during the week, when no one else is likely to be here, and—*voila!* You'll find own private paradise.

Romantic Alternative: CALIFIA PARK, 240 Avenida Califia, is a larger, ocean-terrace park. Though it's not nearly as private as Leslie Park, it enjoys an ocean view and looks down onto the occasional passing train.

INLAND ORANGE COUNTY

Brea

Restaurant Kissing

LA VIE EN ROSE, Brea
240 South State College Boulevard
(714) 529-8333
Expensive to Very Expensive
Lunch Monday-Friday; Dinner Monday-Saturday

This stunning restaurant, designed to be a replica of a Normandy farmhouse, succeeds in every regard. The octagonal steepled ceiling and the small intimate dining rooms with handsome appointments add to the luxurious effect. Relax near a glowing fireplace in the mansion's lounge, while classic French music serenades you throughout the evening. The Provençal menu reads like a dream. Try the poached salmon bathed in tarragon sauce or the pork tenderloin sautéed with apples and Calvados sauce. It isn't easy to get to Brea, but La Vie en Rose is worth the trip.

Fullerton

Restaurant Kissing

THE CELLAR, Fullerton
305 North Harbor Boulevard
(714) 525-5682
Expensive to Very Expensive
Dinner Tuesday-Saturday

The artistic crew from Disneyland designed The Cellar in 1969. What makes dining here so engaging is that the three main dining rooms are located underground. Private, secluded, exclusive booths are placed around a room filled with roaring open fireplaces, magnificent statues, and crystal chandeliers. The cavernous stone walls are decorated with silver lanterns, antiques, artwork, and wine casks. Eating at The Cellar is like being in the French wine country, enjoying classic French/European cuisine. We highly recommend the salmon and caviar dishes, roasted breast of pheasant, and grilled venison medallions with caramelized apple slices.

Be sure to ask your waiter for a tour of the upstairs cellars where the wine is stored. The restaurant carries more than 1,000 different wines from 15 countries, ranging in price from $50 to $1,500.

Romantic Suggestion: The Cellar holds occasional wine-tasting sessions that take place in the wine cellars. You can sample rare French wines, champagnes, and imports from Europe, Canada, and Australia, while learning a great deal about the history of winemaking.

Anaheim

Restaurant Kissing

JW'S STEAKHOUSE, Anaheim
700 West Convention Way, at the Anaheim Marriott Hotel
(714) 750-8000
Expensive to Very Expensive
Dinner Monday-Saturday

Step into JW's and you will be immediately transported to an English country house with high ceilings and 19th-century details. Hardwood floors, fireplaces, and brick walls add to the classic atmosphere. Most tables are set in their own intimate dining room and classical music plays softly in the background. Every room is different, but all are adorned with original artwork, candelabras, fabric wall coverings, and handsome antiques. Choose between the tempting beef and seafood entrées on the menu, such as filet mignon, porterhouse steak, and blackened tuna with papaya relish. Finally, you can draw out the evening over a slice of toffee-crunch Kahlua mousse cake.

MR. STOX, Anaheim
1105 East Katella Avenue
(714) 634-2994
Expensive
Lunch Monday-Friday; Dinner Daily

Mr. Stox is an award-winning restaurant, for both cuisine and wine. Reminiscent of a European chateau, the dark interior is decorated with Renaissance artwork, Oriental carpets, and beautiful flowers. We suggest requesting one of the burgundy leather booths, so you can sit as close to your dining partner as you desire. Then the choices begin. You might try the fettuccine with blackened swordfish, mesquite-grilled veal chop, or the house specialty, sautéed Maryland crab cakes. All the herbs are home-grown, and all the pastas and pastries are made fresh in-house. A pianist plays lovely melodies every night, and the fireside lounge is a tempting place to cozy up after your gourmet meal.

Irvine

Restaurant Kissing

CHANTECLAIR, Irvine
18912 MacArthur Boulevard
(714) 752-8001
Expensive to Very Expensive
Lunch Monday-Friday; Dinner Monday-Saturday

Despite its expansive size, Chanteclair is masterful at creating a feeling of intimacy. The French country interior is divided into five distinctly different dining rooms, four of which have fireplaces. The library is filled with small tables encircling a crackling hearth; the garden room, with its tiled floor and hanging plants, feels light and airy. No matter which room you choose, your evening will be enhanced by classic dishes such as ahi tuna with pan-seared foie gras and veal chop with grilled forest mushrooms.

San Juan Capistrano

Restaurant Kissing

CAFE MOZART, San Juan Capistrano
31952 Camino Capistrano
(714) 496-0212
Moderate to Expensive
Lunch and Dinner Tuesday-Saturday

Adorned in a manner that whispers of the past, Cafe Mozart brings a little bit of Europe to San Juan Capistrano. It is a place to quietly enjoy the glow of candlelight reflected in your loved one's eyes, as a grand piano softly plays in the background. Emerald green and pink accents highlight the dark wood decor as richly as the herbs and spices highlight the delicious continental cuisine. The varied menu is laden with German specialties such as schnitzel, sauerbraten, and Bavarian bread dumplings, plus homemade pasta, vegetarian entrées, and fresh fish. Outside, in a courtyard strung with tiny white lights, lovers dine by a trickling fountain. Many a wistful dreamer has tossed a coin or two in the fountain and had a wish come true at Cafe Mozart.

L'HIRONDELLE, San Juan Capistrano
31631 Camino Capistrano
(714) 661-0425

Moderate to Expensive
Lunch and Dinner Wednesday-Saturday; Sunday Brunch

Just across from the famous Mission San Juan Capistrano is a restaurant with a mission all its own: to be a source of romantic inspiration for anyone who crosses its threshold. Mission accomplished.

Quaint, charming, and decidedly French, L'Hirondelle combines European country elegance with a sense of humor. Along with the lace curtains, crisp white linens, and candlelight, you'll find a delightful mélange of knick-knacks and curios. The walls and shelves overflow with charming old plates, hats, pots, and dolls. Conversation pieces, maybe, but the real focal point here is the hearty cuisine. Most entrées come with soup or salad and are just what you'd find in the French countryside: roast chicken or duckling, filet of sole, and pepper steak flambé. For a finale, feast on cherries jubilee or crêpes Suzette for two.

Inland Empire

Ontario

Restaurant Kissing

CALLA THE FINE DINING, Ontario
700 North Haven, at the Ontario Hilton
(909) 980-0400
Expensive
Lunch Tuesday-Friday; Dinner Monday-Saturday

Due to its location near the airport, the Ontario Hilton caters largely to a convention crowd. Once you cross the bustling lobby into Calla, however, you'll find a quiet, intimate dining room where you can make romance your business of the day. Opt for one of the comfortable booths bordering the small dining room, where you can appreciate Calla's relaxed and soothing atmosphere. The room is decorated with pastel wallpaper and simply framed Erte prints, and every table is topped with a white tablecloth, a small hurricane lamp, and a silver bud vase with a single red rose. Calla's understated elegance is echoed on the menu, which features simply prepared continental favorites.

Several of the selections at Calla are prepared for two, including a Caesar salad tossed tableside and an impressively hearty Chateaubriand. Creamy lobster bisque and a crisp grilled vegetable salad are two wonderful starters. A palate refresher of raspberry sorbet and a fresh sprig of mint, served in a cut glass dish, is served between courses. Our entrées of prawns in a rich, chardonnay cream sauce and a flavorful fillet of blackened sea bass were lovingly prepared and equally enjoyable. Looking to end your romantic evening with a little flash? Try a traditional favorite such as bananas Foster or cherries jubilee for your grand finale.

Riverside

Restaurant Kissing

DUANE'S PRIME STEAK RESTAURANT, Riverside
3649 Mission Inn Avenue, at the Mission Inn
(909) 341-6767
Expensive
Dinner Tuesday-Saturday

Recently restored to its former glory, the Mission Inn is a grand resort hotel that displays several architectural styles with its array of arches, colonnades, gardens, turrets, terraces, domes, and catacombs. In short, this unique hotel is full of secret wonders. Duane's Prime Steak Restaurant, the Mission Inn's formal dining room, offers another magnificent discovery. Step into the sunken dining room, sink into a plush tapestry-lined booth, and take a moment to admire the original redwood beamed ceilings. The collection of fine art includes an original oil painting of Theodore Roosevelt and the Rough Riders charging up San Juan Hill.

Guests are often welcomed with a complimentary sip of sherry and the bruschetta of the day. This hospitality characterizes the entire evening at Duane's. To begin your dinner by candlelight, we recommend the rich lobster bisque with brandy, wild mushrooms, and tarragon. For the main course, you can't go wrong with the tender filet mignon or the supremely fresh ahi with ginger and soy; both are done to perfection. When the dessert cart passes your way, don't pass up the cobbler with fresh pears, blueberries, and raspberries à la mode, a sweet finish to an impeccable meal.

Romantic Note: When Duane's main dining room fills up, overflow tables are set in the lobby. If this happens when you visit, be sure to request a table in the main dining room. The difference in atmosphere is worth the extra wait.

Romantic Alternative: On a warm evening, enjoy an enchanting dinner under the stars at the **MISSION INN RESTAURANT'S SPANISH PATIO** (Moderate). Less formal than Duane's, this beautiful courtyard features a soothing fountain, a blossoming orange tree, and twinkling white lights strung along the balconies of intricately designed terraces above.

MAGNONE CUCINA, Riverside
1630 Spruce
(909) 781-8840
Moderate
Lunch Monday-Friday; Dinner Daily

Don't let the Miami Vice facade fool you. Indoors, Magnone Cucina is a true restaurant of the '90s. Arches and a wall of glass blocks set off a light and airy trattoria that always seems to be bustling with activity. The large dining area is partitioned by plate-glass walls, and the open kitchen at the back is set apart by a counter covered with colorful, hand-painted tiles. At lunch, windows and skylights allow the sun to shine in. If you go at night, ask for a table for two near the fireplace. You'll soon be greeted by a friendly waiter and served warm focaccia with virgin olive oil and balsamic vinegar to nibble while you scan the menu.

Like many other contemporary Italian kitchens, Magnone Cucina offers fresh salads and soups, wood-fired pizzas, and both traditional and original pasta dishes. An old-country staple such as *pasta e fagioli*, a hearty bean and macaroni soup, makes a great starter. For the main course, try a gourmet pizza with shrimp and grilled vegetables or a pasta special such as penne with sausage and red bell peppers in a spicy tomato sauce. If you have any room left for dessert, the classic tiramisu is sure to please.

Romantic Note: While the food and service at Magnone Cucina are excellent, the bustling trattoria atmosphere may not be ideally suited for an intimate dining experience. However, the live jazz on weekends and the casual atmosphere make this a great option for a first date or a relaxed night out on the town.

MARIO'S PLACE, Riverside
1725 Spruce
(909) 684-7755
Expensive
Reservations Recommended
Lunch Monday-Friday; Dinner Monday-Saturday

For years, Mario's has been *the* place where Riverside couples go to celebrate special occasions and spend romantic evenings. A small wooden bridge leads into the intimate dining area, which is divided into a few small rooms with several private booths lining the walls. You'll soon be greeted by a friendly and able server who will explain the daily specials.

Although the antiquated old-world decor may suggest something different, Mario's Place features contemporary Italian cuisine, the finest in the Inland Empire, in addition to traditional dishes. Mario's exceptional entrées include gnocchi in a pesto sauce with crawfish, wild mushroom ravioli in cream sauce, seared ahi in a ginger-soy marinade, and rack of lamb rubbed with rosemary. For the grand finale, and we do mean grand, choose the lemon tart in puff pastry or the chocolate-hazelnut gateau for a literal slice of heaven.

Romantic Note: The bar at Mario's Place offers live jazz every weekend, a real treat for music lovers. While it's more crowded than the main dining room, the atmosphere here is more casual, and couples listening to music can still order from the full-dinner menu.

Redlands

Restaurant Kissing

THE RESTAURANT OF JOE GREENSLEEVES, Redlands
220 North Orange
(909) 792-6969
Expensive
Lunch Friday; Dinner Tuesday-Sunday

Located in the heart of downtown Redlands, Joe Greensleeves is a restaurant full of surprises. Though it's modest on the outside, the inside is absolutely beautiful. Beveled glass windows and a row of green library lamps that extends to the back of the room contribute to an open and elegant effect. The long, narrow dining room resembles the hull of a ship; in fact, the wooden half-shell of a vessel is set into the left side of the building. On the opposite wall, a large fireplace warms nearby tables set for two. The back of the restaurant is lined with cork paneling to absorb noise. The ceiling, shaped like an upturned boat, is strung with rows of tiny white lights and gives the dining room its panache.

Joe Greensleeves is a "chop house" that prides itself on serving prime cuts of beef. However, the menu also lists a fair selection of fresh fish and some of the best soups in town; don't miss the red bell pepper purée or the black bean tureen—both are irresistible. Keep in mind that this place is for serious meat-eaters. If you want vegetables with dinner, you'll have to order them on the side, although entrées are served with generous portions of rich Yorkshire pudding. For dessert, the Reese's peanut butter pie is almost too rich to handle, but give it your best shot.

Lake Arrowhead, Big Bear, and Environs

Whoever wrote about "purple mountains' majesty" must have had in mind the stunning scenery that follows Highway 18 north from San Bernardino to Lake Arrowhead and Big Bear Lake. As you climb to 6,700 feet above sea level, your eyes will revel in the scenic stimulation this region provides. From the time you leave the arid flatlands and begin your coiling climb up the road, you'll behold tableaus of granite-etched peaks and alpine greenery, as refreshing as they are wondrous. Not surprisingly, Big Bear and Arrowhead were once the domain of Hollywood notables and their wealthy cohorts. Now this resort area attracts vacationers who want to wake up in the mountains, play in the winter snow, eat in interesting restaurants, and shop in quaint boutiques between bursts of outdoor recreation.

Big Bear Lake and its environs are more rustic than the Lake Arrowhead area. Big Bear offers sensational camping during the summer and exhilarating downhill skiing during the winter. Both are beautiful areas where you can renew your city-weary souls in Mother Nature's healing mountain air and scenery. Any time of year is ideal for blissful outdoor escapades here.

Romantic Suggestion: In addition to the resorts and bed-and-breakfast accommodations, many private homes and condos are available for rent for a few days or longer. These are usually fully furnished, and some are very luxurious and located in beautiful settings. Most have wood-burning fireplaces in the living rooms and well-stocked kitchens, so you can prepare a cozy dinner for two and enjoy each other's company in complete privacy. **ABC MOUNTAIN ACCOMMODATIONS**, (909) 337-1003, (800) 550-LAKE (Inexpensive to Unbelievably Expensive) is a complete reservation service for Lake Arrowhead and Big Bear, with a whole range of possibilities in every price category, from luxury lakefront homes to rustic cabins, condos, and special honeymoon packages. You do not pay extra for this service; ABC Mountain Accommodations acts like a travel agent and receives a commission from the owner. Two other possibilities are **ARROWHEAD MOUNTAIN RESORTS RENTAL**, (909) 337-4413, (800) 743-0865, which specializes in Lake Arrowhead properties, and **BLUE SKIES RESORT RENTALS**, (909) 866-7415, (800) 442-2422, for accommodations in Big Bear Valley.

Skyforest

Hotel/Bed and Breakfast Kissing

GREYSTONE, Skyforest
831 Kuffel Canyon
(909) 337-9644
Moderate to Unbelievably Expensive
Minimum stay requirement on weekends and holidays

Surrounded by ancient pines in the community of Skyforest, Greystone is a ten-minute drive from Lake Arrowhead. Guest options here consists of four rooms and a separate cottage, all decorated with antiques and floral fabrics in a Victorian style. The Rendezvous Suite features a king-size bed, marble fireplace, and marble bath with a Jacuzzi tub for two (candles included). The restored 1934 cottage is secluded among giant cedars and includes a kitchenette and dining area, fireplace, and a loft with a king-size bed positioned beneath skylights so you can gaze at the stars.

Lake Arrowhead

Hotel/Bed and Breakfast Kissing

CHATEAU DU LAC
BED AND BREAKFAST, Lake Arrowhead
911 Hospital Road
(909) 337-6488, (800) 601-8722
Expensive to Very Expensive
Minimum stay requirement on weekends and holidays

This bed and breakfast has one undeniably special attraction: it peers down onto the lake. Surely this is one reason Chateau du Lac was proclaimed "Bed and Breakfast of the Month" by *Country Inn* magazine—a prestigious honor indeed.

It's very easy to understand, though. Gingerbread on the outside, fairy tale on the inside, this magnificent inn has everything. It's elegant without being pretentious, romantic without being frothy, and let's not forget that to-die-for view. Each of the five guest rooms is expertly appointed, with a stuffed animal here and a throw pillow there to give them a welcoming touch. Though expensive, the Lakeview Suite is worth the splurge for the private balcony, fireplace, full sound system, and spacious bathroom with a Jacuzzi tub for two that has its own view.

Breakfast is served on the terrace or in the formal dining room. Expect to be treated to homemade egg dishes, scones, quiches, omelets, and other gourmet treats. Afternoon tea is also a lavish affair. And if you're going to have a lavish affair, this is the place to have it.

Romantic Alternative: The nearby **CARRIAGE HOUSE BED AND BREAKFAST**, 472 Emerald Drive, (909) 336-1400, (800) 526-5070 (Inexpensive to Expensive) is a New England–style country home nestled amid tall pine trees. The three rooms are not as spacious and luxurious as those at Chateau du Lac, but the country furnishings are charming and the deck off the sunroom offers a great view of the lake. The Lakeside Trail, a few minutes away, can be followed into Arrowhead Village, and guests can take advantage of the owners' membership at a nearby beach club.

EAGLES LANDING, Lake Arrowhead
27406 Cedarwood Drive
(909) 336-2642, (800) 835-5085
Expensive to Very Expensive
Minimum stay requirement on weekends and holidays

Eagles Landing is a modern mountain inn set in an exclusive West Shore neighborhood. Unlike the many frilly bed and breakfasts located in this neck of the woods, Eagles Landing has a more masculine feeling. The four guest rooms are decorated primarily in earth tones. The spectacular and large Lake View Suite, by far the inn's most romantic offering, is done up in rustic early California-style decor. With a sitting room, large bath, full bar, wood-burning fireplace, TV, and refrigerator, the suite has almost everything you could need in order to burrow in and hibernate together for days. From its private terrace you can appreciate a panoramic view of the lake, sparkling by day, reflecting the stars by night.

When morning arrives, so does a hearty country breakfast. Afternoon hors d'oeuvres are complimentary. A large, comfy hammock beneath the pines awaits your indulgence.

LAKE ARROWHEAD RESORT, Lake Arrowhead
27984 Highway 189
(909) 336-1511, (800) 800-6792
Moderate to Unbelievably Expensive
Minimum stay requirement on holidays

Lake Arrowhead Resort's main draws are its location on the lake and its status as the only full-service resort in the area. Guests can enjoy the on-site health spa, lake-view pool and whirlpools, tennis courts, restaurants, and lounge. Unfortunately, the rooms are more sterile than cozy, with wood-veneered furniture, synthetic bedspreads, and thin bath towels. The more expensive lakeside accommodations do feature king-size beds, wet bars, fireplaces, full kitchens, and balconies overlooking the lake.

Romantic Suggestion: The resort adjoins **LAKE ARROWHEAD VILLAGE**, which contains over 50 specialty shops and restaurants in a charming alpine setting.

LAKE ARROWHEAD VILLAGE LODGE, Lake Arrowhead
28041 East Lakes Edge Road
(909) 337-2544, (909) 337-2543
http://www.sbmnet.com/thelodge
Expensive to Very Expensive
Minimum stay requirement on holidays

Located just across the highway from Lake Arrowhead Village, this former hunting lodge was handcrafted by German artisans. Each room is tastefully decorated in a European style with beautiful linens, wicker furniture, and hand-carved four-poster and knotty pine beds. The rates include a full breakfast and late-afternoon wine and hors d'oeuvres, which can be enjoyed by the massive stone fireplace in the Grand Parlor overlooking the lake.

ROMANTIQUE LAKEVIEW LODGE, Lake Arrowhead
28051 Highway 189
(909) 337-6633, (800) 358-LAKE
Inexpensive to Very Expensive
Minimum stay requirement on weekends seasonally and on holidays

From the moment you scale the steps to the lodge's lovely front terrace, set high above the shimmering lake, you can't help but anticipate the night ahead. Elegant Victorian furnishings and a blazing hearth in the beautifully appointed lobby add to the feeling that you've discovered someplace exceptionally special.

Each of the nine rooms seems to perfectly unite old-world charm with modern comforts. Antiques, lace curtains, fireplaces, luxurious private baths, and panoramic lake views are just part of what you'll find here. VCRs, video cassettes, microwave popcorn, and hot chocolate are also provided for those who like to curl up with a steamy movie classic.

SADDLEBACK INN, Lake Arrowhead
300 State Highway 173
(909) 336-3571, (800) 858-3334

Moderate to Very Expensive
Minimum stay requirement on weekends

This restored historical landmark features 34 guest rooms and 20 cottages with queen- or king-size beds, stone fireplaces, and double whirlpool baths. The furnishings are a blend of Victorian, mountain, and country styles, complemented by Laura Ashley linens and fabrics. The inn is situated at the entrance to Lake Arrowhead Village, which is convenient but not exactly remote. Just off the lobby is the wonderful new restaurant, **TAPESTRY** (see Restaurant Kissing).

Restaurant Kissing

BELGIAN WAFFLE WORKS, Lake Arrowhead
28200 Highway 189
(909) 337-5222
Inexpensive
Breakfast and Lunch Daily

If you'd like a hearty breakfast—or if you just have a sweet tooth—follow your nose to the Belgian Waffle Works, dockside at Lake Arrowhead Village, for mouthwatering waffles served a multitude of delicious ways. This petite country-style restaurant is situated right along the shore, so scoring a window seat may be difficult during high season. Take heart, though: a few terrace tables are added in the summer, creating an ideal spot for taking in the view, the food, and some maple-flavored kisses.

TAPESTRY, Lake Arrowhead
300 State Highway 173, at the Saddleback Inn
(909) 336-2017
Moderate to Expensive
Lunch and Dinner Monday-Friday; Brunch Saturday-Sunday

Tapestry, located on the ground floor of the historic **SADDLEBACK INN** (see Hotel/Bed and Breakfast Kissing), is a welcome new addition to Lake Arrowhead. Guests are welcome to relax by the fire in the comfortable lounge and enjoy an aperitif before dinner. Try to get one of the romantic, intimate booths framed by curtains and upholstered in floral tapestry fabrics, or one of the tables placed next to the floor-to-ceiling French windows facing the lake. The eclectic menu includes Italian appetizers such as caprese salad (mozzarella and roma tomatoes with basil) and calamari; "good ol' American cooking," like Mickey's meat loaf and New York steak; and gourmet dishes, such as marinated pork tenderloin with a grilled vegetable salad and mountain mashed potatoes in a molasses glaze. Later, you can step outside, breathe in the invigorating mountain air, and do a little stargazing.

Blue Jay

Restaurant Kissing

CASUAL ELEGANCE, Blue Jay (Agua Fria)
26848 State Highway 189
(909) 337-8932
Expensive
Dinner Wednesday-Sunday; Sunday Brunch

Whenever we asked the whereabouts of Lake Arrowhead's most romantic restaurant, we were always pointed in this direction. Located in the center of a small mountain hamlet, this cottage is aglow with candlelight and the brilliance of a glittering hearth. The dining rooms are tiny—barely fitting three or four tables—so even when every chair is filled, your need for intimacy is never threatened. The menu changes weekly, but you will undoubtedly find gourmet offerings of meat, seafood, and pasta. Dinner is a long, leisurely affair, presented in true French fashion with the salad served last and sorbet between soup and entrée. This gives you a chance to enjoy your surroundings: antiques, lace curtains, and spotlighted oil paintings. Better yet, it provides the opportunity to look into each other's eyes and savor an evening destined to be unforgettable.

Big Bear Lake

Hotel/Bed and Breakfast Kissing

APPLES BED & BREAKFAST INN, Big Bear Lake
42430 Moonridge Road
(909) 866-0903
Expensive to Very Expensive
Minimum stay requirement on weekends

An acre of pine trees embraces this Victorian home. The 12 guest rooms are all individually decorated, but each has a king-size bed with down comforter, a gas fireplace, and an old-fashioned rocking chair or recliner; four have Jacuzzi tubs for two. A complimentary full breakfast is served in the large dining room and includes homemade baked goods, French toast, honey-apple sausages, and other delights. The large gathering room, with its wood-burning stove and library loft, is filled with comfy overstuffed furniture and is the ideal place to curl up with a homemade dessert before going to bed.

Romantic Alternative: **BEAR MANOR CABINS**, 40393 Big Bear Boulevard, (909) 866-6800, (800) 472-BEAR (Inexpensive to Expensive) has 16 rustic cabins with private baths. These accommodations are not as luxurious as those at Apples, but many have fireplaces and kitchenettes, and all offer total privacy.

NORTHWOODS RESORT, Big Bear Lake
40650 Village Drive
(909) 866-3121, (800) 866-3121
Moderate to Unbelievably Expensive
Minimum stay requirement on weekends and holidays

Within walking distance of the village at Big Bear Lake, this full-service resort offers 139 spacious rooms and suites with custom-designed rustic furnishings; some also have fireplaces and lake views. During summer months, the heated pool and spa are a popular place for couples to relax, and in winter the ice-skating pond is a great place to practice skating *à deux*.

Restaurant Kissing

IRON SQUIRREL, Big Bear Lake
646 Pine Knot Boulevard
(909) 866-9121
Moderate
Lunch and Dinner Daily

Though you'd never guess from its name, the Iron Squirrel has plenty of romantic dining potential. Candlelight, dark wood, linen tablecloths, and lace curtains distinguish Big Bear's most intimate hideaway. There are three small dining rooms and many booths for quiet conversation. The sumptuous French cuisine, highlighted by delicious seafood, pasta, lamb, and veal dishes, will satisfy every appetite.

Big Bear City

Hotel/Bed and Breakfast Kissing

GOLD MOUNTAIN MANOR HISTORIC
BED AND BREAKFAST, Big Bear City
1117 Anita
(909) 585-6997, (800) 509-2604

http://www.bigbear.com/goldmtn
Inexpensive to Very Expensive
Minimum stay requirement on weekends

If you're looking for a romantic mountain hideaway, it doesn't get much better than this. The astutely renovated mansion with maple floors and beamed ceilings contains five exceptional guest rooms, each with a character all its own, and two suites. What the rooms have in common are wood-burning fireplaces, antique furnishings, and unusual beds with attractive linens. Most of the rooms have private baths but several are shared, so be specific when making reservations. Of the two suites, we recommend the Ted Ducey Suite with its Jacuzzi tub. Breakfast is a tantalizing affair that will keep you going strong on a morning hike through the national forest, just one block down the road. In the evening, sit side by side on one of the glacier-carved boulders that overlook Big Bear Lake and watch the setting sun.

Fawnskin

Hotel/Bed and Breakfast Kissing

WINDY POINT INN, Fawnskin
39015 North Shore Drive
(909) 866-2746
Moderate to Very Expensive
Minimum stay requirement on weekends and holidays

Mountain lore has it that a young, handsome man stricken with a terminal illness devoted his last days to building a place so beautiful, so compelling, so intimate, that no romantic could resist. Like the director of a great love story, he proceeded to set the stage. First he found the land, a beautiful secluded point along a glistening azure lake. Though it was not for sale, he convinced the owners to sell and allow him his dream. He then found the best craftsmen, and with no more than the ideas in his head, he expertly designed and decorated the tranquil oasis now known as the Windy Point Inn.

This is the only bed and breakfast in the area set directly upon the shore, and it's easy to see how that fact directly influenced the inn's design. Everywhere you look you'll find window seats and private decks—anything to help take in the incredible views. The decor is elegant and sophisticated, combining high-tech furnishings, rustic antiques, and eclectic pieces of art. Nowhere is this better illustrated than in The Peaks, the very expensive but unbelievably luxurious master suite. Beyond romantic, it was designed so that no matter where you are in the suite you can enjoy the dramatic lake views. Above your pillows, a strategically placed skylight practically brings the stars into the bedroom. There's a fireplace in the corner, a sunken Jacuzzi tub, a double-headed shower that doubles as a sauna, and a private deck with a tree growing right through it (after all, this is an environmentally protective resort).

In the morning, a full gourmet breakfast is served in the beautiful living room area beside a blazing hearth. Listening to soft classical music and gazing out the wall of windows at a flawless lakefront view, you will probably feel the way we did. Windy Point Inn must have been created by someone incredibly special.

"*Soul meets soul on lovers' lips.*"

Percy Bysshe Shelley

Palm Springs and Environs

Palm Springs was almost left out of the original collection of kissing places. This man-made, concrete oasis is made up of straight slabs of highways and roads that crisscross vast stretches of overdeveloped, monotonous flatlands filled with trailer parks, suburban housing ventures, condominium complexes, shopping strips, spa resorts, hotels and motels, and jade green golf courses. Rising abruptly from this real estate explosion are the towering, rocky summits of the San Jacinto mountain range. The contrast between the natural rugged beauty of the land and the urban sprawl can be disconcerting.

But for Californians (and snowbird Midwesterners) who love golf, heated fresh air, celebrity sightseeing, and outstanding resort accommodations, Palm Springs is more than an oasis—it's a spiritual sanctuary. Of course, the underlying reason for this fervent attachment to the desert is its sultry, omnipresent sunshine and abundant underground water supply. These wellsprings keep the developed areas green while the sun keeps everything else, for as far as the eye can see, burnished with tan, gold, and olive green. Although Palm Springs itself may not be romantic, it can be the setting for a literally heartwarming holiday.

Palm Springs

Hotel/Bed and Breakfast Kissing

CASA CODY BED AND BREAKFAST COUNTRY INN, Palm Springs
175 South Cahuilla Road
(619) 320-9346, (800) 231-CODY
Inexpensive to Expensive
Minimum stay requirement on weekends and holidays

Although billed as a bed-and-breakfast inn, this charming complex offers more seclusion and privacy than most B&Bs. In fact, many of the rooms have fully stocked kitchens, private patios, and fireplaces. Founded in the 1920s, Casa Cody has been completely redecorated in a charming Santa Fe style, complete with tile floors, throw rugs, and colorful towels in the bathroom. Two pools and a whirlpool spa are on the beautifully landscaped grounds, and continental breakfast is served outside each morning. Some guests choose to stay for months, because the accommodations are so comfortable and the surroundings are so serene.

INGLESIDE INN, Palm Springs
200 West Ramon Road
(619) 325-0046, (800) 772-6655
http://www.prinet.com/ingleside
Expensive to Unbelievably Expensive
Minimum stay requirement on weekends

Ingleside Inn's brochure promises everything you could want in an exclusive getaway; unfortunately, the slightly tacky decor does not live up to that promise. The guest suites encircle a lush garden that requires some manicuring. The rooms are lavishly decorated with period furnishings, and some have fireplaces and private patios, but the poorly lit interiors are in need of remodeling and general sprucing up. Also, the bathrooms are dated and some of the furniture could use recovering. There is a lovely outdoor pool surrounded by lawn and shade trees, but it's right off the front entrance, so you don't have much privacy.

Romantic Warning: The restaurant on the property, **MELVYN'S** (Expensive), is also on the tacky side, so we recommend going to one of the places reviewed in Restaurant Kissing rather than dining in.

KORAKIA PENSIONE, Palm Springs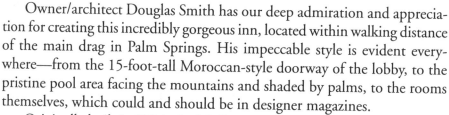
257 South Patencio Road
(619) 864-6411
Inexpensive to Expensive; No Credit Cards
Minimum stay requirement on weekends

Owner/architect Douglas Smith has our deep admiration and appreciation for creating this incredibly gorgeous inn, located within walking distance of the main drag in Palm Springs. His impeccable style is evident everywhere—from the 15-foot-tall Moroccan-style doorway of the lobby, to the pristine pool area facing the mountains and shaded by palms, to the rooms themselves, which could and should be in designer magazines.

Originally built in 1924, the Mediterranean-style villa now has a North African desert feel. The details are perfect: handmade feather beds, adobe walls, wood accents, and antique furnishings. Even the baths have custom touches and look as if they should be in a showroom. Best of all, the prices are very reasonable for the quality and size of the rooms, many of which are suites with separate living rooms and stocked kitchens. In addition, a gourmet continental breakfast is included with your stay. Korakia Pensione is a brilliant new option for those in search of a romantic escape.

VILLA ROYALE, Palm Springs
1620 Indian Trail
(619) 327-2314, (800) 245-2314
http://www.prinet.com/vroyale
Moderate to Very Expensive
Minimum stay requirement on weekends

Talk about an oasis in the middle of an oasis! From the moment you arrive, Villa Royale will make your hearts beat faster and refresh your city-weary minds. The decor combines rural grandeur with eclectic European flair. The 31 guest rooms, each with its own private entrance, front a series of inner courtyards enhanced by meandering brick paths, vine-covered stone arches, urns filled with flowering bushes, and bubbling stone fountains. Two swimming pools and a hot tub are hidden by towering palm trees. No two rooms are alike, but all are decorated in imported furnishings and fabrics, with firm beds and plush down comforters. Many of the suites have cozy sitting areas, stone fireplaces, French doors, and private patios and spas. There isn't a corner of this villa that isn't soothing and gracious.

Romantic Note: Villa Royale calls itself a bed and breakfast because of the complimentary morning meal served poolside in the center courtyard. Unlike other bed and breakfasts, however, it also has an intimate restaurant. EUROPA (Expensive) serves continental cuisine for lunch and dinner except in summer, when it's closed.

Restaurant Kissing

ST. JAMES AT THE VINEYARD, Palm Springs
265 South Palm Canyon Drive
(619) 320-8041
Expensive to Very Expensive

Owner and head chef James Offord has moved the former Cafe St. James to larger quarters down the street, and the new space is a dream. Beautiful wall coverings by local artists set off Offord's collection of exotic masks and other artifacts, including a large Buddha and a model of a witch doctor from Indonesia. The Green Room, located in the back, is the most intimate, with comfortable (and cozy) bench seating built into the wall and a glorious view of the glassed-in wine cellar. On cooler evenings, the outdoor patio is a romantic alternative.

Billed as "international gourmet cuisine," the menu still carries the popular curry dishes, as well as seafood, pastas, and New York steak grilled with wild mushrooms, cognac sauce, and a touch of cream. The award-winning wine cellar holds nearly 200 selections from throughout the world, and the prices are surprisingly reasonable for the quality. You'll be tempted to linger over an exotic after-dinner drink and enjoy the seductive surroundings.

Outdoor Kissing

INDIAN CANYONS, Palm Springs
South Palm Canyon
(619) 325-1053, (619) 325-5673
$5 per person

On South Palm Canyon, three miles south of East Palm Canyon Drive.

Hiking trails, running springs, and waterfalls can be found only a few miles from the heart of Palm Springs in three canyons that used to be inhabited by the Agua Caliente Cahuilla Native Americans. This is a wonderful destination for a nature hike and a picnic lunch (which you'll want to bring with you, since there aren't many dining options here). These canyons are on record as having the most Washingtonia palm trees in the world, and they stretch for miles past indigenous flora and rocky gorges. As you explore, take advantage of the many opportunities to step off the beaten track and into each other's arms.

Romantic Note: THE TRADING POST next to the parking lot is rather touristy, but does carry handmade Native American crafts. If you can tolerate the kitschy ambience it might be passable, but it is not recommended for anything more than a browse.

PALM SPRINGS AERIAL TRAMWAY, Palm Springs
Highway 111 and Tramway Road
(619) 325-1391, (619) 325-1449
$16.95 per person, round-trip

Follow North Palm Canyon Road north out of town to Tramway Road. Turn left up the mountain to the tram.

This is the longest tramway in the world, which in itself is not a particularly moving statistic. The tourist concession stands are unimaginative and bleak. None of that, of course, has anything to do with kissing and tender moments. What has everything to do with snuggling close is the 15-minute, 12,800-foot ascent to perilous, rocky cliffs with astounding views and a temperature as much as 40 degrees below that of the desert floor. Here you'll find a winter wonderland of cross-country skiing and sledding, a summer paradise of endless hiking trails dusted with desert hues of gold and green, and the unsurpassed exhilaration that comes from being on top of the world. For the adventurous, camping facilities provide the ultimate in outdoor romance.

Romantic Warning: This ride is not inexpensive. To really get full value from this stirring sightseeing attraction, come prepared to spend the day. But if you only have a few hours, the more romantic and less expensive option is to check out **INDIAN CANYONS** (see previous review).

Rancho Mirage

Hotel/Bed and Breakfast Kissing

THE RITZ-CARLTON, Rancho Mirage
68-900 Frank Sinatra Drive
(619) 321-8282, (800) 241-3333
Unbelievably Expensive
Minimum stay requirement

Kissing in the desert doesn't get any better than at this top-flight luxury hotel. From the impeccable service to the opulent furnishings to the gorgeous locale in a secluded mountain wildlife reserve (complete with bighorn sheep, coveys of quail, and roadrunners), we were hooked. The luxurious rooms have all the necessary amenities, including spacious, well-stocked bathrooms and his-and-her bathrobes. Nearby, a steaming Jacuzzi tub overlooking the bluff and an Olympic-size pool beckon. The fitness center boasts state-of-the-art equipment, a variety of spa services, and a spotless, luxurious bathhouse with separate sauna and steam rooms. Tennis courts are a few feet away; horseback riding and golf can be easily arranged. But our favorite activity occurs after sundown: cheek-to-cheek dancing to the live jazz combo in the lounge after dinner.

Speaking of dinner, "south of the border" dishes and gourmet meals featuring ingredients from the desert region are served in the Ritz's two restaurants. **THE DINING ROOM** (Expensive) is formal, elegant, and closed during the summer. **THE CAFE** (Moderate to Expensive) has a spectacular view of the pool and the desert below, and an equally spectacular menu. Begin your meal with chilled gazpacho and a wild mushroom empanada. Also try the seafood ravioli with salmon, shrimp, and scallops in lobster sauce, or the papaya and watercress salad with marinated chicken in a lemon-ginger vinaigrette.

Romantic Note: If you're traveling with children, you'll appreciate Ritz Kids. This special program of supervised activities includes nature walks, arts and crafts, and outdoor games that keep your children occupied all day, so you can relax and enjoy each other.

Romantic Suggestion: Ask the concierge to arrange a two-hour jeep tour with DESERT ADVENTURES, 67-555 Highway 111 (East Palm Canyon Drive), Cathedral City, (619) 324-JEEP ($69 per person) through the nearby mountains or INDIAN CANYONS (see Outdoor Kissing in Palm Springs). Cuddle up in back under a blanket while your guide intertains and informs you about the terrain and the Native American culture of the desert.

Restaurant Kissing

CHART HOUSE, Rancho Mirage
69-934 Highway 111 (East Palm Canyon Drive)
(619) 324-5613
Expensive
Dinner Daily

It's obvious why a number of architectural awards have been bestowed on this dramatic building set into a desert hillside. Inside, a beautifully curved wooden ceiling meets stone walls adorned with large original artwork. Tables are placed in intimate alcoves, and many are framed by semicircular wooden beams for greater intimacy. Natural light streams in from an outside garden, and soft instrumental music plays in the background. This is a very cozy setting for gazing into each other's eyes.

Fresh fish and steak dishes are the house specialties, and dinners include a first course from the salad bar. Two highlights are the New Zealand rack of spring lamb and the coconut crunchy shrimp. Even though the setting is first-class, casual dress is encouraged, so you have the best of both worlds.

The Chart House doesn't take reservations, except from hotel concierges, but the bar area is lovely if you need to wait. Try to get one of the booths.

Palm Desert

Hotel/Bed and Breakfast Kissing

TRES PALMAS BED AND BREAKFAST, Palm Desert
73135 Tumbleweed Lane
(619) 773-9858, (800) 770-9858
Moderate to Expensive
Minimum stay requirement on weekends

Although this newly opened bed and breakfast is just a few blocks away from a major shopping mecca, the quiet, residential neighborhood could fool you into believing it's your own weekend home in the desert, but with none of the hassles. The Southwest-style decor is highlighted by Navajo rugs, handsome wooden furniture, and Native American artwork. All four guest rooms have private baths, queen- or king-size beds with down pillows, and color televisions. In the backyard, you can bask in the sun along with the pet turtles and tortoises, or cool off in the large pool next to the Jacuzzi tub. Continental breakfast and afternoon snacks are served in a dining room that adjoins the spacious living room.

Restaurant Kissing

JILLIAN'S, Palm Desert
74-155 El Paseo
(619) 776-8242
Expensive to Very Expensive
Call for seasonal hours.

For romantic ambience and great food, Jillian's should be at the top of your list. The serene and regal interior is reminiscent of an elegant Spanish villa, with a number of small, intimate dining rooms arranged around an outdoor patio in the middle. Whitewashed walls contrast with dark wooden beams and high-backed tapestry upholstered chairs.

The food is out of this world. Appetizers range from grilled shrimp in champagne sauce to wild mushroom strudel. Tasty pasta dishes include fettuccine with slivered Norwegian smoked salmon and spaghetti with prosciutto, asparagus, and mushrooms. Each dish comes as a main course or you can order a sampler of three different pastas. The entrées here are mouthwatering, especially the rare seared ahi tuna and the Renaissance pork, but save room for a sweet finale. The raspberry crème brûlée and the chocolate mousse trilogy aren't made any better in France. Adjourn to the piano bar for an after-dinner drink and you can continue the seduction.

Outdoor Kissing

THE LIVING DESERT, Palm Desert
47-900 Portola Avenue
(619) 346-5694
$7.50 admission
Call for seasonal closures.

On Portola Avenue, south of El Paseo and just past Haystack Road.

A wonderful way to learn more about the desert habitat, while enjoying an outdoor stroll hand in hand, is to spend an hour or two at the Living Desert Wildlife and Botanical Park. Its 1,200 acres house exhibits of Native American culture, hiking trails, and many of the world's rarest animals and plants. Our walk took an hour and we saw only a handful of other people. Desert flowers, fascinating cacti, and unusual shade trees are well tended and labeled, and add to the feeling of being on safari in an exotic land. Close-up views of mountain lions, wolves, coyotes, bighorn sheep, golden eagles, and other rare desert animals also contribute to the sense of adventure. If it's hot outside, it is best to go in the early morning or midafternoon to avoid the high temperatures at midday. The park closes at 4:30 P.M.

Romantic Suggestion: A five-minute drive from the Living Desert, **CEDAR CREEK INN**, 73-445 El Paseo, (619) 340-1236 (Inexpensive) is a charming place to refresh yourselves afterwards, especially if you can snag a table on one of the two outdoor patios surrounded by foliage (one faces a small fountain). The interior is not nearly as appealing. Situated in the middle of blocks of expensive shops, this casual restaurant serves sandwiches, salads, and delectable desserts in the afternoon. A more formal dinner menu begins at 4:30 P.M.

Desert Hot Springs

Hotel/Bed and Breakfast Kissing

TWO BUNCH PALMS, Desert Hot Springs
67-425 Two Bunch Palms Trail
(619) 329-8791, (800) 472-4334
Unbelievably Expensive
Minimum stay requirement
Call for seasonal closures.

Other resorts pale in comparison with this pinnacle of spa tranquility and self-indulgence. Guests check in for high-class pampering in one of the 44 private villas spread out on more than 100 lush, verdant, wooded acres. The villas, havens of bliss and comfort, are spacious, with plush furnishings and details. Secluded rock grotto pools, fed by mineral hot springs, are the ideal place to unwind and rediscover each other. Tennis courts and a swimming pool complete the picture, so you never have to leave the property.

Swathed in satiny golden hues cast by lovely stained glass windows, Two Bunch Palms' restaurant, **THE CASINO** (Moderate to Expensive) is an evocative setting for culinary and interpersonal magic. A complimentary continental breakfast of fruit, freshly baked goods, cereal, juice, tea, and coffee is served in the dining room and on the adjoining terrace overlooking the beautiful grounds. Order a picnic lunch box to enjoy by the large pond in the middle of the property. The area by the pond is shaded by large trees and encircled by a well-tended lawn dotted with chairs that invite you to curl up and soak in the serenity of your surroundings. (Your reverie will probably be temporarily interrupted by the adorable rabbits that have the run of the place.)

Though all of this is enough for any two people who need time to unwind, Two Bunch Palms is also a spa, and the services here will heal you mentally and physically. Options include Swedish and Japanese massages, aromatherapy, reflexology, body wraps, mud baths, and many other exquisite treatments that sound as exotic as they feel and can melt years of stress from every inch of your bodies. One of the most romantic possibilities is the Roman Tub Rejuvenator ($98 per person), an hour-long massage followed by a lavender Epsom salt bath by candlelight. The sensations you'll take home with you after a few days here are meant for sharing.

Romantic Note: Only registered guests are allowed on the property, but others can avail themselves of the spa facilities and stay for lunch afterwards. Plush, large bath towels are plentiful, but you'll want to bring a bathrobe or purchase robes and other Two Bunch souvenirs in the resort's shop.

"A soft lip would tempt you to an eternity of kissing."

Ben Jonson

Idyllwild

At an elevation of 5,500 feet, this small resort village is tucked in the San Jacinto Mountains between Los Angeles and Palm Springs. Unlike some other Southern California mountain resorts, this one has managed to remain small. Beautiful scenery, clean pine-scented air, and four distinct seasons contribute to Idyllwild's charm. Hiking is one of the major draws, with hundreds of miles of trails ranging in difficulty from a casual stroll to Devil's Slide, a seven-and-a-half-mile trek up 4,400 feet. On your travels you may spot deer, coyotes, bobcats, and a variety of colorful birds.

A more than adequate supply of shops and boutiques will entice those who don't want to get too far away from shopping, and a small movie theater in the center of town shows recent releases. Many of the accommodations are bed and breakfasts, and the prices are less expensive than other places in Southern California, averaging around $85 per night. Most of the restaurants are more rustic than classically romantic, but we've highlighted a few that caught our attention. Whatever you choose to do in Idyllwild, we can assure you of three things: you'll be close to the mountains, close to the stars, and close to each other.

Hotel/Bed and Breakfast Kissing

CEDAR STREET INN, Idyllwild
25880 Cedar Street
(909) 659-4789
Inexpensive
Minimum stay requirement on weekends and holidays

Located a few blocks from the center of town, Cedar Street Inn is a country Victorian lodging surrounded by lovely gardens. The hospitality here is not limited to guests: we were charmed to see squirrels drinking out of the fountain as blue jays flocked to a nearby bird feeder on the wooden deck. Constructed from two 1930s homes, the inn offers delightful surroundings and personal comforts in otherwise rustic Idyllwild. Each of the eight guest rooms has its own bath, deck, queen-size bed, and private entrance, and six have fireplaces. Pick a room to fit your personality, from The Cottage, decorated in white with floral accents, to the Captain's Quarters, with its New England nautical decor, river-rock fireplace, and claw-foot tub. The parlor is stocked with books, games, and puzzles, and warmed by a roaring fire in the winter.

FERN VALLEY INN, Idyllwild
25240 Fern Valley Road
(909) 659-2205
http://www.ids.net/wknd/calif/fernval.htm
Inexpensive to Moderate
Minimum stay requirement on weekends

Embraced by towering cedars on the outskirts of town, the Fern Valley Inn offers 11 rustic cottages connected by stone pathways and furnished with antiques, quilt-covered beds, and corner fireplaces. These are not luxurious accommodations, and they lack phones, but the room rates are very reasonable for the setting. The pathways also wind through a rose garden and up to a secluded, heated outdoor pool (the only one we're aware of in Idyllwild).

STRAWBERRY CREEK INN, Idyllwild
26370 Highway 243
(909) 659-3202, (800) 262-8969
Inexpensive to Expensive
Minimum stay requirement on weekends and holidays

This rambling 1941 home is tucked in a grove of pine and oak trees only minutes away from the center of Idyllwild. Owners Diana and Jim Goff have lovingly created a refuge for city-stressed couples to rediscover peace and quiet, and, ultimately, each other.

Whether you stay in the main house or in one of the rooms that border the courtyard, you'll find a queen-size bed and a private bath for your comfort. What you won't find are televisions and phones. *Ahhhh.* Beginning to relax? Each room has a different decor, from the rustic mountain-lodge feeling of the San Jacinto Room to the Victorian ambience of Helen's Room. We recommend opting for one of the rooms with fireplaces in the winter.

A delicious breakfast is served in the glassed-in porch of the main house. After breakfast you can curl up on an overstuffed sofa in the living room, play a board game, browse through nostalgic photographs, or select a novel from the book-lined shelves. There are plenty of extra touches, like "Granny," the soft-sculptured doll who sits in her rocker, and the bowl of chocolate kisses left out on the coffee table. If you're planning on sneaking a kiss (chocolate or otherwise), be forewarned that nothing gets past Granny. The good news is that when you decide to head back to your room, Granny stays put.

Restaurant Kissing

ANTONELLI'S, Idyllwild
26345 Highway 243
(909) 659-5500
Moderate
Dinner Wednesday-Sunday

This contemporary, casual Italian restaurant is a new addition to the Idyllwild scene. Bright and airy, its natural-style interior is highlighted by hardwood floors warmed by throw rugs, paneled walls adorned with dried flowers, and a beamed ceiling overhead. Soft instrumental music plays in the background. In addition to an excellent selection of pasta dishes, Antonelli's offers a variety of mouthwatering choices at reasonabe prices. Try the raspberry chicken salad, ribeye steak, or baked Alaskan salmon. Then top off the evening with a decadent tiramisu for two.

RESTAURANT GASTROGNOME, Idyllwild
54381 Ridgeview
(909) 659-5055
Moderate to Expensive
Lunch Monday-Saturday; Dinner Daily; Sunday Brunch

Upon entering Restaurant Gastrognome, you'll be asked if you'd like to sit in the dark, snug cafe, with its tiny windows bordered with snow in the winter, or in the open, spacious dining room, with its enormous fireplace. We prefer the dining room: although the cafe is cozy, the tables are a little too close together. Throughout the restaurant, however, the wood paneling, dark burgundy color scheme, and candlelit tables provide a warm and inviting shelter for lovesick mountaineers. When the weather permits, the charming outdoor patio is an ideal spot for lunch or an aperitif before retreating inside for dinner.

The menu presents more difficult choices, from a wide range of steak, chicken, seafood, and pasta dishes. The fiery chicken on cilantro pasta with almond butter sauce is scrumptious—a definite favorite—and the service is attentive.

UPTOWN CAFE, Idyllwild
54750 North Circle Drive
(909) 659-5212
Inexpensive
Breakfast and Lunch Daily

If all that fresh mountain air starts getting to you and you find your-selves craving a cappuccino or a latte and maybe even a contemporary work of art or two, head over to the Uptown Cafe. It's a nice mix of city hip and mountain rustic, with knotty pine paneling, open beams, colorful collectibles, and expansive windows looking out to pine trees.

Curl up on a cushioned couch in front of the river-rock fireplace or sneak outside to the corner table on the enclosed sunporch. The outdoor deck is definitely the place to be on weekend evenings, when you'll be serenaded by live guitar music. The simple, healthy menu specializes in East Indian and Mediterranean dishes such as tandoori chicken salad with baby greens, and pasta with roasted eggplant and sun-dried tomatoes. Uptown Cafe also prepares picnic lunches—perfect provisions for an affectionate ramble in the woods.

Temecula and Julian

Temecula

Vineyards draping sun-drenched hillsides, hot-air balloons filling the skies with crayon-bright color, connoisseurs sipping wine in a provocative stone courtyard—these scenes abound throughout the Temecula wine country. While this may not be Napa Valley, the hills here are bursting with sweeping vistas and ripening grapes. The best part is that it's only an hour's drive from San Diego and Los Angeles, although the atmosphere is worlds away.

Hotel/Bed and Breakfast Kissing

LOMA VISTA BED AND BREAKFAST, Temecula
33350 La Serena Way
(909) 676-7047
Moderate

The Loma Vista Bed and Breakfast is nestled in the heart of the Southern California wine country. The attractive Mission-style hacienda is probably too contemporary to be considered endearing or cozy, but it is decorated with personality and charm. Several of the rooms have private balconies that look out onto the citrus groves and vineyards that blanket the valley. The Loma Vista is also minutes from downtown Temecula, a colorful (though somewhat touristy) frontier town decked out in Western garb. Your stay here includes a generous champagne breakfast served in the dining room or on the flower-clad garden patio, and nightly cheese and wine presented in the living room.

Restaurant Kissing

CAFE CHAMPAGNE, Temecula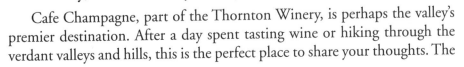
32575 Rancho California Road, at the Thornton Winery
(909) 699-0088
Moderate to Expensive
Lunch Daily; Dinner Tuesday-Sunday

Cafe Champagne, part of the Thornton Winery, is perhaps the valley's premier destination. After a day spent tasting wine or hiking through the verdant valleys and hills, this is the perfect place to share your thoughts. The contemporary Mediterranean-style villa is surrounded by beautifully landscaped grounds, cascading fountain and all. Inside, it has a traditional European country mood that is both elegant and comfortable. The cobblestone courtyard is the best spot for an intimate afternoon or evening meal, with a terrace that looks out over the abundant vineyards. The international cuisine here is eclectic but remarkable, and designed to complement wine or champagne. Start your meal with an appetizer such as the roasted poblano chiles stuffed with Muenster cheese and drizzled with relleno sauce, or perhaps the curried butternut squash soup with apple chutney. Then move on to the chicken breast with ricotta cheese and pancetta stuffing, glazed with a rosemary-mustard demi-glace. Sensational.

Julian

Tiny Julian is little more than a four-street town set high in the Vallecito Mountains in the middle of the Cleveland National Forest. Things move at a slower pace out here, the skies are a bit bluer, and the mountain air is incredibly fresh and revitalizing. Coiling backroads take you through pine-covered meadows and past well-tended orchards. The four seasons are distinct, with blossoms in the spring, dry parched earth in the summer, lush fruit and fall foliage in autumn, and brisk air and snow-sprinkled scenery in winter. A century ago people journeyed to Julian in search of gold; nowadays they come seeking peace and quiet, both of which can be found in ample supply.

Julian also excels in another arena: apples. Julian produces an abundant apple crop for the entire San Diego region. Apple pie à la mode and fresh cider will be the first of your pleasant discoveries here in the vibrant fall harvest months.

Romantic Note: Although Julian offers plenty of scenery and solitude, choices are limited when it comes to finding romantic restaurants and accommodations. There are only a few notable spots, but mostly the assortment of bed and breakfasts, inns, and restaurants range from nondescript to run-down.

Hotel/Bed and Breakfast Kissing

ARTIST'S LOFT, Julian
(619) 765-0765
http://www.julianbnbguild.com
Moderate
Minimum stay requirement on weekends

Take two wildly creative artists, give them a spectacular plot of land in the mountains, let them fulfill their own unique concept of a bed and breakfast, and you have a retreat that appeals to all the senses. There are only two guest rooms here and a cabin, but each is a special gift. A large collection of the owner's artwork is on display in the Gallery Room, and the bed in the Manzanita Room is crowned with a large manzanita branch that has been strung with tiny white lights. Both rooms have private entrances, woodburning stoves, queen-size beds, sitting areas, private baths, and an abundance of peace and quiet. Mornings bring a sumptuous breakfast accompanied by freshly squeezed juice.

A new addition to the property is the Cabin at Strawberry Hill. The name is a bit misleading: "cabin" is just too ordinary a term for this unique hideaway, with its towering ceiling, wood-burning fireplace, eclectic kitchenette (where breakfast fixings are provided), cedar paneling, king-size bed, and one of the most intriguing bathrooms you will ever see. French doors open to a screened porch that makes the surrounding meadows and trees a vital part of the interior. No matter where you stay at the Artist's Loft, you can be assured that the owners have created an environment where relaxation and romance are an art form.

Romantic Note: The Artist's Loft is an environmentally friendly inn; the owners ask that guests refrain from smoking on the property and they discourage the use of perfume, cologne, and hairspray during your visit.

JULIAN HOTEL BED AND BREAKFAST, Julian
2032 Main Street
(619) 765-0201, (800) 734-5854
Inexpensive to Expensive
Minimum stay requirement on weekends

Little has changed since this wood-framed hotel opened its doors in 1897. Authentically Victorian, the 13 rooms are best described as snug, with tiny private bathrooms. The detached "Honeymoon Cottage" behind the hotel has a fireplace and more space, but it's borderline rustic and a bit drab. The hotel is on Julian's main street, which can be busy during high season, obliterating any sense of a journey into the past. In the morning a hearty, nicely prepared breakfast of fresh fruit, eggs Florentine, and homemade breads is served in the parlor.

THE JULIAN WHITE HOUSE
BED AND BREAKFAST, Julian
3014 Blue Jay Drive
(619) 765-1764, (800) WHT-HOUSE

http://www.julianbnbguild.com
Moderate
Minimum stay requirement on weekends

This beautiful country home is set amidst sprawling trees in the rolling countryside. The appealing Colonial-style wood-framed exterior is graced by white pillars, a sweeping veranda, and long-branched trees that keep things well protected from the summer sun. Inside, everything is fastidiously maintained, and the decor is decidedly Victorian.

The four guest rooms are individually decorated. The French Quarter Room has a New Orleans theme, complete with feather masks and Mardi Gras memorabilia; the Blue Room features a double goose-down feather bed piled high on an antique Victorian frame; and the East Room is a lovely Victorian confection embellished with white and blue Laura Ashley linens. Our favorite is the Honeymoon Suite, which holds a four-poster queen-size rice bed with a white voile canopy, a wooden love seat for two, and a claw-foot bathtub that surveys the pine-covered hills. Breakfast is quite a performance, with such tempting dishes as thick old-fashioned oatmeal pancakes, eggs Benedict, or a rich, cheesy vegetarian quiche.

ORCHARD HILL COUNTRY INN, Julian
2502 Washington Street
(619) 765-1700, (800) 716-7242
Expensive
Minimum stay requirement on weekends

Only a handful of places ever warrant a higher lip rating than we can provide, and this is one of them. Every nuance and detail here is endearingly romantic, in every sense of the word. Set on a hillside overlooking the rustic town of Julian, the inn and its handful of cottages are embraced by meticulously tended gardens, swaying pinery, and strategically placed picnic tables and lawn furniture. Twelve suites in the main building are lovingly filled with soothing pastel colors, fresh American country decor, down comforters, and TV/VCRs. Most have whirlpool tubs, fireplaces, private patios or decks, cozy furnishings, idyllic views of the countryside, and, most important, an intimate mood. Particularly heart-stirring for dreamlike interludes are the five Craftsman-style cottages scattered about the property. Each unique mini-home has an enticingly cozy atmosphere, all the gracious appointments of the suites, and an abundance of country-perfect character and space.

Breakfast is a culinary event at Orchard Hill Country Inn, with fresh breads, pastries, and elaborate egg dishes or ricotta-stuffed pancakes. Enjoy your morning repast at individual tables arranged around a massive beach-stone hearth aglow with a morning fire, or dine outside on the tiled terrace with stupendous views in the background. Our only hesitation about recommending this place is that your hearts will break when you finally have to leave.

RANDOM OAKS RANCH, Julian
3742 Pine Hills Road
(619) 765-1094, (800) BNB-4344
Expensive
Minimum stay requirement on weekends

Random Oaks Ranch is truly a great find. Set in the midst of an equestrian estate, the two cottages are very luxurious, private, and beautifully decorated. Elegant from start to finish, the resplendent English Squire Suite is paneled with mahogany and decorated in hunter green; its flawless antiques and impressive mantel firmly establish a stately, luxurious feeling. Enjoy the wood-burning fireplace from the partially canopied bed, crisp with snow-white Battenburg linens, or slip into the Jacuzzi tub on your own private deck.

The smaller Victorian Garden Cottage is decorated in burgundy with white woodwork and gingerbread moldings. The queen-size Victorian bed is only steps to the French doors that open onto a private patio, complete with wicker furniture and a soothing spa. Regardless of which room is yours, you will be treated to an extensive heart-healthy breakfast in the morning.

The ranch is a mile or two outside of town in a pretty wooded area enveloped by fragrant pine and shade trees, with wildflowers scattered throughout. Although this is a horse ranch, the beautiful creatures are here for guests to pet, not to ride. That's OK, though, because their occasional whinny simply adds to the delicious feeling that you are far, far from home.

SHADOW MOUNTAIN RANCH, Julian

2771 Frisius Road
(619) 765-0323
Moderate; No Credit Cards
Minimum stay requirement on weekends

Shadow Mountain Ranch is the product of an overactive imagination. On one hand it is an authentic dude ranch, with horses, cattle, ducks, and chickens (regrettably, the ranch's horses are not for riding); on the other hand it's an inn where the rooms are filled with waggery and whimsy. One room has a secret passage that leads to the hot tub. Another room is actually a tree house built for two, though its open toilet is sure to give modest people nightmares. Or consider the Enchanted Cottage, a Bavarian-style bungalow complete with an arched wooden doorway, a wood-burning stove, and a snuggly bay-window seat overlooking the meadows. There are six guest rooms in all, including a structure the owners have proudly dubbed the Gnome Home. (This one you've got to see for yourselves.)

A stay here comes with a hearty ranch breakfast, afternoon tea, and a complimentary glass of sherry or warm vanilla milk at the end of the day. There are plenty of trails to hike and trees to climb, so feel free to let the kid in you go wild—it's never too late to become childhood sweethearts.

Romantic Note: Be sure to book far in advance if you want to get a reservation at this popular location.

Restaurant Kissing

JULIAN GRILLE, Julian
2224 Main Street
(619) 765-0173
Moderate
Breakfast Sunday; Lunch and Dinner Tuesday-Sunday

When you're practically the only game in town, it's hard to find motivation to improve. Located in a 1910 country building aglow with twinkling lights, the Julian Grille has an inviting, cozy atmosphere; unfortunately, it's in need of renovation and general upkeep that probably won't happen. The dining area has a homey, rustic feeling, but the pink linens and lace-covered windows seem out of place. Your best option is to request a table near the fireplace or on the enclosed patio. The all-American menu of roast beef sandwiches, hamburgers, fisherman's stew, and smoked pork chops is not exactly exciting, but everything is decent and filling.

ROMANO'S DODGE HOUSE RESTAURANT, Julian
2718 B Street
(619) 765-1003
Inexpensive to Moderate; No Credit Cards
Lunch and Dinner Wednesday-Monday

Besides JULIAN GRILLE (reviewed above), Romano's is the only other game in town when it comes to restaurants. The log cabin–style diner sports lace curtains, checkered tablecloths, and a zesty Italian menu. It isn't fancy, but the food is hearty and the rustic atmosphere is rather quaint, reminding us of an Old West town sprung to life.

Outdoor Kissing

COUNTRY CARRIAGES, Julian
(619) 765-1471
$20 per couple for a half-hour ride; $45 per couple for an hour ride

For Southern Californians accustomed to surf and sun, this is a winter fantasy come true. Imagine whisking down a snow-covered mountain road in an old-fashioned horse-drawn carriage. Snuggled close together, you and your beloved can hold hands beneath a fluffy down quilt while a brisk mountain breeze nips at your cheeks. Although romantic carriage rides are available any time of the year, winter is the most spectacular time to enjoy snow-dusted Julian. Most couples choose to be picked up at their hotel or bed and breakfast, dropped off for dinner, then swept off once again for a moonlit drive. The ride may last less than an hour, but the memories will surely last a lifetime.

"*To be thy lips is a sweet thing and small.*"

e. e. cummings

San Diego and Environs

San Diego County has some of the most beautiful (and crowded) beaches in California, or, for that matter, the world. It is a place where palm trees grow like dandelions; the weather is reliably sunny, with temperatures in the mid-70s; and small, eclectic towns dot the 70 miles of coastline. From the laid-back attitudes of Oceanside and Cardiff-by-the-Sea to the gentrified sophistication of La Jolla and Coronado, each city has a charm all its own. Regardless of which coastal community you visit, you'll quickly realize that romance awaits around each corner, particularly during the less-crowded off-season. Indoors and out, discoveries await: a hot-air balloon ride in Del Mar is a balcony seat to a brilliant sunset, a hike in the **TORREY PINES STATE RESERVE** (see Outdoor Kissing in La Jolla) can be an exquisite way to be close to nature and each other, and dinner in La Jolla is almost always served with a breathtaking ocean view.

When it comes to city life, San Diego also has an overabundance of riches. Its moderate climate is said to be the best in the country, with a consistent breeze that keeps the area from getting too hot. Its glistening bay and beaches are breathtakingly beautiful (at least, the areas not owned by the Navy or the port authority). Best of all, this coastal city is just minutes from the mountains and the desert—meaning you really can have it all here. Couples looking for an urban experience will find plenty of opportunities for romantic big-city exploration. Even the tourist spots are delightful: don't miss Sea World, the **SAN DIEGO ZOO**, or **BALBOA PARK** (see Outdoor Kissing in San Diego). But there is much, much more, and it is all accompanied by fabulous restaurants, panoramic vistas, and world-class hotels.

COASTAL SAN DIEGO

Oceanside

Outdoor Kissing

HARBOR BEACH, Oceanside

Take the Oceanside Harbor Drive exit and go west at the four-way stop. Turn left at the Harbor Beach sign and veer left at the fork in the road. There is a parking lot next to the beach.

About a quarter mile north of the Oceanside Pier lies Harbor Beach, a tiny stretch of shoreline sandwiched between two jetties. Although no one particular quality distinguishes this sunbathing spot from others, it has some features you should know about. First of all, Harbor Beach is fairly quiet. Because it is located at the tweezers' tip of San Diego County, not everyone is willing to travel the distance. Nevertheless, it is well worth the drive. The sand is incredibly white, and strolling down the rock jetties provides a scenic opportunity for reflection as the waves crash at your feet and surfers glide effortlessly toward you. Also, as its name implies, Harbor Beach rests along the docks, making it an excellent spot from which to watch the boats and the weekend sailors who navigate them. And, last but not least, the beach is right next to Cape Cod Village, a small shopping area reminiscent of an old whaling village, complete with a lighthouse. The village has several shops to browse in and some delightful eateries with outdoor patios where you can take in the view. Combine all of these elements and they add up to a fun and invigorating way to spend a day by the sea.

Carlsbad

Hotel/Bed and Breakfast Kissing

FOUR SEASONS RESORT AVIARA, Carlsbad   **Unrated**
7447 Batiquitos Drive
(619) 438-0562
Moderate

Situated on a bluff overlooking the Batiquitos Lagoon, the Four Seasons Resort Aviara holds great promise as a luxurious retreat and romantic destination. Although the hotel was still under construction when we visited, we did get a sneak preview of the restort: its delightful dining room, beautiful golf course, and elegant clubhouse are all open to the public. The hotel is scheduled to open in summer 1997.

First impressions count for a lot, and even in construction this hotel site looks grand. A perfectly manicured golf course embraces the white adobe clubhouse, and lush landscaping trims the cobbled drive. Pass through the elegant lobby to the dining room, where sweeping views of the golf course and the lagoon will take your breath away. Enjoy terrace dining under the shade of an umbrella, or choose to eat in the main dining room where you can watch people try their luck on the links. No matter where you sit, the view is sure to be stunning, the food delicious, and the service accommodating. If this resort lives up to its promising beginnings, the Four Seasons Resort Aviara might just be the romantic equivalent of a hole in one.

PELICAN COVE INN, Carlsbad
320 Walnut Avenue
(619) 434-5995, (888) 735-2683
http://www.pelican-cove.com/pelican
Moderate to Expensive
Minimum stay requirement on weekends

We fell in love with Pelican Cove Inn, a Cape Cod–style home neatly trimmed with burgundy accents and gray paneling. The attractive rooms, all with private entrances, are filled with fluffy feather beds, gas fireplaces, and hand-tiled baths; two suites have spa tubs. The snug, almost cramped, size of the rooms is a drawback that seriously affects the inn's romantic potential. Not that you'll want to spend much time in your room: the sparkling blue Pacific is a mere sea breeze away. The owners will be happy to supply you with beach towels, chairs, and picnic baskets during your stay. Fortify yourselves for a day of fun in the sun with a gourmet breakfast served in the inside dining nook, on the lovely garden patio, or in the heartwarming gazebo.

SEASHORE ON THE SAND, Carlsbad
2805 Ocean Street
(619) 434-6679
Inexpensive to Expensive
Minimum stay requirement

In many ways Seashore on the Sand is just a nice, quiet apartment building with attractive studios and one- and two-bedroom apartments—not outstanding, but pleasant, with lots of space and comfort, as well as fireplaces and private patios or decks. However, this becomes a rare find once you take into consideration the fact that each unit has a mesmerizing view of the Pacific Ocean and your back door opens to a relatively empty white sandy beach. What could be better than a home away from home where you can feel the sea breezes all around you and relish scintillating sunsets? Not much, which is why you should consider yourselves lucky if you can get a reservation during high season.

Encinitas

Restaurant Kissing

PANNIKIN, Encinitas
510 North Highway 101
(619) 436-5824
Inexpensive to Moderate
Breakfast and Lunch Daily

Talk about a great place to wake up and smell the coffee! Though it looks like a cross between a barn and large country home, this enchanting cafe was once a train station. Now painted a cheery yellow, it's home to an art gallery, a gourmet kitchen shop, and a link in the Pannikin cafe chain. Most of the Pannikins have interesting decor, and this one is no exception. Its loft is eccentrically adorned with a tuba, an abstract nude, and old farm equipment dangling from the high beamed ceiling. One nook even has a collection of old red vinyl theater-style seats. The best spots for a romantic tête-à-tête are under a brightly colored umbrella on the outdoor patio or up high on the veranda, where towering trees cast crisp, cooling shadows.

Outdoor Kissing

QUAIL BOTANICAL GARDENS, Encinitas
230 Quail Gardens Drive
(619) 436-3036
$3 admission
Open Daily, from 9 A.M. to 5 P.M.

From Interstate 5, head east on Encinitas Boulevard one-half mile to Quail Gardens Drive. Turn left and go a quarter mile; the gardens are on the left.

Quail Botanical Gardens has one of the most diverse plant collections in the world, flaunting more than 5,000 species of exotic trees, palms, ferns, and flowers. You can spend hours strolling down the gardens' meandering paths, past lily-covered ponds and surging waterfalls. As you rest on one of the many wooden benches encircled by blossoming greenery, serenaded by singing birds, you will feel tranquil and thoroughly romantic.

Romantic Note: Free guided tours are given every Saturday at 10 A.M., or by appointment.

Cardiff-by-the-Sea

Restaurant Kissing

THE BEACH HOUSE, Cardiff-by-the-Sea
2530 South Highway 101
(619) 753-1321
Moderate
Lunch Monday-Friday; Dinner Daily; Brunch Saturday-Sunday

This unassuming seafood restaurant offers a dining experience brimming with scenic potential. That's because it is so close to the beach you can practically reach out and touch the frothy waves below. The main dining area downstairs is open and airy, a casual place where large picture windows frame an indescribably beautiful ocean view. Upstairs is a more formal and elegant retreat paneled in dark woods and decorated in emerald and white. A mirrored wall reflects the sparkling shore. As the evening progresses and sunlight is replaced by candlelight, you won't have to give up the stunning view, thanks to spotlights that illuminate every crashing wave.

Outdoor Kissing

GLENN PARK, Cardiff-by-the-Sea

Take Highway 101 to Chesterfield, and then turn west onto San Elijo. The park is on the left.

Glenn Park isn't just a pretty place overflowing with shade trees and grassy knolls. It's truly a slice of Southern California life. On the tennis courts, bronzed seniors clad in fluorescent pastels engage in lively contests. A few yards away, flat-topped teenagers dart and dash after a basketball. The playground is sprinkled with young parents and their inquisitive toddlers. Though this is not a large park, it has plenty of pretty paths to wander and benches awaiting a lovers' tryst. Better yet, spread out a blanket, curl up together, and just enjoy watching the world go by.

Del Mar

Hotel/Bed and Breakfast Kissing

L'AUBERGE DEL MAR RESORT AND SPA, Del Mar
1540 Camino Del Mar
(619) 259-1515, (800) 553-1336
Expensive to Unbelievably Expensive

Twenty or so years after the original turn-of-the-century hotel was torn down, L'Auberge Del Mar has gallantly risen from the rubble. Luxurious, glamorous, and tasteful, the hotel staves off pretentiousness by cultivating a warm French country atmosphere. The lobby, with its enormous fireplace and scattering of overstuffed floral couches and chairs, is oriented toward sweeping French doors that open to admit swift ocean breezes and a majestic view of the glittering coastline below. Fortunately, each of the 123 guest rooms shares in this glory. While it would be a dream come true to wake up in L'Auberge's Valentino Suite (named after the famous lover who frequented the original hotel), you can save about $300 if you go down a notch or two to one of the more modest rooms on the third floor (modest is a relative term in this context); each of these rooms has a vaulted ceiling and a fireplace.

The inn has tennis courts, private hot-air balloons, a first-class spa, and an outstanding restaurant. **THE DINING ROOM AT L'AUBERGE** (Moderate to Expensive) has gained quite a reputation for its Sunday brunch and daily afternoon tea, but every meal here is a distinguished event. The setting is both sumptuous and refined, and the creative kitchen staff produces some of the most succulent fresh fish and meat dishes in the area.

THE ROCK HAUS, Del Mar
410 15th Street
(619) 481-3764
Inexpensive to Moderate

In real estate, location is everything. This turn-of-the-century country home, settled into the pine-covered hills of Del Mar, is just a stone's throw from Highway 101, and two or three more throws from the Pacific Ocean. The Rock Haus is one of the only bed and breakfasts left along the coast, and while it could use some sprucing it up, it has an unpretentious atmosphere that is relaxing and cozy. Only four of the ten rooms here have private baths, but all of the rooms have their own pleasurable mood. The Huntsman is bold and masculine, decorated in tartan and warmed by a wood-burning hearth. The Wicker Garden is more delicate, with peach accents, flowery curtains, and white wicker furnishings. The Whale Watch has a nautical motif, with a decent view of the sea. In the morning a continental breakfast of freshly baked muffins and granola is served on the glass-enclosed sunporch.

Restaurant Kissing

CAFE DEL MAR, Del Mar
1247 Camino Del Mar
(619) 481-1133

Inexpensive to Moderate
Lunch Monday-Friday; Dinner Daily; Brunch Saturday-Sunday

Cafe Del Mar is the place to visit when you want to slow down and watch the world go by. Located in the heart of the city, the cafe is decorated in shades of emerald and white, surrounded by huge panels of glass, and has a partially convertible roof. Foliage is everywhere; you'll feel like you're having lunch in a greenhouse. If you come here during the day, you can watch the quaint community of Del Mar go about its daily business. If you wait until twilight, you can enjoy the cafe's delicious pasta or fresh grilled items under the glint of a star-filled night.

EPAZOTE, Del Mar
1555 Camino Del Mar, in Del Mar Plaza
(619) 259-9966
Moderate
Lunch and Dinner Daily; Sunday Brunch

Del Mar Plaza is one of the most exquisite miniature shopping malls you are likely to find anywhere. Not only is the distant view of the ocean breathtaking, but the cascading terraces, fountains, precious boutiques, and assortment of restaurants provide a premier collection of options for a variety of tastes and budgets. Leading the list of desirable dining spots is this Southwest-style restaurant, replete with stunning decor, the best view in the complex, and an extremely talented, creative kitchen. The smoked chicken relleno with wild mushrooms, Brie, and tropical fruit salsa is remarkable, as is the pumpkin-seed pesto marinated salmon in a corn husk with red pepper salsa. Just about every dish is intriguing, and the service is amiable. Seating on the deck is the best, but anywhere is suitable for a casually romantic dining experience.

IL FORNAIO RESTAURANT, Del Mar
1555 Camino Del Mar, in Del Mar Plaza
(619) 755-8876
Moderate
Lunch and Dinner Daily; Sunday Brunch

Il Fornaio is probably one of the most attractive "chain-type" restaurants to be found anywhere. Perched on a hill above the sparkling Pacific (you can pretend it's the Mediterranean), this branch is a striking spot for lunch or dinner. The interior combines Italian tradition and California style with wood and marble accents. Outside, an attractive glass-enclosed balcony dotted with umbrellas offers distant ocean views. Besides whipping up a breathtaking sunset night after night, Il Fornaio also manages to conjure up all the distinctive tastes and smells of old Italy. From the *pasta efieno con gamberetti* (spinach and egg linguine sprinkled with shrimp) to the Valentino *vestito di nuovo* (a three-tiered chocolate masterpiece), the food is like an Italian aria. However, the best news is that the prices are *più bellisimo*, which translates into "affordable."

JAKE'S DEL MAR, Del Mar
1660 Coast Boulevard
(619) 755-2002
Moderate
Lunch Tuesday-Saturday; Dinner Daily; Sunday Brunch

Sitting at a window table at Jake's is like looking through a kaleidoscope. As the minutes pass, the ocean scene before you changes constantly. By day, you'll see children frolicking in the surf, sandpipers darting in and out of the breakers, and surfers bobbing on the horizon, waiting for the next wave. Watch long enough and you'll see families give way to lovers, and the sparkle of the sunlit sea replaced by the sparkle of the stars.

Jake's menu consists of fresh fish, meat, and pasta dishes. Though it's set right on the Del Mar coastline, there is nothing pretentious here. The decor is a simple mix of light wood and lush greenery; the view takes center stage. Jake's has become a very popular place for Sunday brunch, so expect to wait before being seated. Then sit back, relax, and enjoy the seascape over a leisurely breakfast.

PACIFICA DEL MAR, Del Mar
1555 Camino Del Mar
(619) 792-0476
Moderate
Lunch and Dinner Daily

Pacifica Del Mar is a popular Southern California dining experience with a modern, upscale interior. Since its opening back in 1989, Pacifica Del Mar has quickly gained a reputation for its sensuous seaside locale, modern, upscale interior, and choice California cuisine. The main room is decked out in black and white, but softened by ocean-inspired bursts of color. Each night soft jazz floats through the room and out onto the romantic glass-enclosed terrace. The chef works wonders with seafood. The pan-sautéed sea bass with crab-garlic potatoes and fried beets is sensational, as is the baked halibut stuffed with seafood mousse on curried rock shrimp risotto drizzled with a piquant curry sauce.

SCALINI, Del Mar
3790 Via De La Valle, Suite 301
(619) 259-9944
Moderate to Expensive
Dinner Daily

Come to Scalini at sunset and you'll have a balcony seat for one of San Diego's most captivating sights. Set just above the polo fields and facing the exclusive estates of Fairbanks Ranch, this is a great place to watch the early-evening parade of hot-air balloons soaring high over Del Mar. After the balloons settle back down to earth and the colors of sunset give way to night, the restaurant displays a charm all its own. The interior is draped in floral pastels and furnished with dark wood antiques, and the terrace is an ideal place for a warm-weather repast. The rich Italian fare is quite satisfying, especially the great veal dishes.

STRATFORD COURT CAFE, Del Mar
1307 Stratford Court
(619) 792-7433
Inexpensive; No Credit Cards
Breakfast and Lunch Daily

The Stratford Court Cafe is nestled in a charming Del Mar neighborhood, just off the main drag. It is a delightful spot to enjoy a light breakfast or lunch in a garden crowned with trees and cooled by ocean breezes. We highly recommend the tables on the wooden deck set amid the profuse greenery surrounding this large Cape Cod–style house; it's perfect for a leisurely, loving interlude.

In addition to enhancing the already verdant yard with an abundance of flowers and a natural-looking waterfall, the new owners have expanded the menu to include such delicacies as freshly baked strawberry-banana bread, pesto quiche in a Parmesan crust, and curried autumn squash soup. Although the menu changes daily, the cafe's extensive list of coffee drinks and fruit smoothies remains consistent. On occasion, you'll find a classical guitarist serenading the sunset here on weekends, adding one more special touch to an already glorious close encounter.

Outdoor Kissing

HOT-AIR BALLOON RIDE, Del Mar
Skysurfer Balloon Company
(619) 481-6800, (800) 660-6809

Expensive
$125 per hour on weekdays; $135 per hour on weekends

Almost every evening of the year, the skies above Del Mar burst with brilliant color as the sun melts into the sea. One of the most romantic ways to view this awesome display is from the basket of a hot-air balloon. As the massive balloon fills with hot air and carries you upward, the sea below takes center stage. At the end of your evening flight, champagne and hors d'oeuvres complete the fantasy. Sure, it's expensive and frivolous, but your heightened feelings afterward will be priceless.

SEA GROVE PARK, Del Mar

At the corner of 15th Street and Coast Boulevard.

Every once in a while it is difficult to reveal a place you'd rather keep to yourself. What a dilemma. But if you promise to keep it just between us, well, that's a different story. If you wander down 15th Street in Del Mar, you'll come across a tiny patch of paradise known as Sea Grove Park. Poised above the ocean, this is an ideal spot in which to curl up with your sweetheart, a bottle of wine, and a fresh, crusty loaf of bread. Mother Nature conducts a symphony of colors here nightly as the sun goes down and the surfers wait for their next ride into shore.

La Jolla

La Jolla means "the jewel" in Spanish, and given the Pacific Coast location, such a name is no exaggeration for this densely populated, upscale, seaside town. Its rugged coastline is splashed with white sand beaches and foamy azure waves; the rolling hillsides are dotted with palatial mansions and winding roads; and the downtown area is replete with art galleries, posh boutiques, and fine restaurants. Some people consider La Jolla too nouveau riche and pretentious, while others think that it's merely extravagant. What no one would argue is how thoroughly Californian it is, and how romantic. There is enough kissing territory to keep you busy from dawn to dusk: checking out Windansea Beach, hiking through **TORREY PINES STATE RESERVE** (see Outdoor Kissing), and strolling along the grassy knolls above the beach are just a few options.

Hotel/Bed and Breakfast Kissing

BED AND BREAKFAST INN AT LA JOLLA, La Jolla
7753 Draper Avenue
(619) 456-2066, (800) 582-2466

Moderate to Very Expensive
Minimum stay requirement on weekends and holidays

No other bed and breakfast in La Jolla has the polished warmth of this inn, but then, there aren't that many bed and breakfasts in town. It's easy to see how it was once a source of inspiration for composer John Philip Sousa, who lived here during the '20s, but that was before so many cars went buzzing by on the nearby main street. Each room is decorated in a different theme, from Victorian to Latin to Oriental, and all have private baths. Though most of the detailing is quite nice, some rooms are in need of refurbishing (swaying lamps, chipped side tables, and dingy carpets do not meet anyone's definition of deluxe). In the morning, a light breakfast is served in the inn's quaint but elegant dining room, or you can choose to have breakfast delivered to your room. Wine and cheese are offered from 4 P.M. to 6 P.M. With a day's notice, the innkeeper will be happy to pack you a picnic lunch for an amorous afternoon at the beach.

THE EMPRESS HOTEL, La Jolla
7766 Fay Avenue
(619) 454-3001, (888) 369-9900
Expensive

This rather ordinary, almost nondescript hotel may have a less than desirable location several blocks from the water, but it does offer four surprisingly luxurious suites that were created exclusively for romance. Large soaking tubs, plenty of space, kitchenettes, and attractive decor make staying in one of these specific units a relaxing, almost posh experience. The other amenities mentioned in the brochure are lackluster at best, including the continental breakfast and mediocre exercise room. But who needs any of that when you are either at the ocean or in one of these suites?

LA VALENCIA HOTEL, La Jolla
1132 Prospect Street
(619) 454-0771, (800) 451-0772
Expensive to Unbelievably Expensive
Minimum stay requirement on weekends and holidays

It's hard to miss a pastel pink hotel, even when it blends in better than you'd think along this promenade of upscale shops and restaurants. In fact, you would almost swear it matches the glowing sunsets La Jolla is known for. La Valencia was built in the '20s, and it soon became a star-studded landmark due to its premier stretch of shoreline. Continuing renovations and impeccable attention to detail has maintained the property's glamour and flourish. There are 100 lavish guest rooms and suites to choose from, all decorated in classic but lavish European style. You can enjoy the shimmering view from your room or visit the posh lobby, where a pianist often provides the proper mood for sunset.

Although there isn't much to complain about at this hotel, the one thing you need to know is that everyone else knows about this place too. It often seems crowded and bustling, with little elbow room for guests. Once you're past the reception area, however, that feeling diminishes quickly and your California getaway begins.

Romantic Note: La Valencia has three restaurants, but **THE SKY ROOM** (see Restaurant Kissing), on the top floor of the hotel, is the one that will make a lasting impression.

SCRIPPS INN, La Jolla
555 Coast Boulevard South
(619) 454-3391
Moderate to Expensive
Minimum stay requirement on weekends

Scripps Inn barely squeaks into the bed-and-breakfast category. Sure, this remodeled 1942 lodge serves a continental breakfast, but you have to come down to the tiny lobby; pile a tray full of croissants, muffins, coffee, and juice; and take it all back to your room. Why include it then? Although the accommodations are simple, the inn resides on a premier piece of oceanfront property. All the rooms are cozy, but we recommend the two units with fireplaces, private terraces, seaside vistas, and plenty of privacy.

Restaurant Kissing

AVANTI, La Jolla
875 Prospect Street
(619) 454-4288
Moderate to Expensive
Dinner Daily

The interior of this stylish restaurant is sheer drama, a striking mixture of black and white, mirrors and chrome, with splashes of brilliant color to brighten the room. It is very chic and upscale, with a lively singles atmosphere after hours that doesn't always lend itself to quiet moments. Still, the continental menu is very good, and consistently so, with a number of northern Italian specialties ranging from steak and seafood to pastas and vegetarian items. Perhaps the best part is after dinner Thursday through Sunday nights, when a live Brazilian band fills the dining room with a pulsating beat.

BROCKTON VILLA, La Jolla
1235 Coast Boulevard
(619) 454-7393
Inexpensive
Call for seasonal hours.

In a town known for restaurants with breathtaking ocean views, this one has created quite a stir. In contrast to its upscale neighbors, the Brockton Villa is proof positive that romantic dining can be achieved on a budget. Situated directly across from Scripps Park, this century-old beach house was recently converted into a place where sun worshippers gather to sip flavorful gourmet coffees, eat light and healthful meals, and enjoy an unrivaled view of La Jolla Cove. Whether in a swimsuit or a pinstripe suit, ordering cappuccino or calamari, you will be warmly welcomed and made to feel that, for a time, this is your home too. Each small wooden table is adorned with clusters of wildflowers and surrounded by mismatched chairs. The best seating is outside, where the view is almost endless. Mornings are often the most crowded as locals and tourists alike line up to enjoy hearty breakfasts and lattes. In the late afternoon, they return to enjoy simple but savory meals and watch the sun vanish into the sea.

CINDY BLACK'S, La Jolla
5721 La Jolla Boulevard
(619) 456-6299
Inexpensive to Expensive
Dinner Daily

Among the shops and restaurants lining La Jolla Boulevard is a pink neon sign summoning gourmets and romance seekers to visit Cindy Black's. Inside, the dining room's stucco walls are painted pale rose and the ceiling a soft mauve. Fragrant floral arrangements fill the room, while tables are topped with pure white linens, softly glowing candles, and silver bud vases with freshly cut flowers. The menu boasts a variety of interesting dishes that are creative without being intimidating. Standouts include grilled marinated vegetables served with a spicy hummus sauce, lobster tails poached in cognac, and a choice filet of beef cilantro peppercorn. For dessert, order the house soufflé, which changes nightly. Local favorites include the chocolate caramel soufflé and the white chocolate decadence.

While the food here is beautifully presented and the service is attentive, the brightness of the dining room, the proximity of other tables, and the noise level may detract from an otherwise four-lip romantic experience. Ask for one of the more private tables along the back wall and you won't be disappointed. For lovers on a budget, Cindy Black's features a "Plat du Jour" menu. Served Monday through Friday from 5:30-6:30 P.M., the dinner includes a house salad or soup, a choice of three entrées, and dessert for $12.95 per person. Sunday-night prix fixe dinners offer additional main-course selections and a choice of dessert for $15.95.

THE COTTAGE RESTAURANT, La Jolla
7702 Fay Avenue
(619) 454-8409
Inexpensive to Moderate
Call for seasonal hours.

Everything about this beachside bungalow is brimming with romance. The outside is set off by a white picket fence, lots of colorful flowers, and a sea of pastel and floral umbrellas shading the tables on the brick patio. Inside, pastel watercolors of the La Jolla shore accentuate the cheerful, albeit extremely casual atmosphere. Hot coffee and waffles smothered with bananas and strawberries highlight a beachcomber dining experience just too good to miss (unless the wait is too long, which it can be at traditional mealtimes).

CRABCATCHER, La Jolla
1298 Prospect Street
(619) 454-9587
Moderate to Expensive
Lunch and Dinner Daily; Sunday Brunch

Because La Jolla is one of the world's most beautiful cities, it is also one of the most popular. Many a couple, in search of quiet romance, has retreated to this pleasing restaurant as a refuge from all the hustle and bustle. Everything about the Crabcatcher is soothing: the soft music, the muted pastel decor, and a view that is so stunning you can't help but forget the commotion you left behind and savor the here and now. Ask for Table 7, a tiny retreat by the window, and you will feel as though you have the surf and sun all to yourselves. As you may have guessed by the name, the Crabcatcher specializes in seafood—and only the freshest will do. There is also a variety of meat and pasta dishes, but the fish and the view are the reasons to be here.

GEORGE'S AT THE COVE, La Jolla
1250 Prospect Street
(619) 454-4244
Inexpensive to Expensive
Lunch and Dinner Daily

George's at the Cove is yet another popular La Jolla oceanfront restaurant with a dazzling view. What makes this place special is the fact that it is divided into three separate dining facilities that cater to several different tastes and budgets. The main dining room is the most formal and is noted for its superb California cuisine, fresh fish, and pasta; **GEORGE'S CAFE AND BAR** and the relatively new **OCEAN TERRACE** are more laid-back and both serve a menu of lighter, less expensive entrées enhanced by ocean breezes and spectacular coastline views.

MAITRE D', La Jolla
5523 La Jolla Boulevard
(619) 456-2111
Very Expensive
Dinner Tuesday-Saturday

Not to be confused with today's trendy French bistros, Maitre D' prides itself on old-world elegance and a dining experience that recalls the grand restaurants of days gone by. Step through the elaborate portals and the maitre d' will greet you as if you're members of the royal family. After being seated side by side at a table for two, spend a minute taking in the court-like decor: red velvet walls punctuated by oil paintings in gilded frames, tables beautifully set with antique crystal from czarist Russia, and fragrant floral arrangements styled by the maitre d' himself. Open the menu and forget any thoughts of calorie counting, because you just can't count that high! The traditional continental cuisine skimps neither on taste nor on richness.

Often an aperitif of champagne with a few drops of raspberry nectar is served even before you see the menu. Enjoy a fresh Caesar salad while your waiter prepares your entrées tableside. Dover sole deftly deboned and served with a light white wine sauce is excellent. Traditional steak Diane, flamed with brandy and sautéed with mushrooms, shallots, and cream, is cooked to perfection. Most of the flaming delights for dessert are prepared for two. Classic baked Alaska is festively served with pistachio ice cream cake, topped with an airy meringue, and flamed with cognac. But the evening isn't over yet; French-pressed coffee and a three-tiered tray loaded with truffles and Swiss chocolates are the crowning touch. Don't be surprised if the maitre d' presents you with fresh flowers and invites you to return again and again. We guarantee you'll look forward to accepting his gracious offer.

MARINE ROOM, La Jolla
2000 Spindrift Drive
(619) 459-7222

Moderate to Expensive
Lunch Monday-Saturday; Dinner Daily; Sunday Brunch

Separated from the sea by only a narrow stretch of sand, this steak-and-seafood restaurant is as close as you can get to the ocean without getting your feet wet. In fact, during high tide don't be surprised to find frothy waves lapping at the windows. Over its more than 50-year history, the Marine Room has been washed out twice during violent storms. Each time it was lovingly restored and its one-inch-thick glass panes were reinstalled. It's this tenacity that has drawn couples, generation after generation, to the Marine Room's premier corner tables. Unlike many seaside restaurants, which look out onto a black void after sunset, the Marine Room illuminates its stretch of beach so you're never without a mesmerizing ocean view. The food at times can pale in comparison to the view, but at other time it soars. Fresh fish here is always superior, and the desserts are excellent.

MILLIGAN'S BAR & GRILL, La Jolla
5786 La Jolla Boulevard
(619) 459-7311
Inexpensive to Expensive
Lunch Monday-Saturday; Dinner Daily; Sunday Brunch

Romance is in the eye (and the heart) of the beholder. What delights one couple may disappoint another. Some like their restaurants casual; others desire a more elegant atmosphere. Milligan's is the perfect answer for both tastes. The main floor feels formal, with its dark wood paneling, rich leather booths, and etched glass panels. Mirrored ceilings, illuminated by art deco sconces, reflect images of people in love. The polished decor of this dining area is flawed only by the nude portraits around the room, which seem out of place in such a regal setting. Request a table upstairs, however, and you'll discover a lighter, more casual atmosphere, plus an ocean view that will take your breath away. Everything here is bright and festive: the walls and table-cloths are white, and modern murals provide welcome splashes of color.

The menu is absolutely American. Milligan's is famous for its country-fried steak, but if you prefer you can get your fillet drizzled with béarnaise sauce. Milligan's also offers an enticing Sunday brunch, complimentary sunset hors d'oeuvres in the upstairs bar Tuesdays and Thursdays, and jazz nightly so you can sip and swoon.

SANTE RISTORANTE, La Jolla
7811 Herschel Avenue
(619) 454-1315

Moderate to Expensive
Lunch Monday-Friday; Dinner Monday-Saturday

Though this restaurant is charming by day, it becomes even more special at night when the oak-shaded terrace is illuminated by twinkling lights that mingle gently with the evening stars. And while most couples prefer to sit in the flower-covered brick courtyard, the dining room is also desirable, even without the balmy breeze and fresh air. The decor, in subtle shades of gray and beige, combines modern chic with bits of old Italy. This tasteful interior is matched by a menu that wins over critics and patrons alike. The chef uses nothing but the finest ingredients, many flown here from Europe on a daily basis. It all adds up to an outstanding meal in a very romantic context.

THE SKY ROOM, La Jolla
1132 Prospect Street, at the La Valencia Hotel
(619) 454-0771
Expensive to Unbelievably Expensive
Dinner Monday-Saturday

This tiny room has an enormously beautiful ocean view and only ten small tables to share it. Each is bathed in candlelight and set with the finest silver and Wedgwood china. Awash in shades of mauve, this lovely French restaurant is constantly embellished by the sky's ever-changing palette. Having dinner at the Sky Room is truly like floating on a cloud.

TOP O' THE COVE, La Jolla
1216 Prospect Street
(619) 454-7779
Expensive
Lunch and Dinner Daily; Sunday Brunch

Table 6, set its own private alcove, is the spot every romantic couple asks for when dining at Top O' the Cove. In fact, it's often booked weeks in advance. This coveted corner of an elegant gingerbread cottage on the sea is like a balcony seat over La Jolla's shimmering shoreline. Through an open window you can feel the sea breeze on your face. Of course, almost every table in Top O' the Cove is a ticket to an unforgettable meal. Though the double waiter service is a bit pretentious and overeager, the atmosphere and gourmet California cuisine are excellent. There is also a bistro terrace where you can sip cocktails at sunset and dine on light cuisine that's even lighter on your wallet. We'll drink to that!

TRATTORIA ACQUA, La Jolla
1298 Prospect Street
(619) 454-0709
Moderate to Expensive
Lunch Monday-Friday; Dinner Daily; Brunch Saturday-Sunday

If ever a restaurant resonated with Italian country splendor, this is it. Romance radiates from a series of charming and graciously appointed rooms that embrace a brick patio with a distant view of the dazzling ocean. But rustic elegance is only a small portion of this trattoria's distinction; the Mediterranean-inspired cuisine exceeds all expectations. Earthy and flavorful dishes such as pan-roasted stuffed quail or onion and Gorgonzola cheese tart are all flawlessly prepared and artistically presented. Portions are generous, so it takes real will power to leave room for dessert, but do your best: what the kitchen can do with sugar, flour, and chocolate is sinful.

Romantic Suggestion: Try to avoid the dinner rush by dining before 7 P.M. or after 9 P.M. Trattoria Acqua's kitchen can lose some of its finesse when overwhelmed.

TRIANGLES, La Jolla
4370 La Jolla Village Drive
(619) 453-6650
Expensive
Lunch Monday-Friday; Dinner Monday-Saturday

Located in the executive center of the Golden Triangle, this popular destination hosts power-lunches by day and candlelit dinners by night. The handsome dining room features private, high-backed booths and white-cloaked tables for two lining the walls. Although plantation shutters successfully block out the busy outside world, the best seats in the house are in the bar at the far end of the restaurant.

The elaborate bar—exquisitely carved from tiger oak wood—was built nearly 100 years ago in Canada, and spent most of its life in a Montana hotel before being acquired by Triangles' owner at an auction and brought to San Diego. This beautiful centerpiece adds to the ambience of the bar, where dim lighting and cozy candlelit tables present a more intimate setting than the main dining room. Here, couples can order from the full menu of continental-inspired fare. We started with Triangles' famous mussel bisque and discovered the reason for its popularity. Everything here is simply prepared and satisfying. If you're looking for comfort food, try Triangles' baked meat loaf on mashed potatoes with rosemary gravy; if you prefer lighter fare, we recommend the fresh seafood and pasta dishes. Triangles is a sophisticated spot for an after-work rendezvous, a quick bite before a movie, or a relaxed and elegant dinner.

Outdoor Kissing

BIRCH AQUARIUM AT SCRIPPS, La Jolla
2300 Expedition Way
(619) 534-FISH
$6.50 admission
Open Daily

Romance does not instantly come to mind when you think about an aquarium and fish. But once you step through this museum's doors, you might change your point of view. Grandly poised on a hill above the La Jolla shore, this venue lets the ocean take center stage. The views from its rocky tide pools and large courtyard are exquisite. And that's not to discount the experience of walking through the museum itself. This is the largest oceanographic exhibit in the United States, with interesting interactive displays, more than 3,000 colorful and exotic fish in enormous aquariums, and a bookstore offering oceans of information on the subject. Learning about the sea and the mysteriously beautiful creatures that inhabit it is a wonderful experience.

LA JOLLA COVE, La Jolla

Heading south on Torrey Pines Road, turn right onto Prospect. Stay to the right and take Coast Boulevard down to the beach.

Walking along the sandy shores of La Jolla Cove, you can understand why this area has been compared to the French Riviera. Although miles of brilliant beaches line Southern California, the water here seems bluer somehow, the sand a bit whiter, and the sunsets more spectacular. Linger over a picnic lunch on the expansive lawn area called **ELLEN SCRIPPS BROWNING PARK**, or dive right into the aquamarine waves. The cove is a perfect place to snorkel or skin-dive, with an abundance of fascinating reefs, caves, and tide pools to explore. And if you're in the mood for a refreshing dip, this one-mile stretch of beach, protected from ocean swells, is great swimming territory. Afterward, find your own private place in the sun on one of the many cliffs overlooking the cove. The view from these vantage points is unrivaled.

TORREY PINES STATE RESERVE, La Jolla
(619) 755-2063
$4 admission

From Interstate 5, take the Carmel Valley Road exit and go west. Turn left onto Torrey Pines; the entrance to the park is on the right.

Tread lightly—this nature reserve spans 2,000 acres of San Diego's most majestic shoreline and is home to the rarest pine trees in the nation (the Torrey pines). In addition, more than 300 other plants and flowers grow wild here, perfuming the air with a bouquet of fragrances. You can spend the day basking in the sun on the reserve's flawless beach or hiking along one of its five winding trails to jutting cliffs, windswept canyons, and awe-inspiring ocean views.

Perhaps the reserve's most beautiful path is the **GUY FLEMING TRAIL**, which fortunately is also its easiest. Two-thirds of a mile long, it meanders past etched sandstone formations and includes some of the park's most stupendous vistas. Torrey Pines is the perfect spot to commune with nature and each other.

Romantic Note: Because this is a state reserve, there is great concern over maintaining the ecological balance. That means no smoking, picnicking, or collecting of flowers or pinecones anywhere in the reserve. For your convenience, picnic benches are located along the beach.

Pacific Beach

Hotel/Bed and Breakfast Kissing

CRYSTAL PIER HOTEL, Pacific Beach
4500 Ocean Boulevard
(619) 483-6983, (800) 748-5894
Expensive
Minimum stay requirement seasonally

The Crystal Pier Hotel, built in 1927, is not really a hotel, but a series of small cottages built along the Crystal Pier. While that may sound like the perfect backdrop for an amorous retreat, be forewarned: in order to appreciate your stay in this historic hotel, you must first ignore a few very unsightly flaws. To start with, the front office is fairly tacky, and the original cottages look as though they haven't seen a new coat of paint in years. Most are in desperate need of remodeling, and all too often the scent of the sea is overpowered by the redolence of mildew. Also, the area is popular with families and teens, and their presence can be jarring for couples looking for quiet bliss. But there is good news—there are six new cottages at the end of the pier. These rooms are modest but pleasantly appointed, and each has a small kitchen. Unlike the older cottages, the newer ones have patios that are fenced in for maximum privacy. There is nothing here to obstruct your view of the coastline and the sparkling Pacific all around you. From this vantage point, the sun seems so close you'll swear you could reach out and touch it. In the morning, the first thing you will hear is the sound of the waves surging beneath you and the sea gulls announcing a glorious new day.

PACIFIC TERRACE INN, Pacific Beach
610 Diamond Street
(619) 581-3500, (800) 344-3370
Expensive to Unbelievably Expensive
Minimum stay requirement on weekends

Having a place to call your own on the beach, even a densely populated beach, is an attraction that is hard to ignore. But finding accommodations that meet the needs of visual splendor as well as romantic comfort isn't easy. Although the Pacific Terrace Inn isn't a premier destination, it has possibilities, and its location on the beach is strictly sensational. Most of the rooms here are just hotel-standard, but the large one-bedroom suites with whirlpool tubs for two and kitchenettes are surprisingly appealing for couples in need of a coastal getaway. Nevertheless, the view out to the ocean from your private terrace is the real attraction here, and a stupendous one at that.

Restaurant Kissing

LAMONT STREET GRILL, Pacific Beach
4445 Lamont Street
(619) 270-3060
Inexpensive to Moderate
Dinner Daily

Do you love dining near the beach but find that all too often the best restaurants have restrictive dress codes and high-tone atmospheres? The Lamont Street Grill is an energizing alternative. This affable beach bungalow combines refinement with welcoming, casual California style. You can dine on a patio illuminated by a glowing fireplace and flickering white lights strung on a spreading oak tree, or sit in one of the small pastel dining rooms bathed in candlelight. There are plenty of private nooks and crannies and corner tables to choose from, and everything from fresh fish to fresh pastas will stimulate your taste buds. When you've finished dinner, the chocolate-dipped fresh fruit is on the house.

Outdoor Kissing

FANUEL STREET PARK, Pacific Beach

From Interstate 5, take the Grand/Garnet exit, follow Grand west to Fanuel, and turn left. The park is at the end of the road.

Fanuel Park is a special place for a special kind of lovers: parents. Just because you have kids doesn't mean you can't or shouldn't enjoy the romantic side of life. This bayside jewel is just one shining example of the kind of daytime outing that will please everyone in the family. There's an expansive playground, a nice lawn for picnicking, and a striking view of the Riviera Shores. It's an ideal spot to sunbathe, or to skate, stroll, or bicycle along the path that winds around the cove. Anyone can appreciate the beauty of Fanuel Park, but for romance-hungry parents it's a dream come true.

Romantic Alternatives: Other scenic spots with swing sets in the greater San Diego area include **GLORIETTA BAY PARK** (a half mile southeast of the Hotel del Coronado on Orange Street), **TIDELANDS PARK** (located at the base of the Coronado Bridge), and **POWERHOUSE PARK** (north of 15th Street on Coast Boulevard in Del Mar).

KATE SESSIONS PARK, Pacific Beach
4000 block of Fanuel Street

From the Pacific Beach area of San Diego, take Grand Avenue west from Interstate 5 and turn right onto Lamont. Kate Sessions is on your right as you head up the hill.

If you've ever wondered what it's like to peer down on San Diego from on high, take a trip to Kate Sessions Park, which overlooks some of the city's most astounding scenery. The unencumbered panoramic view stretches from the ocean to the mountains, across to Coronado, and beyond. Bring a picnic basket and someone you love: there's nothing like snuggling on a blanket as the water sparkles below, the birds serenade from the trees, and the clouds slowly drift by.

MISSION BAY PARK

Call or stop by the Visitors Information Center, located at the corner of East Mission Bay Drive and Clairemont Drive, (619) 276-8200, for detailed information on Mission Bay recreational equipment rentals.

It isn't uncommon for San Diegans to look up or down the coast to find romantic things to do. Everyone needs to get away and escape their day-to-day surroundings. But what about the beauty that lies in one's own backyard? Maybe it's time to take a second look. Start with Mission Bay Park.

When was the last time you rented a jet ski, sailed a catamaran across the sun-sequined water, or cycled the length of Sail Bay? How about a picnic at Crown Point, a bonfire on Fiesta Island, or some kite flying at Tecolate Shores? The possibilities are endless. This enormous marine park spans more than 4,600 acres, offering 27 miles of shoreline, 19 of which are sandy beaches. By day or by night, Mission Bay offers fun and romance served on a sparkling aquamarine platter. Go on, indulge yourselves.

Shelter Island

Hotel/Bed and Breakfast Kissing

KONA KAI CONTINENTAL PLAZA
RESORT AND MARINA, Shelter Island
1551 Shelter Island Drive
(619) 221-8000, (800) KONA-KAI
Expensive to Unbelievably Expensive

Not too long ago, Shelter Island was known for its tacky hotels with an overdone Polynesian motif. But look out, Gilligan! The beautifully remodeled Kona Kai offers romance seekers a peaceful island hideaway with all the luxuries of a full-service resort.

Located at the western point of Shelter Island (which is really a peninsula), the Kona Kai is surrounded by the cobalt waters of San Diego Bay. The resort's architecture recalls a lavish Mexican hacienda, with a gurgling fountain in the circular drive, lush landscaping, and rich bougainvillea that contrasts strikingly against the creamy white stucco walls. The early California style extends into the lobby, where high vaulted ceilings, handcrafted furnishings, a large fireplace, and pale adobe tiles welcome guests into a cavernous but comfortable romantic haven.

The surrounding beauty of San Diego Bay influenced the design of this sprawling, 11-acre resort. Each of the 211 rooms features French doors opening onto a balcony or patio with breathtaking views of the bay or marina. The room sizes range from standard to suites, with two-bedroom townhouses also available. Decorated in pastel fabrics and weathered wood, the standard rooms offer couples plenty of room for a weekend stay. In-room conveniences include cable television, coffeemakers, valet service, and room service, while suites include microwave ovens and refrigerators. Although hand-painted Mexican tile adds an element of charm to every bathroom, ours was very small, with awful fluorescent lighting and a bothersome shower curtain.

Active couples can take advantage of the Kona Kai's myriad resort facilities, which include a heated pool overlooking the marina, spas, lighted tennis courts, a state-of-the-art health club with sauna, and a sandy beach with volleyball and bicycle rentals. If you prefer to relax on your romantic getaway, treat yourselves to a soothing massage. Indulge in the lavish Sunday brunch at **EL EMBARCADERO RESTAURANT** (Moderate), where guests enjoy contemporary Mexican cuisine and sweeping bay views. The kitchen is headed by a master chef who is a three-time Gold Medal winner at the International Culinary Olympics.

Romantic Suggestion: For a unique experience, check out the **GONDOLA DE VENEZIA**, (619) 221-2999 ($62 per couple). Docked at the marina of the Kona Kai, these authentic Venetian watercraft allow lovers to appreciate the beauty of Shelter Island's tranquil waters and the San Diego skyline beneath the stars. The one-hour cruise includes Italian music, hors d'oeuvres, and a bucket of ice with two glasses; all you need to bring is your choice of beverage and your special someone.

Outdoor Kissing

SHELTER ISLAND PARK, Shelter Island

Take Rosecrans Street south to Shelter Island Drive and turn left.

Located on the east side of Shelter Island Drive, this park has a nice long path that stretches along the bay, ideal for jogging, bike riding, or a leisurely stroll. Spread out a blanket or sit beneath one of the covered awnings blossoming with bougainvillea, and watch boats large and small sail out of the harbor and head for the high seas. While this is a popular spot for fishing, it's an even better place to reel in a kiss or two.

Point Loma

Restaurant Kissing

VENICE CAFFE AND BAR, Point Loma
2910 Canon Street
(619) 222-5888
Moderate
Lunch and Dinner Daily

It's a shame the food quality does not equal the intimate ambience of this Italian restaurant. The interior is polished but unpretentious, with a main dining area decorated in an attractive blend of whites and creams, with ivy topiaries and wrought-iron accents. It's hard to choose between a cozy corner table inside or a seat beneath the stars on the charming brick patio, where a small fountain is guarded by a large tree strung with tiny white lights. Although the ambience is endearing, the food is disastrous, so we do not recommend dining here. Instead, come here for coffee and dessert at the cafe, which is a safe and romantic bet. The cafe consists of a large marble-countered bar surrounded by stylish wrought-iron bar stools, an L-shaped banquette with a half-dozen or so tables, and a tiny table for two flanked by overstuffed chairs placed strategically in front of an enormous hearth (the most sought-after seats in the house).

On most nights, you'll find live music in the cafe. Unfortunately, this means having to surrender some of the intimacy you may have hoped for and accepting the fact that a boisterous yell is more practical than a loving whisper. Although jazz connoisseurs may decide to endure the enthusiastic crowds on Friday and Saturday nights, Tuesdays and Wednesdays feature more sedate and soothing piano music that is more conducive to affectionate conversations.

Outdoor Kissing

CABRILLO NATIONAL MONUMENT, Point Loma
$4 per car, $2 per person on foot

Take Rosecrans Street to Canon, and turn right. Go left on Catalina and follow the road to the end of the point.

If the drive to Cabrillo National Monument leaves you in a pensive mood, don't be surprised. Heading toward the tip of the Point Loma peninsula, you'll first pass Fort Rosecrans National Cemetery, where the white tombstones of nearly 50,000 San Diego war heroes are poignantly set against the sparkling blue sea and large American flags billowing in the ocean breeze. Soon the winding road leads you to a picturesque point, first discovered by Portuguese explorer Juan Cabrillo in 1542. High atop its rugged, jutting cliffs, you'll marvel at the beauty of the expansive view before you. On clear days you can see everything from the hills of Tijuana, across the border to the south, to the San Bernardino Mountains, more than 200 miles northeast. While the view is magnificent from the deck of the Cabrillo monument, a little sleuthing will uncover more intimate benches with equally lovely vistas. As you gaze down upon the city and the Coronado shores, you can't help but wonder how they looked when Cabrillo first set foot here, before hotels and skyscrapers marred the landscape. Walk up the hill to the old Point Loma lighthouse, which stands alone on the edge of the scenic point, and you may just get a sense of what such serenity must have been like.

After you take in the amazing views of the San Diego area, study its history, both human and natural, at the visitor center. Here you'll find a theater that shows films about whale migration, tide pools, and Cabrillo's voyage. On your way back, turn left on Cabrillo Road and head down to visit the tide pools. Unfortunately, a Coast Guard station and its high barbed wire fences detract from the natural beauty, but this is still a great spot to admire the sea life in the pools and take in a glorious San Diego sunset.

Coronado

This peninsula is connected to the mainland by a strip of land called Silver Strand Beach. The two best ways to get here are via the Coronado Toll Bridge, which soars high above the downtown skyline, and via a ferryboat cruise across the silvery bay. Once you arrive, the palm-tree-lined streets, the winding bike trails, the manicured neighborhoods, the sandy beaches, and the sweeping vistas will keep you occupied for hours, if not days. This perfect little peninsula is San Diego's own personal Oz, and a great place for fun, sightseeing, and, of course, romancing.

The fare for the Coronado Ferry is $2 each way. The ferries leave downtown every hour on the hour, starting at 9 A.M. The last boat returns from Coronado at 9:30 P.M. Sunday through Thursday, and 10:30 P.M. Friday and Saturday.

Hotel/Bed and Breakfast Kissing

HOTEL DEL CORONADO, Coronado
1500 Orange Avenue
(619) 522-8000, (800) 468-3533
Expensive to Unbelievably Expensive
Minimum stay requirement on weekends and holidays

The century-old Hotel del Coronado is a place of legendary liaisons. Case in point: in 1920, the Prince of Wales met the woman of his dreams during a visit here. He later abdicated his throne as the king of England to marry the former Coronado housewife, and the two became known as the Duke and Duchess of Windsor. From its towering turrets to the artistically carved wooden interior, the Del (as it is known by locals) was once as beguiling as it sounds. Now it is an intense tourist attraction; little about the original structure has changed since Marilyn Monroe filmed *Some Like It Hot* on its golden beaches back in the late 1950s.

All the rooms are more second-hand than antique, and most are dimly lit with old, worn fixtures that contribute to an almost depressing atmosphere. Due to demand, two ocean towers were added to the original hotel in 1980, but they offer little in the way of style and refinement and eradicate any sense of Victorian charm. In fact, they are motel-standard at best. Still, guests at the Del can take advantage of the huge expanse of beach bordering the back of the hotel, plus two swimming pools, three restaurants (more notable for convenience than quality), tennis courts, dozens of shops, and a health spa.

LE MERIDIEN, Coronado
2000 Second Street
(619) 435-3000, (800) 737-8077
Expensive to Very Expensive

Spanning 16 waterfront acres, this beautiful resort rests at the foot of the Coronado Bridge and lays claim to one of the most breathtaking views this side of the Riviera. All of its 300 rooms, suites, and villas are decorated in French country style, and each one is embellished by a private terrace with lovely vistas of the bay and the downtown skyline. Roam the hotel's perfectly manicured grounds and you'll discover six tennis courts, three swimming pools, and two bubbling whirlpools awaiting your indulgence. Should you wish to pamper yourselves further, visit the hotel's renowned European spa, which offers saunas, skin and body treatments, exercise equipment, and fitness classes.

    Romantic Note: Two of the city's most inviting restaurants are located at Le Meridien. **L'ESCALE** (Expensive to Very Expensive) serves French food with California flair (dishes are both rich and deliciously light), but its real draw is a stupendous view of San Diego's bay and downtown skyline. **MARIUS** (Very Expensive) provides an elegant ambience and exceptional Provençal cuisine.

LOEWS, Coronado
4000 Coronado Bay Road
(619) 424-4000, (800) 815-6397
http://www.loewshotels.com
Expensive to Unbelievably Expensive

For a luxury resort, you can't do much better than Loews. Concealed in a very exclusive, quiet neighborhood of bustling Coronado, just south of the **HOTEL DEL CORONADO** (reviewed on previous page) and directly across from **SILVER STRAND BEACH** (see Outdoor Kissing), this is indeed a premier destination. Loews is perched on its own private peninsula, so most rooms have incredible views of the bay. The guest rooms are beautifully decorated, especially the lavish seaside villas, which are all in the Unbelievably Expensive category but worth the splurge if your budget can survive the indulgence.

Romantic Note: The hotel's award-winning seafood restaurant, AZZURA POINT (Moderate to Expensive), is located on the second floor and enjoys spectacular views of the bay. This quaint, casual dining room and lounge has loads of romantic promise for an evening of dinner and dancing above the bay.

Restaurant Kissing

CHEZ LOMA RESTAURANT, Coronado
1132 Loma Avenue
(619) 435-0661
Moderate
Dinner Daily; Sunday Brunch

Chez Loma is housed in a century-old Victorian home that is done up in shades of pink and teal and bordered with a bright row of flower boxes. Inside, floral wallpaper complements the fresh flower arrangements that fill the air with a faint sweetness. Chez Loma's award-winning cuisine is continental, while its atmosphere is vibrant and unpretentious, making it a favorite for special celebrations and private tête-à-têtes.

Its menu consists of fresh fish, meat, and poultry dishes, and the desserts are wonderful. However, it's the view of the docks and the Coronado Bridge that is bound to get most of your attention—aside from the person you're with, that is.

Outdoor Kissing

BAY VIEW PARK, Coronado
At the corner of First and I Streets.

This festive little park is such a well-kept secret that even many locals don't know it exists. Now it can be your secret as well, to share with someone special. However, if your definition of a park includes room to wander, find a different park. Bay View is about the size of a small house lot. In fact, that's what it was before the city turned it into a green knoll in the heart of a charming, albeit exclusive, neighborhood. The space is now filled with generous shade trees and inviting stone benches that look out onto the glittering bay and downtown skyline. It's a delightful place to confide words of love on a starry night.

SILVER STRAND BEACH, Coronado
In front of the Hotel del Coronado.

Sometimes the beach is the worst place to kiss. Even if you still feel inspired to smooch after stepping over glistening hard-bodies, skirting around packs of teenagers, and trying to talk over a blasting radio, chances are you'll be interrupted by the thump of a Frisbee on your head. Surprisingly enough, there is a long, wide stretch of white sand that is usually uncrowded, even on weekends. Though it may seem too beautiful to believe, the Silver Strand Beach is not a mirage. It is a very real beach that seems to have been set aside for long hand-holding rambles, complete with cool waves lapping at your toes and the warm sun lingering on your face and shoulders. It is a wonderful place to kiss. It is also a difficult place to leave.

Chula Vista

Restaurant Kissing

JAKE'S SAN DIEGO BAY, Chula Vista
570 Marina Parkway
(619) 476-0400
Moderate
Lunch Monday-Friday; Dinner Daily; Sunday Brunch

Jake's San Diego Bay is part of a restaurant chain known for its spectacular settings, and this waterfront location at the Chula Vista Marina definitely meets that criterion. Housed in a gray, wooden boathouse-like structure, Jake's is decorated in a nautical motif. Photographs of long-ago regattas adorn the walls, and replicas of antique crafts hang from the ceiling. While the large dining room may be a little too noisy for quiet conversation, Jake's outdoor patio offers a peaceful retreat where you can appreciate the waterside view.

Jake's menu lists standard American seafood and popular international entrées, but for the most part preparations are rather lackluster and ordinary. The enormous Hula Pie, fudge-topped macadamia nut ice cream in an Oreo cookie crust, is the only standout. While the service and view are outstanding, the food alone is not enough to justify a visit. Still, if you're looking for a casual place to watch the sun set over the water, Jake's may be just the place. Begin a romantic evening over cocktails or end it over dessert, accompanied by the sounds of a rollicking surf.

CENTRAL SAN DIEGO

Mission Valley

Restaurant Kissing

PREGO, Mission Valley
1370 Frazee Road
(619) 294-4700
Inexpensive to Moderate
Lunch Monday-Friday; Dinner Saturday-Sunday

Prego is part of a new breed of trattorias that have popped up all over the city. Elegant and sophisticated, they offer delectable, beautifully presented Italian cuisine. From the outside, Prego looks like a grand country villa. Behind its wrought-iron gate, you'll find a romantic patio enhanced by a bubbling fountain and vine-covered walls. The inside is large, with plenty of intimate nooks and corners. Wonderful smells emanate from the open kitchen, and it's easy to second-guess your order as you watch the waiter pass with someone else's food. Everything looks so appealing! The menu consists primarily of pastas and gourmet pizzas, but includes a variety of tasty fish and meat dishes as well.

Old Town

Hotel/Bed and Breakfast Kissing

HERITAGE PARK BED AND BREAKFAST INN, Old Town
2470 Heritage Park Row
(619) 295-7088, (800) 995-2470
Moderate to Very Expensive
Minimum stay requirement on weekends

This century-old bed and breakfast is more interesting than romantic, although a relatively authentic Victorian boardinghouse just may be your cup of tea. Time seems to have stood still here. Upon entering, you are whisked into a staged world of vintage charm and hospitality. This Queen Anne mansion has 11 guest chambers, each decorated in what is supposed to be old-world style, but occasionally descends to second-hand. Some rooms have detached bathrooms, while others have extremely small ones that are meant for one person at a time. What is appealing are the antiques, turn-of-the-century photographs, feather beds, and claw-foot tubs. The most popular rooms are the Turret, with a cozy tower sitting area, and the Victorian Rose, which overlooks the rose garden. Afternoon tea is served in the cozy parlor, where vintage films are shown nightly. Breakfast is a lavish affair, with an assortment of pastries, fresh fruit, and tempting entrées such as pecan-glazed French toast and baked apples.

Romantic Suggestion: Nearby **PRESIDIO PARK** is a place of great natural beauty and historical significance—the first Spanish settlers called it home in 1769. The park offers a tremendous view from its position on the hills overlooking the bay. Its more than 40 acres are abundantly green, making this a favorite spot for strollers, cyclists, and picnic connoisseurs. Unfortunately, at times this park is also a spot for drug deals and cruising, so be aware that daytime is the preferred time to visit.

Restaurant Kissing

BERTA'S, Old Town
3928 Twiggs Street
(619) 295-2343
Moderate
Lunch and Dinner Daily

Eating at Berta's is like being invited to someone's lace-curtained bungalow—someone who serves Latin American cuisine with a gourmet flair. The menu offers dishes such as Guatemalan shrimp (shrimp smothered in a spicy salsa of baked tomato, jalapeño peppers, green onion, and garlic) and *tallarines vatapa* (pasta with a Brazilian peanut-coconut sauce that incorporates ginger, tomatoes, and chilies). Your lips and your taste buds will shout "*Olé!*"

CAFE PACIFICA, Old Town
2414 San Diego Avenue
(619) 291-6666
Moderate
Lunch Tuesday-Friday; Dinner Daily

If you wander outside **OLD TOWN STATE PARK** (see Outdoor Kissing) and down a sidewalk lined with Mexican restaurants and gift shops, eventually you'll come to this quiet restaurant. Although it doesn't fit in with the rest of historical Old Town, Cafe Pacifica, with its strands of white lights reflected from mirrors and windows, is a great place for fresh seafood, California-style. The rigatoni with grilled sea scallops and Sicilian pesto, the salmon and sweet corn cakes with a savory herb butter, and the grilled sea scallops with Chinese plum sauce are more than enough to convince you to forgo enchiladas and burritos for a more contemporary atmosphere.

CASA DE BANDINI, Old Town
2754 Calhoun Street
(619) 297-8211
Inexpensive
Breakfast, Lunch, and Dinner Daily

This 1829 adobe hacienda was once the home of Juan Bandini, who brought the waltz to California from Mexico City. We recommend asking for a table on the patio, although this large area is usually full. Teal-striped umbrellas keep the sun off during the day, heaters help keep you feeling cozy at night, and the birds singing in the palm trees complement the songs of the festive mariachis strolling by the tables. If you choose to sit inside, you'll be seated in a tapestry-covered chair, where you can admire Mexican artwork and antiques. The walls are painted with colorful accents, and the stained glass windows reflect even more color. While the setting is pretty, the food is neither authentic nor outstanding. But you can still sip icy margaritas and drink in the atmosphere at the same time.

Outdoor Kissing

OLD TOWN STATE PARK, Old Town

From Interstate 8, take the Taylor Street exit and follow the signs to Old Town State Park.

Six square blocks of old San Diego have been preserved as a state historic park. The spacious streets, off-limits to cars, are lined with shops, restaurants, and vintage buildings from the Mexican and Early American periods. This is a tourist attraction, and like all tourist attractions, it can be loud and crowded. But if you go during the week or during off-season, you'll find that it can be quite peaceful—and especially affectionate and relatively authentic at night.

The park's bright spot is **BAZAAR DEL MUNDO**, (619) 296-3161. This courtyard is lined with shops and galleries literally bursting with colorful treasures from Latin America. Flowers seem to erupt from every nook and cranny.

Hillcrest

Restaurant Kissing

CAFE ELEVEN, Hillcrest
1440 University Avenue
(619) 260-8023
Moderate
Dinner Tuesday-Saturday

Cafe Eleven has a warm and attractive quality despite its location in a modest shopping plaza near a busy street. Tiny tables and cozy banquettes fill the narrow dining rooms. The decor is crisp and contemporary, with recessed lighting that creates a subtle glow and jazz music that plays in the background. The walls are lined with colorful paintings by local artists, but the cafe's French country cuisine—such as Long Island duck roasted with apples and onions and served with a green and pink peppercorn sauce—may be the real masterpiece here.

CALIFORNIA CUISINE, Hillcrest
1027 University Avenue
(619) 543-0790
Moderate to Expensive
Lunch Tuesday-Friday; Dinner Tuesday-Sunday

Although the name of this restaurant sounds like the title of a magazine article, the dishes here embody all the best qualities of Southern California dining. Menus change daily to take advantage of the freshest ingredients and are presented in Lucite frames, which is appropriate because the chef treats every dish like a work of art. That attention to detail extends beyond the kitchen to every aspect of the restaurant. The intimate dining room is filled with flowers and glowing candles, and one entire wall is covered with original artwork. A covered patio area with a tent-like roof provides outdoor dining year-round. On warmer evenings, the best seats in the house are in the outer patio area, where you can propose a toast to romance beneath the stars. Most of the tables here are set for two, and all of them are spaced well enough apart to allow for quiet conversation. Despite the restaurant's location on a busy section of University Avenue, the only background noise you'll notice is the faint duet of outdoor fountains and softly played love songs.

The menu is almost too enticing for words: It will be a challenge to decide between the crab cakes prepared with fresh yams and served with a grainy Dijon aioli, the pistachio-crusted pork tenderloin accompanied by a fresh vegetable and fruit salsa, and the fresh salmon lacquered with ginger and black pepper and served over a sherried sweet potato purée. We ended our meal here with a cranberry torte served warm and topped with home-made caramel ice cream: sheer ecstasy. Every sumptuous detail at California Cuisine will be music to your lips.

MONTANAS AMERICAN GRILL, Hillcrest
1421 University Avenue
(619) 297-0722
Moderate to Expensive
Lunch Monday-Friday; Dinner Daily

Don't let the down-home name fool you: Montanas American Grill is strictly for urban cowboys. Step inside this sleek restaurant and ask for a table for two in the wine room at the back. If there is a wait, saunter up to the rich mahogany bar and take a moment to admire the elaborate floral arrangements and unusual lighting system. Soon, a friendly host will show you to a smooth, dark granite table and present you with a menu that features nouvelle American cuisine.

Montanas is popular for its consistently good food. You'll find some traditional favorites here, such as juicy cheeseburgers and BBQ ribs, but also more ambitious entrées such as venison chile, smoked turkey sausage, mixed greens with Asiago cheese and spicy pecans, and delicious smoked duck cakes served with roasted red pepper sauce. Desserts are equally smashing. The hot apple cobbler with sour-mash cream and the chocolate torte with vanilla cream and caramel sauce left us speechless. (All the better for kissing!)

Romantic Warning: While the delicious food, excellent service, and chic decor are sure to please even the most discerning city slickers, at times Montanas' noise level may remind some of a wild stampede. Be sure to stand firm in your boots when asking for a quiet table at the back. Your romantic dinner will be much more pleasant.

Uptown

Restaurant Kissing

BUSALACCHI'S RESTAURANT, Uptown
3683 Fifth Avenue
(619) 298-0119
Moderate to Expensive
Lunch and Dinner Daily

Busalacchi's is divided into a half-dozen tiny sections, each aglow with candlelight and romantic detailing. You can dine in front of a flickering fireplace at a cozy window table for two, or on the enclosed terrace. This was once a private home, and it has maintained that intimate atmosphere. The air is fragrant with Italian spices and the aroma of Sicilian specialties. Busalacchi's is a favorite of even the most finicky critics.

FIFTH & HAWTHORN, Uptown
515 Hawthorn Street
(619) 544-0940
Moderate
Lunch Monday-Friday; Dinner Daily

Due to its location near the Old Globe Theater, this staid restaurant has long been a favorite stop for those on their way to an evening show. With the recent introduction of a "Wine Dinner for Two," it may become a preferred destination for affectionate encounters as well. Housed in a relatively small building, Fifth & Hawthorn meets many of our heartfelt requirements. The dining room is separated from the entry by a wall of glass blocks and maintains a cozy, yet intimate atmosphere. Each table is crowned with a white tablecloth, fresh flowers, and glowing candles, and the room is filled with couples speaking in hushed tones. And no wonder: they have struck romantic gold.

Fifth & Hawthorn's "Wine Dinner for Two" is possibly the best deal in town. It includes a choice of appetizers to share, soup or salad, a variety of entrées, a dessert to share, and a bottle of either chardonnay or merlot. This four-course feast costs under $40 per couple. You might start by sharing a rock shrimp quesadilla, followed by a delectable duck soup with crispy wontons. The main course, perhaps Cajun catfish or spicy seafood fettuccine, is sure to be a savory treat, and the remarkable crème brûée makes an inspired finale. Fifth & Hawthorn also offers a full menu with light suppers and full-sized entrées. With the Wine Dinner, however, you can enjoy a romantic dinner and still have money left over for the theater.

LAUREL RESTAURANT AND BAR, Uptown
Laurel Street and Fifth Avenue
(619) 239-2222
Expensive
Lunch Monday-Friday; Dinner Daily

One of the hottest new spots in town, Laurel boasts one of the prettiest restaurant interiors in San Diego. Soft, glowing lights illuminate the sunken dining area, where plush booths, a curving bar, and a private wine room await. The tables are simply adorned with white tablecloths, luminous votive candles, and terra-cotta pots planted with fresh herbs. Love songs played on a baby grand piano set the mood for romance, and lovers can swoon to late-night jazz Friday and Saturday nights.

Although the decor is stunning, the staff suffers from some serious attitude problems. Laurel's hip reputation has gone to their heads, and the service is so haughty and rude we found it difficult to enjoy our meal. So, don't worry if you can't get in: the poor treatment and inconsistent cuisine are nothing to get excited about.

Downtown San Diego

Hotel/Bed and Breakfast Kissing

BALBOA PARK INN, San Diego
3402 Park Boulevard
(619) 298-0823, (800) 938-8181
http://www.travel2000.com
Inexpensive to Moderate
Minimum stay requirement on weekends

While location isn't everything, it is something, and it is the best reason to make Balboa Park Inn part of your San Diego visit. This eccentric, sprawling bed and breakfast has more than 30 rooms in three separate houses. There aren't many bed and breakfasts in the San Diego area, and this one has a superior location at the entrance to remarkable and captivating **BALBOA PARK** (see Outdoor Kissing). The eclectic decor ranges from tacky to peculiar, with second-hand furnishings, animal motifs, gilded mirrors, and, believe it or not, lawn furniture. Yet the rooms, for the most part, are nicely maintained, and some guest quarters have fireplaces, kitchens, large beds, living rooms, whirlpool tubs, and plenty of space. This isn't a premium property, but it is a reasonable consideration for the location and the space.

HORTON GRAND HOTEL, San Diego
311 Island Avenue
(619) 544-1886, (800) 542-1886
Moderate to Very Expensive

The Horton is the result of a resourceful merging of two century-old hotels. Both were slated for demolition when an earnest and wise preservationist bought them from the city for a dollar apiece. Brick by brick, the hotels were dismantled and the materials were stored in a warehouse; finally, in 1986, they were resurrected side by side a few blocks from the original site and connected by a courtyard with a glass atrium. Although authentically refurbished, the interior is too slick to be truly Victorian and too affected to feel alluring. Still, if your frame of mind is such that Victoriana of any kind tickles your fancy, you may want to climb the winding oak staircase to one of the 110 guest rooms, each individually decorated with real antiques and quaint Victorian touches. All the rooms have private bathrooms and gas-burning fireplaces. Most have high ceilings and high platform beds, and feature balconies overlooking the city lights or the atrium. If you make reservations here, be sure to specify which side of the hotel you'd prefer. The left wing is more frilly and feminine; the right wing, once the Kahle Saddlery Hotel, has more masculine decor.

Romantic Note: The hotel's **IDA BAILEY'S RESTAURANT** (Moderate to Expensive) is named after the city's first female entrepreneur, a madam whose bordello was said to be located on this very spot. Like its namesake, the restaurant is lusty and sensual, but that influence is diminished by tour groups and small groups of private parties. Because Ida Bailey's is a favorite spot for weddings and get-togethers, the noise from the restaurant's courtyard can carry over into the rooms.

HYATT REGENCY SAN DIEGO, San Diego
One Market Place
(619) 232-1234, (800) 233-1234
http://www.hyatt.com
Expensive to Unbelievably Expensive

If you don't mind the atmosphere of a massive hotel complex, the fine, chic style at the Hyatt Regency will serve your needs well. While such hotels are usually impersonal, the employees here go out of their way to make your stay a pleasant one. The doorman will greet you warmly, the bellhop will eagerly gather your suitcases, and the concierge will all but do handstands to make sure your every need is attended to.

This hotel is the tallest waterfront building on the West Coast, and the views from the higher floors are breathtaking. While the south-facing rooms have vistas of the Coronado Bridge, they also look down onto the industrial areas that mar much of the coastline beyond. The rooms with the best views are those facing Mission Bay and the La Jolla coast.

If you should ever desire to leave your room (and many do not), there's certainly plenty to do. Since the hotel is located on the marina, you can walk along the docks or stroll through the romantic (albeit touristy) **SEAPORT VILLAGE** just next door (see Outdoor Kissing). But you need not leave the hotel at all. You can take advantage of the swimming pool, tennis courts, spa and health club, world-class restaurants, and a cocktail lounge that boasts

the best view in town (see Restaurant Kissing for reviews of SALLY'S RES-
TAURANT AND BAR and TOP OF THE HYATT).

U.S. GRANT HOTEL, San Diego
326 Broadway
(619) 232-3121, (800) 237-5029
http://www.travel2000.com
Expensive to Unbelievably Expensive

   Dedicated to a former U.S. President by his son, the U.S. Grant Hotel
was once the haunt of dignitaries and movie stars. Now it is a nice downtown hotel in need of some venture capital to bring it up to par. The guest
rooms are furnished in Queen Anne reproductions and some have excellent
city views, but the ambience is fairly standard and the bathrooms are unimpressive. However, many of the hotel's suites offer both a hydra-spa bath
and a fireplace. Afternoon tea in the lobby, accompanied by the lilt of soft
piano music, is a nostalgic salute to the romance of yesteryear.

WESTGATE HOTEL, San Diego
1055 Second Avenue
(619) 238-1818, (800) 221-3802
Expensive to Unbelievably Expensive

   You should know ahead of time that there's nothing casual about the
Westgate. It makes great efforts to project an elegant, even ornate European
character. Although the rooms are embellished with many elaborate 18th-
century details, the furniture is an odd mixture of Levitz and enviable gilded
period pieces. What a juxtaposition. Even the lobby displays this same con-
fusion. Space isn't a problem here; the rooms have tall ceilings and feel more
than roomy. In some ways the Westgate is beautiful, and in other ways it's
exceptionally tacky. You will have to decide for yourselves.

   Romantic Note: The hotel's restaurant, **THE FOUNTAINBLEU
ROOM** (Moderate to Very Expensive), is gilded, flamboyant, and absolutely
dripping with awards. This is the place to come for an unforgettable culinary
experience. The tuxedoed waiters are doting but a bit haughty (white gloves
and all), so you'll want to think twice about your manners. For a private,
formal meal it is one of the best places in town.

Restaurant Kissing

ANTHONY'S STAR OF THE SEA ROOM, San Diego
1360 North Harbor Drive
(619) 232-7408

http://www.gofishanthonys.com
Expensive to Unbelievably Expensive
Dinner Daily

While Anthony's remains a favored spot for celebrations of the heart, and the waterfront view *is* magnificent, the food, service, and dated decor leave much to be desired. (Our server was completely officious, and the tiny portions of food were singularly unimpressive.) The seafood-oriented, seasonal menu features less than a dozen entrées. Some may call the decor "old world," but by most standards it is in need of a major face-lift. When making reservations, you may be asked to have the males in your party wear a jacket; you will notice upon arrival that only about two-thirds of the men dining are thus attired. Enforcement of the rule is sporadic, much like the quality of the food.

BELLA LUNA, San Diego
748 Fifth Avenue
(619) 239-3222
Moderate
Lunch Monday-Friday; Dinner Daily

Bella Luna is Italian for "beautiful moon." As the name suggests, this is a place where the two of you can dine on celestial Italian food while gazing at the heavens above. The most romantic tables are those on the outside patio, lit by glowing candles and warmed by a plastic tent and space heaters. The inside dining room is narrow, with large windows overlooking the street. Closely spaced tables are topped with white tablecloths and dried flowers in terra-cotta pots, and the high ceiling is painted to look like the sky. While dining indoors at Bella Luna may not offer much intimacy, the bustling atmosphere and excellent cuisine will really get your hearts pumping.

Everything on Bella Luna's menu is authentic and prepared fresh daily. Once you've been seated, your amiable waiter will bring warm focaccia and a dish of virgin olive oil, balsamic vinegar, and Parmesan cheese. Among the impressive dishes, you'll find a flavorful taglierini primavera (a fine linguine with fresh vegetables) and a rich cheese ravioli with fresh tomato and basil. When you're finished, stroll through the historical neighborhood and share a kiss beneath the beautiful San Diego moon.

BISTRO BACCO, San Diego
420 E Street
(619) 233-3377
Moderate to Expensive
Lunch Monday-Friday; Dinner Daily

Unlike many of the cramped trattorias in the historical Gaslamp Quarter, Bistro Bacco has a large, beautiful dining room with adequate space and a quiet atmosphere, perfect for a loving dinner for two. A number of tapestry-covered tables are situated around a series of arches and columns, a large colorful mural, and an open kitchen gleaming with hammered copper. The decor is truly stunning, so the chef is forced to compete with the interior designer. For now the designer is ahead, but only by a nose. The menu lists a wide selection of appetizers, salads, pizzas, fresh fish, and pastas. Highlights include a mixed salad topped with a champagne vinaigrette and feta cheese; savory roasted chicken pizza with smoked mozzarella, sun-dried tomatoes, and roasted pine nuts; and tasty linguine with clams, oregano, white wine, and Italian parsley. Rich chocolate mousse is a luscious way to end your meal. Portions are large, and the attentive servers do their utmost to see to it that you enjoy your meal.

CAFE LULU, San Diego
419 F Street
(619) 238-0114
Inexpensive; No Credit Cards
Breakfast, Lunch, and Dinner Daily

Cafe Lulu is an upscale cappuccino bar decorated more like a modern art gallery than a coffeehouse. As you enter, notice the broken mirror, the glass-and-stone collage at your feet, the unique art, the large exotic bouquet, and the interesting blend of rippled glass and neon light in the far corner. While Cafe Lulu offers the usual desserts, baked goods, and light breakfast items found in most coffeehouses, the menu also boasts such tantalizing treats as raspberry baked Brie. Situated near the heart of the Gaslamp Quarter, this is a great place to start or end your evening.

CROCE'S, San Diego
802 Fifth Avenue
(619) 233-4355
Moderate
Breakfast, Lunch, and Dinner Daily

One of the first restaurants to prompt widespread renovation of this historical area was opened by Ingrid, the widow of singer/songwriter Jim Croce. Instantly trendy for its nightly schedule of live jazz, Croce's soon became popular for excellent international cuisine. For a special dinner setting, ask for a table upstairs, where the atmosphere is quiet and intimate. The walls here are lovingly adorned with Ingrid's personal collection of paintings and photographs, some of which include photos of her late husband relaxing at home. If you want to re-create the dishes the Croces enjoyed, pick up a copy of Ingrid Croce's cookbook, *Thyme in a Bottle.*

Croce's was such an astounding success that Ingrid ended up buying almost half of the block that adjoins Croce's and opened **INGRID'S CANTINA,** 802 Fifth Avenue, (619) 233-3660 (Moderate), featuring Southwestern cuisine and hot jazz at the Top Hat nightclub. While an upstairs table may hold romantic possibilities, the nightclub is too crowded to be considered romantic. People are packed in like sardines at night, and shouting to be heard over the music doesn't prompt much passion. Still, depending on your musical preference, your ears could be pleased with the tunes blasting through the air.

DAKOTA, San Diego
901 Fifth Avenue
(619) 234-5554
Inexpensive to Moderate
Lunch Monday-Friday; Dinner Daily

This is one of the few restaurants downtown that offers something other than Italian fare; in fact, Dakota seems to revel in its American-style independence. The casual downstairs dining area offers both indoor and outdoor seating, while the more intimate upstairs features a full bar and an outside deck. Pop art posters of Gene Autry and Roy Rogers adorn the walls, and each table is covered with a white tablecloth and topped off with a small, black boot that holds a handful of flowers. There's no mistaking this place for another trattoria, and the food here provides another welcome change. Our helpful server pointed out that the most popular dishes are noted in the menu by a small pistol, so we narrowed our choices by focusing on those, and were pleased with the results. The Southwest Caesar salad, wild mushroom fettuccine, and chicken with an orange chipotle glaze were all remarkable.

GRANT BAR & GRILL, San Diego
326 Broadway, at the U.S. Grant Hotel
(619) 239-6806
http://www.travel2000.com
Expensive
Breakfast, Lunch, and Dinner Daily

Cross the elegant lobby of the U.S. Grant Hotel into the Grant Bar & Grill and you'll feel as if you've taken a step back in time. Richly decorated with dark wood paneling and old-fashioned English hunting prints, the Grant Bar & Grill recalls an exclusive men's club of a bygone era. Once you slip into one of the plush, high-backed leather booths, the gracious atmosphere and attentive service will melt away your everyday concerns as you anticipate a truly refined dining adventure. Concentrating on continental cuisine, the kitchen turns out European classics with a contemporary twist. For starters, try the splendid spinach, Belgian endive, and Stilton cheese salad with a very light citrus vinaigrette. Entrées such as a risotto with shrimp and scallops or sea bass Sri Lanka are beautifully presented, the portions are ample, and everything tastes as good as it looks. This is genteel, leisurely dining at its best, with an earnest old-world flair.

Romantic Alternative: The U.S. Grant hosts a less expensive, equally elegant afternoon tea in the chandeliered lobby from 3 P.M. to 6 P.M. every day.

LA PROVENCE, San Diego
708 Fourth Avenue
(619) 544-0661
Moderate
Lunch and Dinner Daily

If you and your loved one yearn for a romantic weekend in the French countryside, but you don't have the time or the resources, visit La Provence. You will absolutely feel transported. Stroll past the bistro tables on the patio and you'll discover a dining room filled with Provençal-style touches. Dried flowers hang from wood-beamed ceilings, colorful fabric frames the paned windows, and rustic wooden furniture invites you to linger. Ask for a booth near the rocky fountain in the corner, sink into a pile of patterned pillows, and let your adventure begin.

La Provence specializes in French cuisine with Mediterranean influences. Unfortunately, items listed on the menu are often translated incorrectly, and you may very well end up with something you aren't expecting. The trick is to clarify things when ordering to avoid any disappointment. As a new restaurant, La Provence needs to improve the uneven service and confusing menu. In the meantime, the pleasant country French decor and authentic coastal French cuisine make a visit worth your while.

MISTER A'S RESTAURANT, San Diego
2550 Fifth Avenue, in the Fifth Avenue Financial Center
(619) 239-1377
Moderate to Very Expensive
Lunch Monday-Friday; Dinner Daily

Mister A's is San Diego's classic destination for intimate dining, as much a part of the city's personality as nearby **BALBOA PARK** (see Outdoor Kissing). This place is expensive, opulent, and possibly even garish (the waitresses wear strapless sheaths of red taffeta, prompting some to call the style of this establishment "early bordello"). However, the dining room offers one of the best views in San Diego, and the service is friendly and attentive.

The dining room is decorated in deep burgundy, accented by rich wooden trim and elaborate golden candelabras. On most nights the aisles are packed with tableside carts at which the waiters flambé practically everything. Fortunately, Mister A's is not all flash. Its continental cuisine is award-winning, and the wine list is extensive. (The maitre d' was almost giddy as he described a rare 1963 vintage.) Nevertheless, the real claim to fame here is the unparalleled vista of the city. You can enjoy it from virtually any seat in the restaurant or while sipping a romantic nightcap in the cocktail lounge.

MOLLY'S, San Diego
333 West Harbor Drive, at the San Diego Marriott Hotel and Marina
(619) 234-1500
Moderate to Expensive
Dinner Daily

Molly's will exceed all your expectations for a perfect evening. The food is exquisite, the service is flawless, and the pianist gladly takes requests. The resplendent dark wood paneling is set off by emerald green velvet chairs and marble accents. Softly lit beveled glass panels separate each booth or table for supreme privacy.

Caesar salad, perfect steaks, and delicious seafood are all sensational and beautifully presented. After-dinner coffee is a regal production, served on a silver platter with all the trimmings: shaved chocolate, orange peel, and whipped cream flavored with amaretto. The desserts are equally grand; the dark chocolate truffles and chocolate-dipped strawberries are sublime.

RAINWATER'S, San Diego
1202 Kettner Boulevard
(619) 233-5757
Expensive
Lunch Monday-Friday; Dinner Daily

Located next to the beautiful Sante Fe train station, Rainwater's is dark, sensuous, and adorned by city lights. The restaurant occupies the second floor of an old Bekins Storage warehouse. Once inside this renovated historical building, guests climb a suspended, tiled staircase with glittering white lights to a quiet, elegant room illuminated by little more than candlelight. Large, cozy booths and tables for two overlook views of the trains and San Diego Bay. The service here is attentive and the American cuisine is superior. It is truly a stately place to dine.

Primarily known as a steak house (its reputation for having the best beef in San Diego is well deserved), Rainwater's also offers fresh seafood, pasta, and poultry for those who prefer lighter fare. We feasted on the special black bean soup with a dollop of sherry, and shared bites of flavorful steak and herb-encrusted sea bass over creamy mashed potatoes with crispy leeks. Want to end your special dinner on a sweet note? Rainwater's award-winning chocolate lasagna is deliciously rich and perfect for sharing, but only with someone you really like a lot.

SALLY'S RESTAURANT AND BAR, San Diego
One Market Place, at the Hyatt Regency San Diego
(619) 687-6080
Moderate
Lunch and Dinner Daily

Adorned in ultra-modern decor, Sally's offers a sophisticated setting for romance. This beautiful bayfront restaurant is encircled by 17 sets of windowed doors, which, when opened, literally make the walls disappear and allow in cooling breezes. Unfortunately, the best views are reserved for the bar area, but there is some patio and window-side seating for restaurant patrons too. If an unobstructed view is not your top priority, you'll find plenty of comfortable booths and intimate tables to call your own. Muted halogen lighting and candlelight give each table its own sensual halo. The menu primarily features seafood, prepared with a distinctive Mediterranean flair. Sea scallops with corn pancakes, linguine with Florida rock shrimp, and paella are just a few of the gratifying entrées.

SALVATORE'S, San Diego   ♥♥♥
750 Front Street
(619) 544-1865
Inexpensive to Expensive
Dinner Daily

A darling of the food critics, Salvatore's is everything an endearing restaurant should be. Its ornate yet subtle dining room is divided by florid pillars and illuminated by gilded sconces and flickering candles. Blush-colored tablecloths sweetly contrast with crisp white overlays, while a gathering of fresh flowers completes the effect. Live music sets a soothing tone nightly, as patrons dine on beautifully presented northern Italian cuisine, including homemade pastas, delicious veal, steak, and seafood. Our scampi with caramelized orange and lemon and the veal scalopini with marsala wine, cream, and porcini mushrooms were superb.

TOP OF THE HYATT, San Diego
One Market Place, at the Hyatt Regency San Diego
(619) 232-1234
Moderate
Lunch Daily

If you've ever yearned for a bird's-eye view of San Diego, let your heart take wing. This lovely cocktail lounge is perched high atop the beautiful Hyatt Regency on San Diego Bay, the tallest waterside hotel on the West Coast. The large, rectangular dining room is furnished with a scattering of oversized chairs and couches, and its floor-to-ceiling windows reveal sweeping vistas of the San Diego coastline on three sides: the ocean glimmering by day, the city lights twinkling by night. The most romantic tables, at the west end of the lounge, are ideal for sipping Dom Perignon ($18 a glass) as you watch the sun set over the Coronado shore.

Romantic Warning: As wonderful as this can be for romance, the smoke that spills into every space can be disagreeable to the point of intolerable if you are not a smoker.

TOP OF THE MARKET, San Diego
750 North Harbor Drive, at the Fish Market
(619) 232-FISH
Expensive to Very Expensive
Lunch and Dinner Daily; Sunday Brunch

If you are searching for a restaurant with a captivating view, look no further. A seat at the Top of the Market may not inspire romance, but it can guarantee you some of the best fish in town. From the terrace vantage point, gaze out onto the harbor and watch as the sun sweeps a final glistening stroke across the water's surface. In very warm weather, you may want to choose an indoor table, because the terrace can get quite warm. Either way, you'll find it a night to remember. The kitchen's fresh-from-the-ocean seafood and tender steaks are legendary, and there is every indication that the kitchen's quality standards are only getting better.

Romantic Note: If informal dining is more your style, you'll find the same view, minus the ambience, downstairs at **THE FISH MARKET RESTAURANT**, (619) 232-FISH (Inexpensive to Moderate). It's usually noisy, crowded, and often frequented by the family set—but shorts and sandals are always welcome.

TUTTO MARE, San Diego
4365 Executive Drive
(619) 597-1188

Inexpensive to Moderate
Lunch Monday-Friday; Dinner Daily

This strikingly chic restaurant is visually impressive. Though polished and slick doesn't always lend itself to cozy and romantic, a series of banquette seats allows for plenty of space and close snuggling. The impressive menu specializes in Italian coastal cuisine, prepared with a California attitude. Mesquite-grilled fish is always exceptional, and the wood-fired pizzas are some of the best in town.

Outdoor Kissing

BALBOA PARK, San Diego

Take Laurel Street east from Interstate 5 and you'll end up right in the heart of the park.

Balboa Park is a romantic adventure waiting to happen, and you won't have to spend a cent in order to come home with a fortune in memories. With more than 1,100 acres of lush tropical greenery that seems to be perpetually in bloom, this is one of those quintessential spots for walking hand in hand, satisfied just with the pleasure of being here and with each other.

No matter how many times you've been to Balboa Park, there's always new territory to explore. It takes hours to stroll the entire grounds, days to see everything in the celebrated zoo, weeks to explore its 11 museums. There are organ concerts to be heard, international cottages to investigate, and plays to attend at its three theaters. A tour of the botanical gardens, followed by a picnic at the reflecting pool, a kiss at the wishing well, and even a ride on an old-fashioned carousel, makes for an idyllic afternoon. A day of exploration at Balboa Park will make you feel like you've grabbed the brass ring.

CORONADO FERRY, San Diego
1050 North Harbor Drive
(619) 234-4111
$2 each way

At the foot of Broadway and North Harbor Drive, at the downtown Embarcadero.

Although Coronado is just a short drive across the bay from the downtown Embarcadero, getting there by ferry makes the trip much more romantic. For $2 each you can leave the car behind, take along a couple of bikes, and head out in search of an unforgettable day. The trip takes only 15 minutes, but it's 15 minutes of gliding across shimmering waters filled with sailboats and catamarans, taking in wonderful skyline views. Though the boat is often very crowded, there's not a spot on deck where you won't feel the sun on your face or the wind in your hair. The ferries leave downtown every hour on the hour, starting at 9 A.M. The last boat returns from Coronado at 9:30 P.M. Sunday through Thursday, and 10:30 P.M. Friday and Saturday.

EMBARCADERO MARINA PARK, San Diego

Take Harbor Drive to Fifth Avenue, turn south, and follow Fifth Avenue until it ends at the park.

A couple of blocks east of **SEAPORT VILLAGE** (reviewed on following page) and right next to the Intercontinental Hotel is a pretty little park that until recently was a wonderfully well-kept secret. Embarcadero Marina Park is a peninsula-like stretch of land that lies practically in the shadow of the Coronado Bridge, looking out onto the docks and a bay overflowing with boats and catamarans. The park has a small pier, a quaint gazebo, plenty of hungry seagulls to feed, and even a workout path that winds around its stretch of shoreline. Although a sit-up here and a pull-up there may be invigorating, most couples seem content just to spread out a blanket and smooch, which can also be a heart-healthy activity.

Romantic Warning: Like it or not, the San Diego Convention Center has become the park's newest neighbor, and it's not uncommon for conventioneers to stumble onto its pristine shores.

GASLAMP QUARTER, San Diego

The Gaslamp Quarter extends from Broadway to L Street and from Fourth Avenue to Sixth Avenue. The most popular night spots are on Fifth Avenue, between E and F Streets.

Ready to jazz up your relationship? Visit the Gaslamp Quarter. Not only can you catch dinner and some incredible jazz here, but you can get a history lesson at the same time. You'll find some of the city's most beautiful Victorian-style buildings in this area. Restored to turn-of-the-century authenticity, the streets of the Quarter are crowded with people (locals and tourists alike), lined with nightclubs, and filled with fabulous restaurants. You can dance the night away, listen to a local jazz band, stop for espresso and dessert, or simply wander the area hand in hand and take in all the sights.

Romantic Warning: Outdoor patio diners beware—although the Gaslamp Quarter is charming and beautifully restored, it is not immune to the aggressive panhandlers who are increasingly filling San Diego's downtown streets. Many restaurants have outdoor seating, but during our breakfast at one popular spot recently, we were asked for money, stared at frequently, and became the subjects of someone's screaming epithets.

SAN DIEGO ZOO, San Diego
(619) 234-3153
$15 admission

At Park Boulevard and Zoo Place.

The San Diego Zoo is not only one of the largest zoos in the world, it's one of the most beautiful. Spanning 100 acres of lush greenery and exotic flora, the zoo is home to more than 4,000 animals. There's too much to see in just one day, but you might want to cuddle up on the double-decker bus tour, enjoy a eagle's eye view from the Skyfari aerial tram, or go it by foot along the zoo's verdant and winding trails. If you think zoos are for kids and tourists only, you are in for a big surprise. A visit with the wild and exotic animals who share the Earth with us is as enriching and joyous as anything in San Diego. Besides, what better way than a day at the zoo to bring out the animal in each of us?

If you should work up an appetite hiking along all those footpaths, skip the concession stands and head over to **ALBERT'S** (Inexpensive to Moderate), the zoo's restaurant. The decor of woven leather, jara wood, and exotic art evokes images of Africa. Window tables look out onto a dense forest of trees and the maze of trails below. The seats on the outdoor patio next to a cascading waterfall are surrounded by tropical flora and rare birds. The menu offers sandwiches, pasta dishes, and meat and seafood entrées. If you are more interested in heart-healthy food, just upstairs from Albert's you'll find **THE TREEHOUSE** (Inexpensive). Here you can choose from a variety of vegetarian items, from stir-fry to Stroganoff, while enjoying lovely views from its open-air decks.

SEAPORT VILLAGE, San Diego
849 West Harbor Drive
(619) 235-4014

From Interstate 5, north or south, take the Airport exit, which merges with Kettner. Follow Kettner south and it will take you right to Seaport Village.

Shopping doesn't make everyone's heart beat a bit faster, but Seaport Village is different. This 14-acre specialty park on the bay is filled with 85 quaint New England–style shops that offer everything from mugs to music boxes, cookies to crystal. And this is one shopping center that offers more than just a way to spend your money. Scattered between the brightly colored shops are babbling brooks, weeping willows, and flower-covered knolls. Mimes and magicians coax smiles from the passersby, sidewalk vendors sell caramel apples and colorful balloons, and a century-old hand-carved carousel offers rides to kids of all ages. The picture is completed by the glistening bay and a sky filled with colorful kites being flown in the small adjacent park.

While you could make it through an afternoon without purchasing anything more than a box of popcorn, it's just as easy to munch your way from one end of the park to the other. There are 13 diverse eateries here, but discriminating romantics may want to wait for a window seat at one of the park's several bayside restaurants. **LUIGI'S ON THE BAY**, 861 West Harbor Drive, (619) 232-7581 (Moderate) is a handsome hideaway in the midst of the village. Embellished by murals of Italian cities and ports of call, the dining room is divided into two tiers, so everyone can share equally in the picture-postcard view. More casual, yet also quite tempting, is the **SAN DIEGO PIER CAFE**, 885 West Harbor Drive, (619) 239-3968 (Inexpensive to Moderate), a New England–style boathouse set on stilts above the water.

INLAND SAN DIEGO

Anyone who has visited San Diego recently knows it is growing in leaps and bounds. As the city continues to spread across the map, we've had to ask a tough question: Can romance be found in suburbia? The answer, to our surprise, is an enthusiastic yes! While discriminating lovers have always headed toward the coast, it appears that romance may also be found as close as their own backyard. With a little detective work, we've found a number of endearing hideaways and welcoming retreats throughout the county. Rancho Santa Fe is home to one of the country's most exquisite resorts and a number of heavenly restaurants. And Escondido, once the last place you'd go for quality time together, is now undergoing a marvelous metamorphosis.

Rancho Santa Fe

Hotel/Bed and Breakfast Kissing

INN AT RANCHO SANTA FE, Rancho Santa Fe
5951 Linea Del Cielo
(619) 756-1131, (800) 654-2928
Inexpensive to Unbelievably Expensive
Minimum stay requirement on holidays

Nestled in the rolling hills of San Diego's most affluent community, the Inn at Rancho Santa Fe has a flawless, magnificent country feeling. More than a dozen stunning adobe cottages are scattered over 20 acres of lush greenery crowded with fragrant eucalyptus trees. All of the rooms are exquisitely decorated, and many come with a fireplace, wet bar, and private patio. If you tire of lounging, take a swim, play a game or two of tennis, or test your mallet skills on the inn's championship croquet court. The hotel also has two restaurants; our favorite is **THE LIBRARY** (Moderate to Expensive), with its book-lined walls and cozy hearth. Recently declared a historic landmark, this inn appeals to a more staid crowd than the **L'AUBERGE DEL MAR RESORT AND SPA** (see Hotel/Bed and Breakfast Kissing in Del Mar). But if your budget allows, the Inn at Rancho Santa Fe makes a wonderful getaway for anyone looking to relax.

RANCHO VALENCIA RESORT, Rancho Santa Fe
5921 Valencia Circle
(619) 756-1123, (800) 548-3664
http://www.integra.fr/relaischateaux
Unbelievably Expensive
Minimum stay requirement on weekends and holidays
Recommended Wedding Site

Tucked away in the lush, rolling hills of Rancho Santa Fe, this plush, secluded hideaway does not have any "rooms," only spacious suites in charming adobe cottages called *casitas*. Each lavish sanctuary features a vaulted ceiling, a fireplace, a wet bar, and a private garden terrace. The crisp white-on-white Southwest decor is accented with pale pastels. Should you ever decide to leave your *casita,* you'll find plenty to do outside. In addition to 18 tennis courts, Rancho Valencia has croquet lawns, walking paths, and a swimming pool. If you overdo things, schedule a massage. You can even rent a hot-air balloon at day's end for an exhilarating ride through the air.

Romantic Note: Begin your night with a truly spectacular meal at the resort's five-star restaurant, **THE DINING ROOM,** (619) 756-3645 (Moderate to Expensive). The dining room is luxuriously romantic: candles flicker at every table and a crackling fire lends warmth to the elegant surroundings. The menu offers a mouthwatering assortment of seafood entrées and appetizers, from baked oysters to pan-roasted whitefish and sautéed sea scallops.

Restaurant Kissing

DELICIAS, Rancho Sante Fe
6106 Paseo Delicias
(619) 756-8000
Very Expensive
Lunch and Dinner Tuesday-Saturday

Perfectly at home in its sophisticated surroundings, Delicias offers exquisite decor, exceptional food, and an elegant atmosphere that's unparalleled in San Diego. The beautiful dining room is distinguished by tapestries adorning the ivory walls and a magnificent floral arrangement on the large crystal table in the center. As you're being seated, the hostess will stop you from simply putting your purse on the floor and place a special wicker stool next to your seat; now that's service. After you've surveyed your surroundings, take a moment to review the California-style continental menu. Fortunately, this restaurant's appeal is more than skin-deep. For starters, you can share the succulent panko fried prawns with Thai peanut sauce and orange-sesame honey. Entrées are equally sensational and artfully presented. Try the fresh John Dory (a type of fish) sautéed with tropical fruit salsa and a buerre blanc sauce, or the Dover sole prepared in a white wine sauce and served with garlic mashed potatoes and sautéed spinach. For dessert, we recommend the decadent baby chocolate cake with cream cheese and chocolate chips, embellished with vanilla ice cream and a rich caramel sauce.

As you leave, take one last look around and decide where to sit the next time you visit. Perhaps, instead of the main dining room, you can request a table on the flower-filled patio. Here, you can sit near an outdoor fireplace and enjoy your meal in a more intimate setting.

MILLE FLEURS, Rancho Santa Fe
6009 Paseo Delicias
(619) 756-3085
Expensive to Very Expensive
Lunch Monday-Friday; Dinner Daily

Elegant Mille Fleurs specializes in continental cuisine so beautiful you are almost reluctant to eat it. Menus change daily to take advantage of the freshest ingredients available and the chef's inspirations. Norwegian salmon in pink grapefruit sauce, veal chop stuffed with goat cheese, mahimahi served with black peppercorn and cognac sauce—the results are always fabulous. Add to this a refined country French decor enhanced by two blazing hearths and you have an evening positively blooming with romantic possibilities.

While a fireside table is definitely heartwarming, even more enticing is the small, private dining room available upon request. This intimate nook is popular with the celebrities who live in the area because it has its own private entrance. Beyond its dark cherry-wood doors, you'll find a circular booth that can seat as many as eight but is ideal for two, and the perfect place to say happy birthday, happy anniversary, or happy anything. When asked if he had any romantic stories to tell about this cozy alcove, the chef replied, with a glint in his eye, "I really cannot tell you. The doors are always shut." *Bon appetit.*

Escondido

Restaurant Kissing

150 GRAND CAFE, Escondido
150 West Grand Avenue
(619) 738-6868
Moderate to Expensive
Lunch Tuesday-Friday; Dinner Tuesday-Saturday

This captivating new cafe lives up to its name. It is simply grand. Although the dining room lacks cozy dark corners and intricate lace curtains, romance abounds in its understated elegance. High ceilings, bare arched windows, and a lovely jade-and-white color scheme are set off by a Chinese slate floor. Traditionalists will be pleased by the white linen tablecloths and fresh flowers at each table. Built-in bookshelves hold dramatic floral arrangements and a vast collection of cookbooks. But the real recipe here is for romance. Take the table for two tucked near a mosaic slate-and-tile fireplace. Or, for more privacy, slip into one of the richly upholstered high-backed booths. There is also seating on the patio, where you can admire a water fountain and palm trees.

The delicate California cuisine served here is almost as wonderful to look at as it is to eat. The tempting salads (such as grilled chicken) and pastas (try the smoked salmon linguine) are complemented by a nice selection of steaks, chicken, and fresh seafood. And let's not forget to mention the featured pianist who plays sentimental love ballads every night. Now, isn't that romantic?

BRIARWOOD, Escondido
29850 Circle "R" Way, at the Castle Creek Inn Resort and Spa
(619) 751-8800, (800) 253-5341
Moderate
Dinner Daily; Sunday Brunch

For those who like to venture off the beaten path, the Briarwood offers classic romance in the backcountry north of Escondido. We suggest the cozy table for two in front of the marble fireplace. From here you can take in the lace curtains, ornate antiques, and chandeliers. The menu includes tarragon chicken, angel-hair pasta primavera, seared ahi and Szechwan shrimp, and chicken Gorgonzola. A Sunday brunch buffet is served from 10:30 A.M. to 2:30 P.M.

Romantic Warning: The Briarwood is part of the **CASTLE CREEK INN RESORT AND SPA** (Moderate to Expensive). It may be a great place to golf and play tennis, but the accommodations fall a little short on the kissing scale: they're basically nice, large motel rooms with a few tole-painted accents on the walls. Better to just make the trip for dinner.

Outdoor Kissing

FELICITA PARK, Escondido
(619) 694-3049

Take Interstate 15 to Via Rancho Parkway. Go west one mile to Felicita Road, then turn north to the park entrance.

If you're looking for a typical Southern California park with perfectly manicured lawns and the latest in brightly colored plastic playground equipment, you won't find it here. What you will find are trees. Dense groves of large oaks keep much of Felicita Park's 53 acres in the shade. There are also vast open meadows where no mowers or edgers have roamed, perfect for spreading a blanket and sharing a picnic. Or take a walk on one of the wooded trails that wind along the stream.

The park can get crowded on the weekends, but it's big enough that you can always find a remote spot in which to snuggle. During the week, don't be surprised if you practically have the place to yourselves.

Romantic Note: Alcoholic beverages that do not exceed 20 percent are allowed in San Diego county parks. So go ahead and bring along that favorite bottle of wine to go with your picnic.

ORFILA VINEYARDS, Escondido
13455 San Pasqual Road
(619) 738-6500

From downtown San Diego, drive north on Interstate 15. Take the Via Rancho Parkway exit and turn right. Drive one mile to San Pasqual Road and turn right. The winery is one mile down on the right.

Most people visit wineries to taste the wines. While we're not suggesting you skip that part of your visit here, we wouldn't want you to leave without getting a taste of the view. Orfila sits on 120 acres overlooking the San Pasqual Valley, and is an excellent destination for a picnic. You can bring your own, or stop by the tasting room and buy a wedge of cheese, a loaf of bread (available on the weekends), and a bottle of wine. Set up your repast at a picnic table, or just spread out a blanket on the stretch of lawn above the vineyard. If it's not being used for a wedding party, you can also picnic in the rose garden.

Rancho Bernardo

Hotel/Bed and Breakfast Kissing

RANCHO BERNARDO INN, Rancho Bernardo
17550 Bernardo Oaks Drive
(619) 487-1611, (800) 542-6096
Expensive

Fore! If you stay here you will have to get used to that word, because during daylight hours you are more likely to hear about pars and birdies than hugs and kisses. Still, this handsome resort offers complete spa facilities, oodles of space, winding paths shaded by towering eucalyptus trees, immaculate lawns, and attentive service. Of the 287 rooms here, the suites are the best, particularly those in the 700 Building. These beautifully renovated, spacious rooms are filled with oversized, plush furnishings, and the decor imparts a contemporary, Southwest feel. The view surveys the golf course, but even if you aren't a fan of the sport, the vista is grand.

Romantic Note: The inn's restaurant, **EL BIZCOCHO** (see Restaurant Kissing), is a bit of dining heaven. Even if you are not planning to stay here, you should dine here if you are anywhere near this part of town.

Restaurant Kissing

BERNARD'O, Rancho Bernardo
12457 Rancho Bernardo Road
(619) 487-7171
Moderate
Lunch Tuesday-Friday; Dinner Tuesday-Sunday

People always say that good things come in small packages. Bernard'O is proof of that. The small dining area is lined with oversized curved booths that face the center of the room, and the walls are graced with beautiful murals that create a welcome feeling of depth. The food, best described as California French, is very good, including such entrées as grilled salmon with asparagus spears and champagne sauce, veal tenderloin with wild mushrooms and port wine sauce, plus pastas and gourmet pizzas. The desserts will tempt you away from any diet: we highly recommend the decadent crème brûlée, the refreshing lemon tart with raspberry coulis, and the list goes on. Bernard'O is the toast of the most discerning critics. Due to its stellar reputation and limited seating, we suggest visiting Bernard'O during the week to avoid the crowds.

CAFE LUNA, Rancho Bernardo
11040 Rancho Carmel Drive
(619) 673-0077
Moderate
Dinner Monday-Saturday

Cafe Luna is simple yet heavenly. Textured, peach-colored walls serve as a backdrop for the gray and marble accents. Padded wrought-iron chairs contrast with the crisp white tablecloths, and linen curtains drape the windows; the floor has been left bare. Everything on the menu is reasonably priced and looks so good you may have trouble deciding what to order. Try the Rosetta—thin noodles rolled with ham and Swiss cheese, and baked in a light béchamel sauce. Indecisive folks will be pleased with the *tris della casa*, a sampler of three different pastas.

EL BIZCOCHO, Rancho Bernardo
17550 Bernardo Oaks Drive, at the Rancho Bernardo Inn
(619) 487-1611
Expensive
Dinner Daily; Sunday Brunch
Recommended Wedding Site

El Bizcocho is a restaurant of interesting contradictions. Despite its Spanish name and California Mission design, it offers first-class French nouvelle cuisine. The tables here are so well spaced and the room so warm and endearing, a couple could feel as though they have this sizable place all to themselves. The service is attentive yet inconspicuous. But more than anything else, El Bizcocho is an exceptional place to kiss. Its enormous picture windows peer out to a lush golf course and stately hillside homes. By dusk, its subtle peach decor takes on a dreamy golden glow. Everything on the menu lives up to this glorious setting. Dishes such as roasted salmon with a tangy mustard crust and roasted duckling carved tableside are all done to perfection. The atmosphere can be a bit stuffy—for example, jackets are required for men, and the clientele is definitely well heeled—but the delectable cuisine and handsome decor are worthy of any personal celebration you may have in mind.

Outdoor Kissing

BERNARDO WINERY, Rancho Bernardo
13330 Paseo Del Verano Norte
(619) 487-1866

From Interstate 15, take the Highland Valley/Pomerado Road exit. Take Pomerado Road east 1.75 miles to Paseo Del Verano Norte. Turn left and go one and a half miles to the winery.

As you follow the directions to this quaint old winery, you may begin to doubt our accuracy. The road goes on and on through the heart of suburbia—hardly the best setting for a secluded interlude. But have faith and keep going. Long before the housing developments sprung up, Bernardo Winery stood where it still stands today. You'll soon forget the less than scenic drive that brought you here, once you turn off the main road and wind down to the rustic buildings tucked among olive trees, ancient vineyards, and lush foliage.

Built in 1889, Bernardo is the county's oldest operating winery. There are no formal tours, but you're welcome to roam through the winery and vineyards at your leisure. Most of the buildings are part of the original winery, and you'll spot old farm machinery and winery equipment from the turn of the century. There are also specialty shops to browse through, and don't forget the tasting room. The staff is very friendly and will answer any questions you may have.

Romantic Option: SOFYA'S, (619) 673-5373 (Inexpensive) is located at the winery. On Wednesdays, Saturdays, and Sundays this restaurant-deli features homemade Russian specialties such as stuffed cabbage and peppers, and Russian ravioli. Sandwiches, soups, and salads are available the rest of the week. The restaurant is open from 11 A.M. to 3 P.M. and is closed on Mondays. Patio dining is available, or you can bring your own lunch and head for the picnic area.

La Mesa

Outdoor Kissing

MOUNT HELIX, La Mesa

From Interstate 8, take Fuerte Drive south to Mount Helix Drive. Turn right and follow the road to the top of the mountain.

At one time Mount Helix was the city's "passion pit" (or, more appropriately, "passion peak"), the place you went to watch submarine races. Times have changed, and it is no longer the relatively innocent place it once was. Now the park is closed after sunset, and you can't even drive to the top anymore because the road is barricaded. The good news is that Mount Helix is still worth the trip on a clear day. The views of San Diego and the El Cajon Valley are sensational, and it's a spectacular spot to witness sunset. You'll find plenty of stony crags on which to sit and ponder the universe, or you can picnic at the top of the amphitheater.

"A kiss is something you cannot give without taking and cannot take without giving."

Anonymous

Index